SHAMAN WISDOM, SHAMAN HEALING

DEEPEN YOUR ABILITY TO HEAL WITH VISIONARY AND SPIRITUAL TOOLS AND PRACTICES

Michael Samuels, M.D.
Mary Rockwood Lane, PH.D.

WILEY

John Wiley & Sons, Inc.

Published by John Wiley & Sons, Inc., Hoboken, New Jersey
Published simultaneously in Canada

Design and production by Navta Associates, Inc.

For general information about our other products and services, please contact our Customer Care Department within the United States at (800) 762-2974, outside the United States at (317) 572-3993 or fax (317) 572-4002.

Wiley also publishes its books in a variety of electronic formats. Some content that appears in print may not be available in electronic books. For more information about Wiley products, visit our web site at www.wiley.com.

Library of Congress Cataloging-in-Publication Data:

Samuels, Michael.
    Shaman wisdom, shaman healing : deepen your ability to heal with visionary and spiritual tools and practices / Michael Samuels, Mary Rockwood Lane.
        p. ; cm.
Includes bibliographical references and index.
    ISBN 0-471-41820-X (cloth)
    1. Shamanism. 2. Mental Healing.
        [DNLM: 1. Shamanism. 2. Faith Healing—methods. 3. Imagery (Psychotherapy).
    4. Relaxation Techniques. 5. Spirituality. WB 885 S193s 2003] I. Lane, Mary Rockwood. II. Title.
        RZ401 .S186 2003
        615 . 8'52—dc21   2002153115

Printed in the United States of America

10 9 8 7 6 5 4 3 2 1

*This one's for the family—Valentino and Tamae Agnoli,
Fred and Keitha Miller, Bill Niman, and the second and
third generations—I'm thankful for a lifetime of love.*

—Michael Samuels

*To Jane Rockwood, my mother; Hope, Larry, Frank,
and Peggy; and in memory of my father,
William Peck Rockwood.*

—Mary Rockwood Lane

CONTENTS

PART THREE

HEAL NOW

ACKNOWLEDGMENTS

I thank the Creator, the directions, my guides, and my spirit animals.

I thank Mary Rockwood Lane and all the healers and shamans we interviewed for this book. I want to thank some two-leggeds, too. For healing: Rolling Thunder, Turtle Hawk, Randy, Ed, Tudor Marinescu, Edmund, Roberto, Paco, Kelly, Dan, the bear dancers, Alan, White Bear Woman, Yashoda, the Hopi people, the Denai people, David Cheek, Irving Oyle, Jose Silva, Kurt Hirshhorn, Sidney Cohlan, Joel Reiter, Richard Bernstein, Stan Terman, Dean Ornish, Bernie Siegel, Christiane Northrup, Michael Lerner, Bill Buchholtz, Emmett Miller, Sam Spivak, Rachel Remen, Frank Lawlis, Geanne Achterberg, Vicki Green, Marshall and Phyllis Klaus, Lewis Sandner, John Small, Jen Anderson. For writing: John Berryman, Kees Bolle, Alan Watts, Nancy Samuels, Don Gerrard, Jim Silberman, Mark Chimsky, PTA, Linda Bennett, Wendy Frost, Hal Bennett, Susan Muldow, Jeremy Katz. For healing art: Christiane Corbat, Vijali, Alex Grey, Marian Weber, Gina Halpern, Anna Halprin, Lee Ann Stacpoole, Dominique Mazeau, Annette Ridenour, Linda Samuels, Kenn Burrows, Kumari Fabio, Mimi Farina, Annette and Petros Dellatolas, Sigrid Hacker, Maurice Tuchman. For houses: Hurford Sharon, Valentino Agnoli, Herry Holdorf, Tara Allen, Harris Wall and the boys, Joseph Saccocci, Ingrid, Uta, Heidi Kramer, Gorgo. And family and friends: Rudy, Lewis, Florence, and Iggy Samuels, Owen Lampe, Stephen Rosenwasser, Jimmy and Carol Katz, Kurt and Karen Willig, Sarah Singer, Andrew Singer, Elizabeth Nelson, and, finally, our editor, Tom Miller, and our agent, Elaine Markson.

—Michael Samuels

I thank my family—Tim Lane, Anneliese, David, and Francesco—and Norman, Jan, Melissa, and Michael Lane. I'd also like to thank Jan Poser, LeeAnn Dodson, Patty Hall, Missy Fox, Tara Emily Allen, Mary Lisa Spano, Jill Sonke Henderson, John Graham-Pole, Tina Mullen, Debbie Olgetree, Judith Comeau, Cynthia Bush, Shelley Waters, Ransom Friedman, Barbara Orban, Gina Zeitlin, Lyn Goodwin, Bill Schaaf, Randy Brower, Selma Wood, Annie Pais, Jana Borino, Celia Cade, Marilyn Thursby, Cathy DeWitt, Fro and Lori Warren, Margaret Tolbert, Jill Lacefield, Wilma Siegel, Linda Wilson, Liz Bedel, Allen and Myrna Neims, Randy Batista, Jean Watson, Martha Rogers, Nell Page, Rodger and Katie Powell, Madeline Austin, Yashoda Yehudit, Sally Hutchinson, Alex Grey, Annette Ridenour, Laurie McLaughlin, Vickie Noble, Stuart Krantz, Christine Feldman, Vijali, Sandra Arey, Carol Reed Ash, Nancy Lasseter, Heidi Kramer, Ana Puig, Christiane Corbat, Albert Alcalay, Linda Samuels, Bernie Siegel, Herb Benson, Joan Borysenko, Sue Bassett, Al Rhoton, Mark Pashayan, Tom Zavelson, Jeff Smith, Anne Morgan, Gail Ellison, Ellie Sommer, Eleanor Blair, Rachel Veronica Williams, Ann Peckman, Fletcher Thorne-Thompson, "Hido," Willie Mae Thomas, Emma Brown, Howard Shapiro, Mary and Frank Presti, Jeremy Katz, Mark Chimsky, Tom Miller, Elaine Markson, and my dear, lifelong friend Melanie Sorensen.

—Mary Rockwood Lane

INTRODUCTION

Shaman Medicine is a guide for anyone who wants to use spiritual and visionary tools to expand his or her own ability to heal. It is a guidebook for both the lay person and the professional healer. If you are ill and want to heal yourself, if you have always known you are a healer, if you are a caregiver to someone who is ill, if you are a simply a person interested in healing, this book will teach you to maximize your ability to heal by adding a dimension of deep spiritual healing to your life. If you are a physician, a medical student, a nurse, a nursing student, a massage therapist, a body worker, an acupuncturist, this book will change the way you practice healing by giving you the mystical and intuitive tools to become a more powerful and effective healer.

Shaman medicine applies to any healing you do, even if it is not usually called healing. If you heal neighborhoods, the earth, your community, it will change the way you work. If you are an artist, writer, musician, dancer, architect, community planner, designer, land developer, or environmentalist, this book will teach you ways to make your work meaningful, sacred, and in harmony with your community and the earth.

A major goal of this book is to open you up to your visionary life, to allow spirit to flow through you. This book is a guide to hearing the voice of the living earth. The spirit of the earth is inclusive of any spiritual belief. You can be of any religion and do shamanic work.

RESEARCHING THIS BOOK

This book on shaman medicine, written by a physician and a Ph.D. nurse, is based on both personal experience and academic

1

research. Michael trained with many shamans, including Rolling Thunder and Peruvian shamans. Both of us have also taught workshops in shaman medicine and trained people to be shaman healers. We both have extensive experience with patients using spiritual, visionary, mystical, and intuitive tools to heal.

This book also comes out of the research we did for our previous books together, *Creative Healing, Spirit Body Healing,* and *The Path of the Feather.* In *Creative Healing* we studied creativity and healing. We did research on how art, writing, music, and dance were powerful healing tools for the individual and for society. We found that the first healer and first artist were one person, the shaman. In *Spirit Body Healing,* Mary's peer-reviewed research at the College of Nursing and Medicine, University of Florida, Gainesville, we demonstrated that people heal with creativity by having a visionary spiritual experience. The *Spirit Body Healing* research told us ways healers can support and promote peak spiritual visionary experiences to facilitate healing. *Spirit Body Healing* led us to the mystical and intuitive tools of the shaman. In *The Path of the Feather* we looked at how the medicine wheel and spirit animals are healing. We demonstrated how medicine wheels could be used to create sacred space, increase visions, and manifest healing. In this, our fourth book together, we merge creativity, spirituality, and shamanism into a new medicine that uses mystical and intuitive tools to heal, and we introduce a new figure in contemporary healing: the shaman healer.

We interviewed healers of all kinds and found themes that were common to each of their stories. This is phenomenological qualitative research, which is done also in the professional health sciences of medicine and nursing. We asked each person, "How do you use mystical and intuitive tools to heal? What is your lived experience of spiritual or visionary healing?" Next we asked them to describe their process in detail and tell how it felt in their bodies to do this work. Sometimes we asked them how they became a shaman healer or how they learned to do this work.

The book includes stories of lay people who became shaman healers, of massage therapists, body workers, psychic healers, and traditional shamans, acupuncturists, homeopathy practitioners, physicians, and nurses. We also interviewed architects, environmentalists, city planners, and healing artists. People we talked to ranged from famous heads of departments in medical schools to Native American healers, from environmental activists to body workers. These healers are our teachers; their actions are now your teaching. What they have in common is personal power and the lived experience of being a healer.

This book is meant to be revolutionary. In it we say that everyone is a healer. Our message is: You can take care of your eighty-year-old mother, your husband, your lover, your community, and the earth with visionary and spiritual tools. You can supplement conventional medicine with mystical and intuitive tools. You can have healing energy flowing from you; you can create a sacred space for your family and others to be healed. That is something new. We say anyone can do this—read this book and you can. The spiritual and visionary tools of the shaman are available to each of us and allow us all to become healers. If you master the skills in this book, you can be a healer who can heal yourself, your family, others, your community, and the earth.

Story: A Medicine Man Heals

In 1968, Michael was a physician in the Public Health Service, Bureau of Indian Health, on the Hopi reservation at Keams Canyon, Arizona. He tells this story:

> I looked deeply into her eyes. She was very beautiful. She was wearing a purple velvet dress with a silver squash blossom necklace resting on her chest. Her sunburned face was framed by her hair, which was pulled back in a bun, and by large turquoise earrings. Her eyes were closed. She was ancient; the wrinkles on her face looked like the canyons on the high mesa, her dark skin

was as rich as the earth. And she was dying. Everything I had been taught as a well-trained Western doctor told me she would die tonight and there was nothing I could do to stop the awesome process.

I admitted her to the hospital from the emergency room. She was carried in by her family; they had brought her in the back of a horse-drawn wagon across the endless mesas through mud, potholes, and cold rain. It must have been a dark and frightening journey. When I saw her, she was not conscious and barely breathing. I examined her; her breath sounds were crackly and almost absent. I touched her skin and it stood up in the tent that signified severe dehydration. She obviously had pneumonia and dehydration, throughout history the old person's friend to take him or her to the other side.

Now she was in bed in her warm hospital room. Her family sat around the bed—some cried, some looked stoic like rocks standing on the hill outside the window watching. I had put in two I.V.'s; one was running fluids, one also had antibiotics flowing into her. In this primitive hospital we had no electrolyte tests, no bacteria cultures. I did not think she could last in the back of our pickup truck for the hours it would take to transport her to a larger hospital. I looked into her eyes and suddenly knew what I had to do. I asked a Native American nurse if there was a medicine man I could call. No Public Health Service doctor I knew of had ever called a medicine man into the hospital; the rules forbade it at that time.

The medicine man entered her room like the wind. He brought in power and light; he carried his drums, his headdress, his rattles, his healing herbs, his medicine bag. The family knew who he was and I could see questions in their eyes. They were both relieved and confused. Why had this doctor brought in a medicine man? Medicine men were very expensive. Who would pay for it? The clash of two cultures sent out sparks. But the medicine man seemed oblivious to it all. He put on his headdress and feathers and chest plate. He painted his face with lightning bolts and white bear paw prints. Then he bent backward and started praying. He looked upward to the sky and sang, he drummed and rattled. The sterile hospital seemed to crack—space and time opened, the room seemed huge with no walls and ceiling, the sky and thunder came in.

Nurses and aides ran toward the room; they stopped at the door as if it was a invisible membrane. They looked into the room in silence. They were all Native Americans themselves and knew this sacred space, this happening deep in their bodies and spirits.

The drumming became all there was. The rattling was beyond hypnotic. It took us all upward in spirals, wide and open, like an eagle flying. The medicine man's eagle feathers brushed over the woman; they flew around her like spirits, they carried off illness, they took out dark shapes, colors flew. He touched her, put an herbal potion on her, sucked her skin. In the drumming, it all blended and swirled. Then the space opened and opened and cracked like lightning, visions spun, song echoed, the drumming and rattling merged into overtones like a heartbeat and breathing. The medicine man stopped, exhausted from hours of drumming, and fell in a chair. He looked ordinary now. An electric softness settled in the room, which was now full of a radiant light that you could actually feel, like the air after a thunderstorm.

The woman sat up in bed like a shot. She opened her eyes and the family ran to her. The medicine man touched her face and quietly left. He looked me in the eyes with a deep understanding that something important had happened. Something left with him and something remained, too. The woman laughed and made a joke in the Navaho language. The family laughed. It was totally different now. In a couple of days, her family took her home. She was completely well.

The next day I saw my forty patients, admitting several to the hospital who had pneumonia and dehydration. I went back to my exhausting routine. I did not know then the profound effect that incident would play in my life. I had absorbed it into my body more than into my rational mind. Even today, I see it more deeply than I did then; each time I look at it, I see more and more. Now I see that during the healing a darkness left her body, and a bright light came into her.

That medicine man was my teacher, and he still is. He showed me what breaking time and space was; he showed me how to heal on a level beyond what I had learned in medical school. And now through this book, he is your teacher, too.

If you examine what the shaman in the story did, you see the roots of modern integrative healing. Contemporary holistic healers use the separate parts of the healing now. The contemporary healer uses prayer, ritual, and ceremony; massage, body work, and energy healing; herbs and medicines. All these were part of the Hopi medicine man's shamanic healing. To increase the power of the modern healer, we need to bring these tools back into healing with intent. We need to bring back into modern healing the power of the shaman to pray, go into visionary space, move energy, bring the soul its life, and change reality.

In the mysterious and visionary places of the shaman's mind lay his ability to see in visionary space. By seeing into the woman's body, he allowed the power of the universe and the power of spirits to come through him. He pulled things out of the woman; he put her soul back. He brought lightning bolts of pure power from the Creator and from the earth into the woman through him.

THE HISTORY OF SHAMANISM

Shamanism is the oldest tradition of making change in the world for healing from a spiritual space. Mircea Eliade, renowned University of Chicago history of religions scholar, defined shamanism as "the technique of ecstasy." In his classic book, *Shamanism: Archaic Techniques of Ecstasy,* he describes shamanism as a magico-religious phenomenon that originated in Siberia and central Asia thousands of years ago. The word comes to us, through the Russian, from the Tungusic *saman.* Throughout central and northern Asia, the magico-religious life of society centered on the shaman. Even now, the shaman remains the dominating figure, for the shaman is the great master of ecstasy. The shaman is magical in his ability to make change and religious in that the change comes from spirit. Eliade believes that even though the term *shaman* comes from the Siberian steppes, shamanism probably originated farther south. The Buddhist lamas to this day have shamanic ritual to heal. They go into an ecstatic state and go to the spirit world, and they take the dead over to the other side. They have drums and do ecstatic ritual. Many Lamaist teachings are shamanic, and scholars can trace the flow of ancient Buddhist philosophy and ritual from the south northward to Siberia. It is likely that Tibetan Buddhism and shamanism come from the same traditions. The shamanic tradition started in Lamaist India four thousand years ago and then spread all over the earth. The shaman is the specialist of the soul.

There have been shamans on every continent and in almost every culture. The shaman is not limited to Native American healing, and in fact is less common there than in other areas. Some Native American people object to people who are not Native Americans using the term *shaman;* they feel their culture is being stolen from them. We apologize for what has been done to Native Americans. But no one people owns the term *shaman*—it is the first term for the spiritual healer of any people. You have the right to this teaching; it is a teaching of the earth and spirits, not of one culture. The earth speaks to all its children.

Eliade defines shamanism as going into a trance to heal. The key event in shamanism is seeing spirits, whether in a dream or awake. Seeing is the most important characteristic of the shaman; divination and clairvoyance are part of the shaman's mystical techniques. A shaman goes inward to the spirit world in a shamanic journey or ecstatic trance. He or she interacts with the spirits in the inner world and then comes outward into the outer world and heals the person's body, the community, or the earth.

The shaman is indispensable in any ceremony that concerns the human soul. In traditional shamanism, the shaman is the healer because he can find a person's fugitive soul and bring it back. In all 310 cultures (except ours) in the Human Relations Area Files at Yale University, illness is believed to be caused by soul loss. So when the shaman brings the soul back, this fits into the causal theory of illness of the culture.

The shaman may also conduct a dead person's soul to the underworld. The shaman's soul can abandon his body, roam to the underworld, and ascend to the sky. Sanctified by initiation and protected by the guardian spirits, the shaman can challenge danger of the mystical geography in sacred space.

The shaman is the man or woman who sees into the sacred world. The shaman goes inward and brings his or her visions of the ancient spirits and spirit animals outward to the world as ceremony and ritual. By this process—most similar to prayer, imagery, and art—the shaman heals himself or herself, others, and the earth. By having visions of healing, and by doing sacred rituals, the shaman makes the visions come true. The shaman goes into the world of the spirits and can act there. The shaman affects the spirits, talks to them, has them as helpers— or, if they are a cause of illness, removes them. That is how the shaman heals.

The older term *ecstasy* in *Shamanism: Archaic Techniques of Ecstasy* describes what is now commonly referred to as an altered state of consciousness, most similar to a trance or a guided imagery state. Eliade said that the shaman commands the techniques of ecstasy because his soul can safely leave his body and travel at vast distances; it can penetrate the underworld and rise to the sky. Through his own ecstatic experience he knows the paths to the extraterrestrial regions. He can go below and above because he has already been there. The danger of losing his way in these difficult regions is still great; but, sanctified by his initiation and furnished with his guardian spirits, a shaman is the only human being able to challenge the danger and venture into a mystical geography.

Shamanism has been around for thousands of years and it has been changing, developing, and adapting to new circumstances and new ideological backgrounds the whole time.

There is nothing pure or primordial about any of these beliefs as they exist today. When you become a shaman healer you join the ancient tradition and become one in a line of shamans going back to before recorded history.

THE NEW SHAMANISM

In this book we present a new view of shaman healing that joins ancient shamanic processes with modern medicine, modern knowledge, and contemporary culture. It is an expanded view of shamanism that takes into consideration our view of the cause of illness—viruses, DNA, bacteria—and scientific research, as well as alternative therapies like acupuncture. For people to understand shamanism today, they need it to make sense in their vocabulary and worldview. The shaman gets messages from the world around him and acts on them to heal. When a shaman says she speaks to the owls, it sounds delusional in our culture. But in shamanism, to listen to an owl is not delusional. To understand shamanism, it is important to differentiate between societal concepts and delusions. For most of humankind's history, listening to animal voices was the dominant paradigm. The reason it was the accepted thought of the culture was that it worked. Shamanism healed people, balanced them with the ecosystem. It helped them hunt, plant crops, predict and deal with weather, and increased the fertility of the people. When a system can explain reality, it provides a map for how to predict events. It gives the people coherence and meaning.

The shaman healer has tools to heal. The tools are different from scalpels, medicines, or syringes. They are mystical tools that come from the inner world of consciousness. To learn to use these tools the shaman healer needs to change his or her consciousness. It is a process of learning to see differently, being in the world in a different way. The shamanic experience is a lived experience, not a theory. Each tool is a way of being in the world, a change in consciousness. It is work on yourself in the inner world.

Diagnosis and treatment are the basic tools of any healer. For a shaman, diagnosis is to listen and see. It is going into the visionary world. Sacred space is the place from which seeing differently comes. Shamanic treatment includes praying and moving healing energy, coming out and changing the path of one's life journey. Both diagnosis and treatment use guided imagery to travel inward and to move energy. Guided imagery is used in both seeing and moving energy; it is the basic tool of the shaman healer. In ancient times it was not called guided imagery; it was ecstatic journeying, seeing into the spirit world. In the terms of modern psychology, the trance, altered states of consciousness, prayer, meditation, and guided imagery are all names for the way the shaman sees and heals. That is why it is probably easier for a modern person to become a shaman, because these tools are deep in our culture; we can all learn them, and they are part of our way of being a healer already.

This book has guided imagery exercises throughout to help you deepen your ability to see and hear in the visionary world. The exercises have a defined form. The first part is abdominal breathing, the second relaxation, the third deepening. The fourth is the subject of the imagery: the intent and content. The fifth is the return to the room and grounding. The final step is an instruction for carrying something forward into your life. Each part is important; as you become more experienced you can shorten the introductions and closings somewhat if you wish. Each time you do a guided imagery exercise, you get better and better and habits form. The relaxation takes place instantly after many practices.

To do the exercises, you can read them and remember to do them in your meditation space. You do not have to remember the exercise word by word, only the form. You can make up the words by yourself. Guided imagery is much more powerful when you make it up. Other ways to do the exercise are to have someone read them to you, or make a tape and play it back.

THE SHAMANIC JOURNEY

Being a shaman is a lifetime journey. It will take many years to deepen your abilities and learn shamanic techniques. This book is a beginning. The journey will encourage you to explore ways of healing in your life; it is about constantly expanding your realms of creativity in healing. As a healer, you can incorporate guided imagery, writing, music, art, and dance; you can expand your traditional techniques to weave an eclectic tapestry of healing. You can learn herbs or body work, or you can follow your innate natural abilities and make your own healing ways. Open yourself to new ways of healing, to understanding that each way has powerful things to offer. Each person will come up with something different. That is why it takes a long time to become a shaman. Native Americans say it takes a lifetime to become a true shaman; many Native Americans will never say they are shamans because that is not humble. Learning to heal with shamanic techniques is a slow process because it is about the ability to see visions and be sensitive to energy. It takes years to become sensitive enough to the environment to be able to see visions and feel energy in your body as you work.

Healing with shamanic tools requires a slow development of body sensitivity. As the healer learns to see visions and follow his or her intuition, the skill grows. The learning is body learning, not theory; shamanism is only learned from doing, exploring, and experimenting within the realm of cosmic creativity and spirits. This book and others like it are valuable guides but they cannot replace doing. To learn sensitivity, practice working with family members and friends, and then with people who are ill. Do it often enough so you remember the practice in your body. Feel it in the body, follow it within yourself. Take workshops where you can do, not just listen to lectures. Train with shamans who teach with experience, not talk.

Go on vision quests to have your own visions. Do guided imagery to have visions. When you lay on hands, pay attention to your visions and intuition. Do all this again and again. You learn every day, from everything. Being a shaman takes a life-time.

PART ONE

CREATE SACRED SPACE

1

YOU ARE CALLED

Mircea Eliade, in his classic *Shamanism: Archaic Techniques of Ecstasy,* describes three stages of becoming a shaman: the election, the instruction, and the initiation. We recognize that after a person becomes a shaman there is a fourth stage: the practice. Election is the calling, how a person starts the shamanic journey. Traditionally, the calling was through dreams, visions, and dialogue with spirits. Instruction takes place in solitude, in dialogue with teachers and in practice with shamans. Initiation often involved a ceremony in which there was an ascent to the sky on a sacred tree or sacred ladder. It involved images of death, dismemberment, and resurrection. It is important to understand that the chosen shaman was an ordinary person, not a professional healer. He or she may have come from a lineage of shamans but the training started afresh each time.

Most historical accounts of the calling say that people who were chosen to be shamans by the Creator became dreamy and absentminded, loved solitude, and had prophetic visions. They sometimes had an illness that was cured by shamanism. The shaman was the original wounded healer.

Part of being a shaman healer is seeing your work as what you are called to do. Shamans believe that something greater has called them to this work. It could be God, the universe, the world, the people. They have heard the calling deep in their soul; they are moving toward it. The shaman says, "This is my calling." The inner voice asks you, "Who is calling you? Whoever called you is who is working with you. Who is that for you? That is the mystery—the mysterious one calls." The call comes from a being who is very large. Being a shaman is from the life force. This whole work is to honor the life force, the human as the life force energy. It is about bringing in the life force to heal.

Some people know they are born to do this work, but for others it is a slower and more difficult path. No matter what they do to avoid it, they end up here. When people are born to this work, shamanism resonates with them whenever they see it. If they find a relevant book, a lecture, a movie, they are riveted to it. It is as if it is home. If they leave it and say they will not do it, a book comes to them, a conference, and they are back, drawn back into this work. What is the attraction of this ancient way of being to a modern person? People say it is who they are in their memories, that they remember an ancient way of being. They say it is simply who they are in their soul. The process of becoming a shaman is their soul retrieval and heals them.

THE BODY OF THE STARS

Sometimes the calling arrives as person who comes to you and invites you to be a shaman. That person may become your teacher or may disappear and never be seen again.

Mary tells us this story:

> One day a strange woman knocked at my door. She wanted to sell me an African ceremonial wall hanging. As she told me about the shaman that once wore this beaded scarf, she mentioned that she, too, was a shaman. Then it was almost like a comedy. She was wearing a long dress and a long scarf as a headdress. She started drumming and chanting, throwing her head back as she chanted. She made me very, very nervous. Suddenly, as she was standing in my living room, the floor turned into a

spiral. I felt like I began to spin and whirl. I felt myself becoming larger and larger, I mean huge. I felt myself pass though the ceiling and go up into the sky. There were thunderbolts crashing and crashing all around my head. I reached up and grabbed a thunderbolt from the stormy sky. I could hear her saying, "It is now time." I threw the thunderbolt into the earth with a sizzling, thundering crash. Space and time cracked. I saw a spirit woman whose body was the stars. I looked up and her body filled the whole sky. I thought, "This is how the ancient people looked up and saw the angels, how they saw the lions in the constellations." Suddenly it was still—I opened my arms slowly as if I was bringing in the light. I called forth the shaman. I heard the words clearly vibrate through my head. Then I was in the sky filled with stars. I was reaching for my spirit lover. It was like the heavens were filled with desire. I will never forget this moment. I knew I was on a shamanic path despite the chanting and dancing of this annoying woman in my living room. This was my first shamanic experience.

A Life Event Makes a Shaman

Your life is your teacher. It is the events of your life that propel you and teach you; they unfold in each moment of each day. You do not need to look outside your life for answers; your life allows your own answers to emerge. Through your life, you know the truth and live your authentic life. An illness, a death, a near-death experience, an accident—all make a shaman.

Often a death or a severe illness makes a person a shaman. This is a traditional path that shamans have walked since ancient times. Did you experience a death that changed who you are and changed your priorities? Did you experience an illness that changed you and made you interested in this work? When you face death and survive, you come out in a different place. In death, you lose everything. What you are left with is essential. It is what you are and want to be, then, that is what you bring to your healing.

Michael's wife, Nancy, died of breast cancer in 1993. He tells this story:

> As she was dying, I heard a voice. It told me, "Don't turn away, pay attention, make memories." I looked into her eyes. She was slowing, becoming unconscious. She spoke to me from visionary space. "I am love. I will be with you always. I will help you love from the other side. I will be with you in all parts of your life. I will always be with you and the boys."
>
> For me, my shamanic work began in earnest after my wife's death. I lived alone in nature. I lived with animals and learned to hear their voices. I fell in love. I found each of the animals in my path became alive and a spirit animal. I took my work to a much deeper level.

HIGHER CONSCIOUSNESS

A river of wisdom flows though your body. When you go into a deeply relaxed state, you allow the sacred healing visions to flow through you more easily. You let your personality rest. Your personality plays a distinctive role in your life. It has defining characteristics that express your uniqueness and individuality. For example, a person may have a preference to wear a red dress to a party or may love to watch football games on TV. If these characteristics are all a person concentrates on, it can cloud and override the crystal-clear river of wisdom that is our oneness. When we construct our personality, we can over-build around the river of the essence of who we are. Then we can't see beauty anymore. Learning to tap into a place that is true and deep takes practice. It is the development of the sensitivity to hear the shaman healer within you speaking. This vibrational energy can resonate within you about your essence, about finding yourself in the deepest level. For one who is called, shamanism is finding your true self.

Deep inside, you know who you are, you know what you are to do in your life. Your life is your offering; it is connected to your inner voice, to God's will, to destiny, to your dream.

You have been given life. Do whatever you want, make choices. God wants you to find yourself and love yourself. This brings fulfillment. You are connected to others; you bring forth His love in the world and it comes to you. Becoming a shaman healer is about fulfilling your own calling. In shamanic work, you learn to heed your own counsel, not the counsel of an external authority. The most meaningful experience is a spiritual experience that resonates with your whole life.

BECOMING IMMERSED IN NATURE

Remember the sensual fireflies? Remember a night with the moon rising, the fireflies darting like shooting stars—the stars above spinning, the fireflies like stars below flashing like your love? As you experience nature, feel how the river flows through your own body, through your own life. As you become interconnected with the elements, as you breathe, live, drink, and excrete, there is a constant interchange with your body and the living earth. You are a living organism, a part of nature. Begin the path to becoming a shaman healer with your own holism with nature. Through interconnectedness, the boundaries blur and the essence of consciousness emerges. The shaman healer is one with the earth, one with the river, one with the trees, one with the wind. The shaman healer allows his or her body to merge deeply into the body of the earth. What emerges from the union is spiritual consciousness, is the light, is the essence of your life. When you begin to go into the visionary world and you see in imagery, conceptual space arises and an incredible visionary consciousness is born within you. When you move into connection to the earth, when you plug into the larger earth body, you experience a heightened level of consciousness.

This is not altered consciousness, but heightened consciousness. When the human blends with earth consciousness, the earth feels in oneness, too. It blends, merges, feels like immersion, not letting go. It is the emerging of the vibrational quality of consciousness, of self. The consciousness of the human body, the earth body, the animal body—this is what humans resonate to when they feel wholeness. This is an essential clear consciousness that stems from oneness with the earth's elements. It is seeing sensitivity, transcending to be sensitive to plants, animals, sounds, and smells. The merging and interconnectedness give the shaman healer the power to heal. The power comes from the earth.

One type of election is the ability to know and see deeply into nature. The shaman knows the natural rhythm of the earth. The shaman learns to know, feel, and sense the earth's vibrations. Shamans walking in the woods see things no one else sees. As the orchid blooms, shamans investigate, discovering and dealing with their world in a deep, sensory way. As the sunset streams its colors across the horizon, their bodies split open. As they hear an owl call, they open their hearts with joy and understanding. The natural experience calls to them deep in their bodies. As a butterfly flutters across a shaft of sunlight in an ancient forest, the shaman knows its path, its pattern, its cycles, its magic . . . and its medicine.

The shaman has respect for and faith in the way things are, and a deep belief in and reverence for regeneration. This belief gives the shaman the great faith necessary to do the healing. The faith is simple; it is seen every day in nature. The shaman has the knowledge that when a tree is harmed, it will grow and heal. This knowledge gives the shaman the understanding that each person he or she works with has an innate ability to heal. The shaman is deeply connected to and knows and respects nature. This allows the shaman to really believe and be a strong facilitator for change. The deep knowledge of the cycle of life that deals with healing, growth, and death happens irrespective of the shaman's power. The shaman knows that people are capable of living life and experiencing illness, and that there is no need to be radical in fixing it. By simply aligning itself with nature, the organism achieves balance and harmony. The life force moves through the creature and it will heal itself. The body will heal by itself, the process facilitated by the shaman creating balance.

In the drought, the shaman is the one who knows the water will return and reminds the thirsty rose that the rain will come. The shaman has the ability to see beyond pain and suffering and know the truth and keep the faith in living. The shaman knows healing is possible and passes that knowledge to the person he or she is working with. Possibly the most valuable thing the shaman does is allow the person to believe he or she will be healed.

Spirit acknowledges spirit. Spirit is like rain, spirit is like water, spirit is everywhere, in every leaf. Native Americans believe that the Creator is in everything—the Creator made everything and everything is the Creator's image. The Creator makes no mistakes; everything is as it should be.

EVERYONE IS YOUR TEACHER

This is a journey where, as you walk on the path, you realize that everyone around you is your teacher. Your life is constantly creating opportunities to go deeper into your quest as a spirit journey. Mary deepened her shamanic journey when her grandmother was admitted to a nursing home for Alzheimer's disease. During her drive back and forth to the small rural community where her grandmother lived, she was able to pause and reflect on her own life. She was able to contemplate who she was, what she was doing, and what she could learn from this experience. Even in her confusion and pain, this experience in life was taking her deeper into herself. There were visits when her grandmother did not even recognize her. Mary would watch the rambling spinning in her head. But somehow she could see more deeply into her grandmother's life and her grandmother became a teacher. She could see into her grandmother's fragmented memories; she could see images, sounds, and echoes. She could glimpse experiences deep in her grandmother's past.

They become alive as she listened. Suddenly, her grandmother was a teacher unraveling the mysteries of the deep strings attached to her, her mother, her grandmother, and her great-grandmother. She could see into the present, back to the past; it became a reflection. Suddenly, Mary saw the wisdom of her own life. She began to live in a different way. The opportunity became a mirror for her own authentic voice. She suddenly could see herself for who she really was.

SOUL RETRIEVAL IS FINDING YOUR AUTHENTIC SELF

Soul retrieval is a technique in traditional shamanic healing in many cultures. In soul retrieval, the shaman goes on a journey into the spirit world to bring back the soul of a person who is ill. The basic belief behind this technique is that illness is caused by soul loss, by a spirit or person taking the ill person's soul. Some shamanic teachings rely completely on soul retrieval as the basic technique. We believe shamanism is much broader and includes mystical and intuitive tools in addition to bringing back the person's soul.

How can we relate to soul retrieval today, when our model of illness is so different? Soul retrieval is connected to the concept of who we are as people and how our spirit resides in our physical bodies in this lifetime.

We have moved past the traditional view of soul retrieval in this age of science. We recontact it again in shaman healing. It is a journey, a search in the darkness through space and time. People who are ill go into the mystery where no one has gone before. They go through precarious circumstances and allow themselves to be taken, eaten, defaced, and stripped, yet have inner strength and faith that they will return home again. The shaman is the one who will take you there. It is a move, a move to return you to yourself. It is the hero's journey to return home. The shaman brings you home to yourself. The shaman shows you the validity of your experience of who you are. In modern psychological terms, soul retrieval shows you your authentic self. It allows you to be at home in your body, in your life, to feel comfortable, to be authentic. When you do what is authentic for you, you are in the place of healing.

Look at Your Life Story and Your Election

In Mircea Eliade's book *Shamanism,* he tells the life stories of shamans in many cultures. Eliade says that the shaman as a child had visions, saw spirits, told people about them, was creative, an artist, a solitary. To use your life as an exercise to find your calling, think about your own life story. Look for events that are connected to being a shaman. Find each one in your past, list them, and put them together as a story of a person on a shamanic vision quest. That is who you are; the story is your story of you as a shaman healer.

Take some time to examine your life, looking at it as your own shamanic journey. There have been events and turning points that are critical in making you who you are, in making you a shaman healer. There were forks in the road where you could have gone one way or another; your destiny is where you are now. Your life has taken you to the underworld, to darkness and suffering. There have been opportunities to look into the face of death. It may have been as simple as the death of a pet, or perhaps it was when your grandmother died. Remember when you encountered death and were aware of it? Remember your life; remember a peak experience that excited and thrilled you, where you stood on the top of a mountain, metaphorical or real, and threw your arms open and realized you are your strengths. In the election journal, you can write down those moments, remember those events. Spend some time connecting the passages to the different phases in your life. Be specific about what different relationships taught you or the circumstances they created for you. What part of yourself did you not realize? Each human you have been in relationship with has given you an opportunity to feel, experience, and define who you are. Spend time in your journal writing about core relationships, your parenting, characteristics you share with your father and mother. Explore where you have grown.

Exercise: Your election journal

Buy a special book, lined or unlined, for your collages, poems, short stories. Write your life story from the point of view of your initiation into the shamanic life. Make a journal that highlights how experiences of election made you who you are.

Write about an experience in nature: Did you have an experience in nature that made you a shaman healer? Did you go into a retreat on a river, on a mountain, in a swamp that changed who you are forever? Write about this experience in light of how it made you a shaman healer. Find the details in it about how you discovered the wind, sounds, smells, feelings of deep sensuous connectedness.

Write about an experience with death: If you have been through the death of a loved one, a family member, a friend, or person you have cared for, go into the experience again now. In your memory, let the experience come back to you, see it, feel it, be there. Do not look away. Make memories. Look at the experience from the point of view of what it did to make you a shaman healer. Write about what happened to make you realize your priorities, who you are, what is important to you, what life and death are, what spirits are.

Write about a peak spiritual experience: If you have had a moment of spiritual enlightenment or a spiritual vision, go back to it now. In your mind's eye, go into the moment and see it, feel it, be there. How did this moment make you a shaman healer? What did it teach you about spirits, about who you are, about the Creator?

Construct in writing your own story of what experiences in your life made you a shaman healer.

What captures your attention, sparks your imagination? These are the whispers of your calling. Whose words do you hear resonate in your soul? What gives you a prickly feeling in the back of your neck? What causes your body to wake up? What is your experience of awe? Take note of what is there in your life. Experience ecstasy, ride ecstasy to what you desire. Ride it to the fulfillment of your desires—ecstasy is the journey of your spirit.

Guided imagery: Become the healer you always wanted to be

Guided imagery is the basic tool to see and listen into the visionary world. It is what a healer experiences in a trance. The trance is the place to see images and hear voices. The images and voice are experienced as thoughts with enhanced quality.

1. Breathing: Make yourself comfortable. You can be sitting or lying down. Loosen tight clothing, uncross your legs and arms. Close your eyes. Let your breathing slow down. Take several deep breaths. Let your abdomen rise as you breathe in and fall as you let your deep breath out. As you breathe in and out you will become more and more relaxed. You may feel sensations of tingling, buzzing, or relaxation; if you do, let those feelings increase. You may feel heaviness or lightness; you may feel your boundaries loosening and your edges softening. As you breathe in, let yourself fill with energy. As you breathe out, let whatever you want to leave, leave you body with your breath.

2. Relaxation: Now let yourself relax. Let your feet relax, let your legs relax. Let the feelings of relaxation spread upward to your thighs and pelvis. Let your pelvis open and relax. Now let your abdomen relax, let your belly expand, do not hold it in anymore. Now let your chest relax, let your heartbeat and breathing take place by themselves. Let your arms relax, your hands relax. Now let your neck relax, your head, your face. Let your eyes relax; see a horizon and blackness for a moment. Let these feelings of relaxation spread throughout your body.

3. Deepening: Let your relaxation deepen. If you wish, you can count your breaths and let your relaxation deepen with each breath. You can picture going deeper into a cave, or a walk into a forest down a long path, or an elevator ride watching the floor numbers, or a long hallway—whatever seems most at home for you. As you deepen, you can allow your body to expand. It can expand to one-third larger than its usual size. As you expand, let space appear between your cells. Let the space fill with energy. Let the energy come up into you from the earth and down into you from the sky. As you breathe in, let the energy grow; as you breathe out, let the energy remain high.

4. The Content: Now, in your mind's eye see yourself doing healing work. It can be the work you already do as a healer or work that you would like to do. Give yourself time to let this image come to you. Start by picturing a place where you can heal. Picture a room, see your body, see a person you are working with. Let an image of a healing situation come to you. See yourself, see a place, see a person.

Now, see yourself doing the healing you have always dreamed of. Give yourself time to let this image come to you. You may see yourself surrounded by light, you may see yourself being guided by God's hands, you may see yourself sitting in the country by a fire, you may see yourself drumming, chanting. You may see yourself laying on hands, going into the person's body in psychic space. It can be anything; this is your shamanic healing path, it is unique to you. Give yourself time to see the entire vision, to see as much of it as you can. Rest there and absorb it.

5. Grounding and closing: When you are ready, return to the room where you are doing the exercise. Press your backside down on the place you are sitting or lying. Press your feet down hard on the floor or ground. First move your feet and then move your hands. Move them around and experience the feeling of the movement. Press your feet down harder onto the floor, feel the grounding, feel the pressure on the bottom of your feet, feel the solidity of the earth. Feel your backside on the chair; feel your weight pressing downward. Now open your eyes. Look around you. Stand up and stretch. Move your body; feel it move.

6. Final instructions for healing: You are back; you can carry the experience of the exercise outward to your life. You will feel stronger and be able to see deeper. You will be in a healing state. You can do this exercise whenever you wish. As you read this book, the visions you have will deepen. Each time you do any guided imagery exercise you will be more relaxed and be able to go deeper and be more deeply healed.

Guided imagery: See your life as a shamanic journey

Make yourself comfortable. You can be sitting or lying down. Loosen tight clothing, uncross your legs and arms. Close your eyes. Let your breathing slow down. Take several deep breaths. Let your abdomen rise as you breathe in and fall as you let your deep breath out. As you breathe in and out you will become more and more relaxed. You may feel sensations of tingling, buzzing, or relaxation; if you do, let those feelings increase. You may feel heaviness or lightness; you may feel your boundaries loosening and your edges softening.

Now let yourself relax. Let your feet relax, let your legs relax. Let the feelings of relaxation spread upward to your thighs and pelvis. Let your pelvis open and relax. Now let your abdomen relax, let your belly expand, do not hold it in anymore. Now let your chest relax, let your heartbeat and breathing take place by themselves. Let your arms relax, your hands relax. Now let your neck relax, your head, your face. Let your eyes relax; see a horizon and blackness for a moment. Let these feelings of relaxation spread throughout your body. Let your relaxation deepen. If you wish, you can count your breaths and let your relaxation deepen with each breath.

Now in your mind's eye you will look at your life as your shamanic journey. Now that you are deeply relaxed let the incidents in your life that drew you to a shamanic worldview come

to you. Give yourself time. You may see a book you read, a conference you went to, a meeting with a person you were caring
for where you saw spirit. You may see a trip to an ancient ruin
or stone circle, a meeting with a shaman or teacher. You may
see a time you spent in nature, a animal you saw that affected
you. Let the images of your life come to you like birds flying
across the sky. Invite them to come. Feel and see them deeply.

When you are ready, return to the room where you are
doing the exercise. First move your feet and then move your
hands. Move them around and experience the feeling of
the movement. Press your feet down onto the floor, feel the
grounding, feel the pressure on the bottom of your feet, feel the
solidity of the earth. Feel your backside on the chair, feel your
weight pressing downward. Now open your eyes. Look around
you. Stand up and stretch. Move your body; feel it move. You
are back; you can carry the experience of the exercise outward
to your life. You will feel stronger and be able to see deeper. You
will be in a healing state. Each time you do any guided imagery
exercise you will be more relaxed and be able to go deeper and
be more deeply healed.

Guided imagery for surrender

Surrender is about accepting your life path as where you are
supposed to be. If you are on the path of becoming a shaman
healer, surrender is accepting that part of you and owning it
and becoming it.

Make yourself comfortable. You can be sitting or lying
down. Loosen tight clothing, uncross your legs and arms. Close
your eyes. Let your breathing slow down. Take several deep
breaths. Let your abdomen rise as you breathe in and fall as you
let your deep breath out. As you breathe in and out you will
become more and more relaxed. You may feel feelings of tingling, buzzing, or relaxation; if you do, let those feelings
increase. You may feel heaviness or lightness; you may feel your
boundaries loosening and your edges softening.

Now let yourself relax. Let your feet relax, let your legs relax. Let the feelings of relaxation spread upward to your thighs and pelvis. Let your pelvis open and relax. Now let your abdomen relax, let your belly expand, do not hold it in anymore. Now let your chest relax, let your heartbeat and breathing take place by themselves. Let your arms relax, your hands relax. Now let your neck relax, your head, your face. Let your eyes relax; see a horizon and blackness for a moment. Let these feelings of relaxation spread throughout your body. Let your relaxation deepen. If you wish, you can count your breaths and let your relaxation deepen with each breath.

Now in your mind's eye see yourself as the healer you want to be. See your body, the place you would like to do your healing, even a person you are working with. See it in detail—see it, feel it, smell it, hear it. Be there as a healer.

Now let yourself surrender to the process you are in. Give yourself fully to the process of becoming a healer. Give your body, your life as a sacred offering to the work that you are doing. Realize that your healing work is sacred. Realize it is a gift to the person, the community, the spirits, and the earth. Realize that you, as a sacred shaman healer, are the way the earth heals itself. You are the hands of God, the healing power of the whole system. As you surrender, let yourself loosen, relax more deeply; let yourself fall into the body of the Beloved as if you are diving into deep space. Do not be afraid; you are in the hands of God. You are weightless, falling into the deepest space, surrendering to something much greater and older than your body and life in this single lifetime.

When you are ready, return to the room where you are doing the exercise. First move your feet and then move your hands. Move them around and experience the feeling of the movement. Press your feet down onto the floor and feel the grounding, feel the pressure on the bottom of your feet, feel the solidity of the earth. Feel your backside on the chair; feel your weight pressing downward. Now open your eyes. Look around you. Stand up and stretch. Move your body; feel it move. You are back; you can carry the experience of the exercise outward to your life. You will feel stronger and be able to see deeper. You will be in a healing state. Each time you do any guided imagery exercise you will be more relaxed and be able to go deeper and be more deeply healed.

2

SACRED PRAYER

STORY: A SHAMAN'S HUT

Michael's home is in a valley between two mountain ranges. You cannot see another house from it. The house sits directly on the San Andreas Fault, the largest, most active earthquake fault in North America. A river flows down in the valley bottom; the fog blows up to the hill below the house and hovers there like a kestrel in the wind. The country road is lined with ancient oak trees. The driveway enters an old apple orchard and winds its way to a resting place below the house. The house was designed by a dear friend, an architect. As you walk up to it, hawks call and dive overhead, deer graze in the orchard, foxes play among the fruit trees. Now that his children are grown, the house is a shaman's hut, the place where he lives, writes, and sees patients. A patient coming up to the house experiences the animals, the wind, the fog, the mountains, the earth. If you came to see him, you would pass a sculpture of a rising spirit, an old bell, and four carved wooden animals: a bear, an owl, a lion, a turtle.

The house was purposely placed on a power place; when Michael moved there he felt that the San Andreas Fault holds tension and harnesses power to heal. He believes the fault literally cracks conventional space. Legends of the Miwok people who lived nearby told that no one lived in this place because it was too powerful. People came there only to be healed. Only the healer could live there. Michael brings people he works with to the hearth of his own home. Inside is bamboo, sacred artwork, roses from the rose garden his wife, Nancy, made before her death, feathers, medicine wheels. The wind blows through the shaman's hut; many doors open and bring the outside in. People come to him and tell him stories. He is the listener. With guided imagery and energy work, using a feather, he heals. In his sacred space he is a shaman healer, not an ordinary physician. "This is my home. It is a way of moving around a personal space that is sacred. Inside this creative soaring space, patients slip through the membrane deeper into the realm of a sacred healing space. They feel at home, but in a different home. They know and believe they are inside the visionary space of a healer."

SACRED SPACE

Sacred space is visionary space; it is nonordinary reality. It is space that is full of meaning, pregnant with power. Sacred space has similar characteristics, so the practitioners who create it usually do similar things. The sacred space itself calls to them and tells them what to do. The ritual is dictated from the space, not the space from the ritual.

Sacred space is connected to your own story of what is meaningful. If you were to walk on a road and find a rock, it might be an impediment and be moved away with annoyance. If you were a Buddhist and were told it was the rock Buddha sat on for his vision, it would be the most sacred space—a place of pilgrimage, full of meaning. When you create sacred space, you find the objects that are most meaningful to you, you bring in light and air, you clean and arrange with love. You make the place a place of love, light, healing energy, and beauty. Each person's sacred space is his or her own, deeply tied to personal meaning; the common threads are beauty, cleanliness, meaningful objects, and careful arrangement. Altars are common to most sacred space. They vary by tradition and content. Sacred space is made alive by prayer and visioning. It is empty without the spirit that infuses it with healing power.

Sacred space involves gratitude and blessings. It starts with giving thanks. It usually has an altar, a place to put sacred personal objects. It often involves fire, a candle, sage, incense. It can have water present in a bowl or fountain. It usually involves a prayer to a higher force: God, the Creator, the Great Spirit. It involves offerings, different for each culture. It often acknowledges the four directions and sometimes it adds two more: up for heaven and down for underworld. It often involves helpers or guides who are invited to come, God, the Great Spirit, angels, spirit guides, spirit animals, nature forces. It is expectant in nature.

In sacred space you feel your own desire in oneness with the earth. The environment is comfortable, you and the person you are working with are comfortable. This creates confidence for both. In sacred space you intentionally change the environment to be one of harmony, peace, and beauty. You focus with light, color, and sound. You care about detail, you put work into it. You do this with intention. What goes in is what comes out. Sacred space in the physical world is clean fresh air, clean water, beauty. It reflects the inner sacred space within you. It is a place of spiritual listening, allowing God to be present, and trusting in faith.

TRADITIONAL SACRED SPACES

All cultures had sacred spaces that were pregnant with meaning for the people. In Greece there were the ancient temples of Delphi and Delos. There were many springs and purification sites. In Europe and Asia there were temples and monasteries, mounds and ancient churches. All are places of pilgrimage for healing. The site itself helped balance body, mind, and spirit. Many sacred sites were medicine wheels—Stonehenge, Avebury, Big Horn. Many involve water. The ancient Roman baths in Bath, England; springs in Tinos, Greece; the waters at

Lourdes in France—all used pure, crystal-clear, flowing water for healing. When you visit an ancient sacred site you feel its power. There is an expectation of spiritual presence at a sacred site.

PRAYER CREATES SACRED SPACE

All shamans, no matter what tradition they are trained in, use prayer to bring in the spiritual forces they work with. We have been told over and over again by all shamans we interviewed that no shamanic work could be undertaken without prayer to a higher power. It is not possible to be in sacred space without giving thanks in an intentional prayer. Shamanic healing includes all spiritualities, all religions; prayer and going inward to the meditative state can be done by anyone. Shamans give thanks, ask for guidance, and pray. This is our prayer for our work to be healing to ourselves, others, and the earth.

A prayer for shamanic work

As we start on our shamanic work, let us pray to those who help us on the way. Let us call for them to come to us, and be with us in this sacred work we are about to do. *(Creator, God, Jesus, Buddha, Our Teachers, She Who Gardens Us from Above, Great Spirit, come to us and help us with this work.)* We thank you for the earth, for our families, and for us as the shaman that we are. We thank you for our spirits and our ability to make this prayer. We thank you for our ability to see visions, and to speak to spirit animals and ancient ones. We thank you for our eyes, our ears, our hands, our bodies, and our lives.

Creator, help us tell the truth and help us understand these words. Help us to know who we are, to receive Her gifts, to act in Her behalf. Give us the power to live with right action. Help us receive the gifts from Her that we wish for, that will balance our lives and the earth. Help us receive the answers to our questions that will inform us on our path and make us true. Help us see, hear, and act with purity of vision and purity of action, to heal ourselves, others, and the earth. Let your healing power come through us to heal.

Now pause a moment and be silent. Center yourself. Thank the powers that you believe in; look at who you are and what you are to do. Pray for you to become the shaman healer who you are. Pray for what you need, ask for your questions to be answered. Go in peace. Now we can begin our sacred work together.

The ancient ones who trained the shaman say to you, "Do this work with commitment, acceptance, and honor. We bless you in your sacred work. We do."

HOW TO CREATE SACRED SPACE WITHIN YOUR BODY

Sacred space is created from within and from without. To create sacred space from within, you create it within your own body. Your body is your temple to enter sacred space. The first step in creating sacred space in your body is to become aware of your breathing. Begin by taking slow breaths in and out, then convert your breathing to abdominal breathing, centered in your belly, grounded in your body. Allow your body to fill up with light as you breathe; this helps you to open. You open up the top of your head and allow an axis to form that connects you with the earth. The axis goes through you from the earth, up through your body, up out of your head to the sky. It connects Mother Earth to Father Sky through the sacred body. It allows the energy of the earth to go through your head; it allows a flow though you from the universal energy of creation and healing.

As you move, as you breathe, God's love, light, and healing energy come through you. In shamanic healing, you do not use your own energy; the universal energy moves through you. It does it itself; something comes through, and you tap into the eternal wellspring of healing energy that flows through all things. This creates spaciousness inside of you and you expand. The sacred space allows you to find a reverence in the detail of the present moment, a reverence in looking at the person you are working with. As you look at the way his mouth is, the way his lips are, the way his eyes move, as you see the little details about his body, you absorb the unique and special beauty of that person.

As you slow down your breathing, you allow yourself a moment to be in a sacred place. You do that with intent. Every moment in sacred space exists in a transient flash. Time slows down; in that moment relish it, observe it, be awake to it. Be awake to how you move though space and time. Be directed, focused, and soft. You can do it; you are moving fluidly. In movement you can be fast—with practice you can move and have grace. In grace, you see yourself and the other illuminated. You actually create a sacred altar within yourself and the other. You do this with prayer. You allow your activities to be your offering. What you offer is your life.

Exercise: Create sacred space in your body

Make yourself comfortable. You can be sitting or lying down. Loosen tight clothing, uncross your legs and arms. Close your eyes. Let your breathing slow down. Take several deep breaths. Let your abdomen rise as you breathe in and fall as you let your deep breath out. As you breathe in and out you will become more and more relaxed. You may feel feelings of tingling, buzzing, or relaxation; if you do, let those feelings increase. You may feel heaviness or lightness; you may feel your boundaries loosening and your edges softening.

Now as you breathe in, let your body expand. As you breathe out, let it stay in the larger state. As you expand, you can feel energy and see light between your cells. The new space created in the expansion fills with God's energy and light with each breath. Feel the energy, the buzzing, the vibration, the movement increase with each breath.

If it is comfortable for you, let your boundaries diffuse a little bit. Let them become softer, more open. Let the love and light of the earth around you come into you, let your love and light go outward the those around you, and heal.

PREPARATION OF THE PHYSICAL SPACE

Preparation of sacred space may involve ritual or it may be influenced by certain traditions and teachers you have worked with. Or it may be totally new, innovative, and your own style. This can involve setting up the room that is specially intended for prayer, mediation, yoga, or healing work. It has many possibilities: building an altar, burning sage, placing objects of reverence with care, making a medicine wheel. These details will be different for every person, but the rituals of preparation with intent are essential. They are important because they change the energy prior to the work that needs to be done. Preparation, purification, and cleansing—that is the first step. This is similar to a surgeon washing hands or a ritual bath. It could be lighting incense in a room for a massage therapist, or playing music for a woman at home with a sick child.

Healers start preparing for the healing work before the person comes to them. Some begin the morning of a treatment, others even the night before. In their sleep they allow their dream time to become a part of their work. They tune in on what they need, where they are, what their function is in helping the other. They read, meditate, center themselves, visualize the process or procedure. They ask, "What can I add, how can I help?" The answer comes as visual and kinesthetic information. It is larger than their body. They prepare the space, move objects around the room to create balance. They may sage the room or clean the room. Some collect wild sage, flowers, dry grasses, herbs. Each act in the preparation, the gathering of materials, is done as a priest would do it. They pray or visualize healing as they collect the sage or altar pieces. They sense who is around. Are there spirits, animals, helpers? They say things; they ask for cleansing, for healing, for help moving energy. They make use of the whole environment for healing with intent and making sacred space.

Tyson, a body worker, described his way of preparing sacred space before a session:

The most important act begins before I enter the patient's room. I see the doorway as a threshold. Before I enter, for a moment I pause. I thank the person for coming to me and having faith in me to be able to heal them. I thank the person for opening himself or herself up to me so healing can take place. I express gratitude in my own mind for being able to do this work and gratitude for the person for coming. I clear my own mind of thoughts and concerns. I go into a place where I am only with what is happening in the next moment and what the person came for. I create a space where I am open like a bowl that will receive anything the person says and be with him or her. I do not think a certain way. It is a protective time in the room with him or her, only the person and me and the spirit.

As a shamanic healing takes place:

I raise my energy level as I am going in the door. I am aware of being within light and tuning into it. It is a conscious decision, then everything gets brighter. The healing light I see comes from the center of everything; we are a part of it. As I walk in, I am conscious of the change of energy in that room. When I think about the person I work with, I say a prayer and hold space. I ask myself, What does the person need? What can I do? And then I feel it. I tune into people, I make myself available. They take what they need. I consciously make myself available so they can get it. That is who I am all the time. I don't think; they flash in. It is intuitive, it comes in, then I know they need something. I feel, I am light, I am giving them light. I am giving someone that essence, letting them take that essence from the universe through me as a shamanic healer.

Exercise: Saging or cedaring a space

Native Americans give offerings to the Creator and use medicines like sage and cedar to prepare sacred space. Plants like sage and cedar are believed to come from the Creator to help humans heal. The plant is used to embody the power the Creator placed in the physical world. Each culture has a story of how the sacred medicines came to them from the Creator.

When the medicine is used in a ceremony, the sacred gift is reenacted and embodied.

To begin a healing, or to begin any ritual or ceremony, burn aromatic sage or cedar bundles to cleanse the site and remove impurities. Sage has traditionally been used by Native American peoples for centuries. You can sage the room or even the entire house if you wish. We burn the sage in an abalone shell or special sage burner. Light the sage and push its rising smoke to the edges of the room with a feather or with your hand. Wave the sage in a clockwise spiral and the house will be different afterward. You can use many varieties of sage, cedar, and herbs to create sacred space. As you sage, say prayers, picture cleansing, thank the Creator—whatever comes to you. What you feel in your heart as you sage is what is important. Do it with intention, with prayer, with peace.

THE SWEAT LODGE

Profound sacred space is often created by ritual. In Native American ceremony it often involves a fire, an altar, and for many tribes a sweat lodge. The sweat is done according to the teachings of the particular group. There is no single right way to do a sweat, but similarities exist between the teachings. There is always a sacred fire made by a fire keeper. The fire keeper prays to the directions, asks for guidance, asks for fire spirit to come and help in the healing. There is an altar that holds sacred objects for the group. There is a lodge built according to instructions and with pure heart. It is a small dome built of branches tied together. It is covered with canvas and blankets in contemporary times; it used to be covered with skins. The doorway is usually to the east and when it is, the fire, altar, and lodge are in a sacred axis pointing from east to west. In many sweats, no one can cross the axis line once the sweat has started; all people come from the northeast side into the sweat. The fire is built and the rocks, referred to as the stone people, are put into it in a prescribed way. The people are saged to purify them, they give an offering, they enter the sweat in a clockwise manner saying the prayer "*Mitakuye oyasin,*" or "All my relations," and go into the lodge to sit. The stones are picked up with a shovel by the fire keeper and handed to a person who uses antlers to place them in the fire pit in the center of the lodge. The water is handed into the lodge in a bowl. Then the door flap is closed. The water is ladled on the red-hot stones. Steam comes up. It becomes very hot. Medicinal herbs are put on the stones for medicine, prayers are spoken.

Each sweat leader directs the sweat in a particular manner for the reason it is done. It can be healing for an individual, for the community, for nature. It can prepare the community for a large ritual like a bear dance or bear healing. The participants sing and pray according to tradition. There are usually four cycles for the four directions. The door is opened between each cycle and more stone people are brought in. The sweat cools a little and then the door is closed. Each cycle gets hotter and hotter. For some sweat leaders, the heat is about suffering and purification. Some sweats are done for the four directions, some with prayers for a meaning in each direction. Some sweats start each cycle with thanks, then a prayer, then songs, then prayers. Others are different. The form of the sweat is up to the leader and the specific tradition.

The sweat is purifying, cleansing, and deeply healing. The spirits come and speak, and people can go deep into a trance. The trance makes the healing visions accessible to the person. The sweat leader keeps the energy up for healing and takes care of the people. There are many traditions for each detail of the sweat—it takes years to learn. It must be done with pure spirit and an open heart.

Guided imagery: Creating sacred space

Make yourself comfortable. You can be sitting or lying down. Loosen tight clothing, uncross your legs and arms. Close your eyes. Let your breathing slow down. Take several deep breaths. Let your abdomen rise as you breathe in and fall as you let your deep breath out. As you breathe in and out you will become more and more relaxed. You may feel feelings of tingling, buzzing, or relaxation; if you do, let those feelings increase. You may feel heaviness or lightness; you may feel your boundaries loosening and your edges softening.

Now let yourself relax. Let your feet relax, let your legs relax. Let the feelings of relaxation spread upward to your thighs and pelvis. Let your pelvis open and relax. Now let your abdomen relax; let your belly expand, do not hold it in anymore. Now let your chest relax, let your heartbeat and breathing take place by themselves. Let your arms relax, your hands relax. Now let your neck relax, your head, your face. Let your eyes relax; see a horizon and blackness for a moment. Let these feelings of relaxation spread throughout your body. Let your relaxation deepen. If you wish, you can count your breaths and let your relaxation deepen with each breath.

In your mind's eye, picture a place where you can do healing work. It can be a room in your house, a place outdoors, an office, a hospital room, an operating room—it can be anywhere you have been or imagine you could be to heal. Before you enter that space, pause a moment and say a prayer. Ask the power you believe in to help you make the space you heal in sacred space. Give thanks to the Creator for this healing moment, for your ability to heal and help someone. Now in your mind's eye see the space becoming sacred. Call in helpers— guides, spirit animals, teachers—to be with you in this healing work. Call in the Creator to be with you in this healing work. Now imagine that the space you are in is filling with light; imagine that the space is becoming brighter and brighter. Imagine that angels and helpers have come to the person you are working with and help them.

Now you can picture the space changing physically. You can imagine an altar, sacred art, sage, Native American art, Christian art, Buddhist art—whatever votives would make the space sacred for your own personal healing work. See what comes to you as you invite the space to change physically and become sacred. You can picture candles, incense, a medicine wheel, paintings or sculpture, things you have found, objects from nature, bones, feathers, rocks. Now you can imagine the place is painted and decorated in a sacred way; you can even imagine its shape changing to round, the lighting changing, the sounds changing. Allow yourself to design your own sacred healing space, even through it may not happen in the outer world immediately. This space is in your virtual reality, in your mind, and it is in resonance with the outer world. Now enter the space and begin your healing.

When you are ready, return to the room where you are doing the exercise. First move your feet and then move your hands. Move them around and experience the feeling of the movement. Press your feet down onto the floor, feel the grounding, feel the pressure on the bottom of your feet, feel the solidity of the earth. Feel your backside on the chair; feel your weight pressing downward. Now open your eyes. Look around you. Stand up and stretch. Move your body; feel it move. You are back; you can carry the experience of the exercise outward to your life. You will feel stronger and be able to see deeper. You will be in a healing state. Each time you do the exercise you will be more relaxed and be able to go deeper and be more deeply healed.

3

HEAL YOURSELF

THE SACRED BODY

Mary tells us how she uses her own ceremony to heal herself:

> When I do my morning ritual, I light fires, as in a Hindu temple. I go into a place in my mind to evoke the goddess with my voice. I do my yoga movements and it creates waves that raise the healing energy. It creates tingling and numbing. I intentionally let go of rage, despair, troubles, anxiety, and fears. It is a letting go. I then evoke power, wisdom, clarity, centering. One of the most powerful practices is to be grounded in my body. I then do shamanic work from a spiritual body that is clear.

The first part of shamanic training is healing yourself. This often requires that you deal with fear and blockages, with resistance and personal issues. The first visit for a person coming to Michael for shamanic training is not so different from the first visit of a cancer patient coming to Michael to be healed. Both visits are about the darkness in a person's lived experience. The shamanic way of being is a lived experience, not a theory. It goes right to a person's early childhood visions. The person coming to be trained is up against their most personal issues of self-confidence, trust, power, and purpose. Being a shaman is about being who you are. That is challenging for anyone. Our teaching is to let it happen, go out in nature, listen to animals and let them take the suffering away. That is the first vision quest.

Healing yourself is an ongoing process that deepens and enriches your ability to be connected and powerful as a visionary healer with other people. Healing yourself has to do with allowing your essence to be expressed and seen. To do this, focus on what your spirit desires so you can move beyond your personality and become larger than your own present life. When you are clear about your own emotional issues, you can function in relationship with another from a place where you have transcended yourself and your own needs. In a relationship of healing with someone else, you need to be able to transcend in a moment, to drop judgments, opinions, and personal idiosyncrasies. To be a healer is not about who you are in your personality and what you want; it is about who the person you are working with is and what he or she needs. To use your energy in communion with that person's energy so he or she can heal requires healing yourself.

The way you heal is to experience your own transcendence. You experience your own ability to have altered states and become large at any given moment. With the experience of transcendence in an altered state, you become larger than yourself. You have a nirvanalike spiritual connection with God. It is like being a bodhisattva; it is like being enlightened. You function from a higher way of being with God, of God, interconnected with God. Everything you do is in communion with God. Everything you do is with total compassion, total love, the wisdom of the bodhisattva. Heal yourself inside your training of whatever kind of healer you are. Shamanic training is a first and foremost a path of healing yourself.

USING THE SPIRIT BODY HEALING PROCESS TO HEAL

The Spirit Body Healing process is an eight-step method taken from research at the University of Florida, Gainesville, on how creativity heals. In our previous book, *Spirit Body Heal-*

ing, we delineate the method in detail. Here we will summarize its main points.

Step 1: Go into your own pain and darkness

Facing your own pain and darkness, bringing it out, is crucial to healing. Inherent in facing pain in Spirit Body Healing is bringing it out and doing something creative with it. Tell the story of your pain to someone you love and trust. When you tell the story, make it vivid with imagery so the other person can feel it and see out of your eyes. Make art with the story of your darkness. Journalize, paint, draw, or write a poem that captures the essence of how dark it was or is for you. Each of us has our own pain and darkness; looking at yours is the first step to healing yourself.

Step 2: Go elsewhere

Facing pain and darkness takes you elsewhere. As you bring the pain out, you go where you bring it to. It is as if concentration and looking at who you are brings you to a place where you are the witness and you can see. Elsewhere is the discovery of freedom from the thoughts that are difficult to control. Going elsewhere leads to many possibilities. Go elsewhere to nature. Nature gives you gifts that are beyond imagination. Go for walks alone or with friends. Go elsewhere in dreams and daydreams. Going elsewhere into nature is shamanic training. The earth and the animals heal you and teach you to heal others.

Step 3: Find your own turning point

The next step is to do something to make the spiritual experience deeper. Do an activity to help you hear the voice of your spirit speaking. When you do activities to illuminate your spirit, you will became open and will be spoken to. The activity could be a vision quest, a walk, gardening, prayer, making art. Doing shamanic healing is an activity to see who you are. The more you do, the more the experience will become real and grow. If you are making art, the series of pieces will allow you to see deeply and change. These voices or images that you will see will be from your own life. You will get ideas, visions, dreams, jokes, or voices. The turning point is the place of deepening.

Start a turning point activity now. Start going on walks, gardening, using humor, helping others, healing. Make a Web site, write joke books, go on a vision quest, do ritual, save a river, walk in nature. Start using prayer, going on retreats, making art, doing meditation, having body work done, using guided imagery, practicing yoga or Qigong, going on a trip. Make art: No matter what else you do, write, draw, paint, sculpt, journalize, dance, play, and listen to music.

Step 4: Slip through the veil

After you allow yourself to be taken into the pain and you merge with the place of darkness, there is a meeting with your own spirit. Let the spirit move from the deepest part within you into your outer life. Within the darkness, let yourself be taken; in becoming your pain, realize that you are not alone. There is something greater than you that is loving life within your own spirit. There is a part of your own spirit that you become connected to.

Slip through the veil. Suddenly, you are within your own body in a place of spaciousness. You can have a dream of God, see Buddha, feel an experience of enlightenment. Slip through the veil into the place of opening. Move out of pain and see your spirit dance. Slip through the veil and glimpse angels, saints, grandparents, or ancestors. You will find yourself suddenly curled up in God's hands, held and comforted. Slip through the veil into the place of the shift of consciousness that is the place of deep healing. The shift starts with going inward, but here it happens for real. When you slip through the veil you go into a deeper state than when you went elsewhere. Go to the place where the spiritual experience lives and is accessible. Go to the other side where the spirit is visible. This is the place of shamanic visions, the place of seeing and listening. Across the veil is the place of shamanic healing.

Step 5: Know the truth and trust the process

In this step, you will know that you are in a flow of a process that is beyond you, and is taking you. You will know the truth of what you are seeing; you will feel the validity of the visions and voices within you. Keep the flow moving; do one act after another quickly. The doorway out of one act is the beginning of the next one. Generate movement quickly. Trust the process—it grows. A process is one step at a time. It is much larger than you are. You cannot imagine what will happen if you do what you love and trust the process. It comes from spirit, from the heart of the living earth. Shamanism is a process that grows. Your trust in the visions you receive and your continued growth is critical. The trust grows as you experience the power of your own visions.

Step 6: Embody your own spirit

Embodiment of the spirit is about merging. Let images of beauty and radiance appear to you. See yourself as strong, beautiful, powerful, or healed. Feel reborn as a brand-new person. Feel enchantment, feel your senses awakened anew. Let yourself feel sounds becoming more intense; feel your whole body and its senses being more sensitive. Feel vitality and recognize it in others. It is described as "the experience of being truly alive." When you are in the world, feel alive in the world. Receive the gift of your own life. Feel a vortex of energy around you that you are part of and merging with. Let yourself see and feel images of light and beauty, feel the enormous feelings of healing. Experience body sensations of energy, buzzing, vibration, calmness, and joy. The sensations feel wonderful. Embodiment in shamanism is merging and seeing out of the eyes of the spirits or animals—seeing out of the eyes of the earth, of the shaman.

Step 7: Feel the healing energy of love and compassion

The Spirit Body Healing method is about feeling compassion for yourself. In Buddhist meditation you go to a place where there is total compassion. You go to a place where you restory your life from compassion and love. Become compassionate for yourself by seeing yourself from a distance, from outside. Stand back and say, "Look at her. She needs." In a moment of witness, of reflection, see what you need to heal. When you see yourself with compassion, you can tend to your body as a sacred body, tend to emotions as natural forces that move through you. You can honor intuitions and insights, be illuminated to find your place in the world. The Spirit Body Healing method is about feeling healing energy. When you feel the energy of the universe flowing through you, you will heal. Shamanism moves healing energy and lets the person you are feel compassion for yourself.

Step 8: Experience transcendence

Experience feelings of oneness, feelings of an immense interconnectedness. Glimpse God or angels; experience the power of the universe or God. Feel yourself in the presence of God and hear the voice of God. Emerge in another dimension, one of great power and beauty. Transcendence is hearing a message from God. You are a vehicle to share love, to communicate love. Experience transformation, see yourself for the first time, discover within yourself a place of ecstasy. Let yourself become filled with power or light.

Invite a vision to come to you. Let your eyes cross; let an abstract shape, like a cloud or a tree stump, that is in natural form trigger a memory of a creative idea from inside you; daydream, meditate. When a vision appears, let yourself see it. Let yourself see beauty, let yourself see spirit. Seeing a vision is a letting go, an acceptance, an honoring, an invitation.

The major goal of shaman healing is for you to experience transcendence. The experience of a peak spiritual event is possible for anyone who wants this to happen. Everything in this book leads up to experiencing transcendence. Going into the darkness, slipping through the veil, feeling energy—all are steps to hear and see visions of pure spirit. Making sacred space, visioning, and moving healing energy are all about transcendence.

USE YOUR BODY AS A VORTEX TO HEALING

Use your body to listen and see, to be in visionary space. This needs to come from clarity within you that is you. If you are in a process that allows negativity to release, you become clear. You need to flow like a river, to see yourself moving. There are three steps to healing yourself. First, create a process that allows you to take notice of negative stuff, of your own dysfunctional patterns. Second, make a commitment to heal yourself with therapy, body work, exercise, fitness, diet change, cleansing. Third, look at your own life and access your personal and individual needs for change and create a process that is intentionally healing for yourself.

STRENGTHEN YOUR BODY

Your body is the focus of this part of shamanic training. An important step in shamanic training is strengthening, purifying, and cleansing your own body. To do this, you need to exercise, eat well, and cleanse. Body cleansing will allow you to access pure essence to do this work. There are many opportunity to create a process of body cleansing. It is an intentional act, and for many it is difficult. It involves participating in a release, purifying, letting go of established habits and patterns that have caused illness.

Cleansing yourself from negativity, anger, and fear works at the physical level in a tangible way. You can do this with a variety of techniques. Use your own life as an experimental laboratory. Use your own experience to expand your repertoire of healing tools. Expose yourself to as many ways of healing as you can and implement portions of methods that interest you, that resonate within you. Your body will open up inner ways of wisdom. Your body will become your teacher.

Choose any process you wish with the intention of purification and cleansing. You will release embedded familiar patterns of being to create a clear spirit body that resides within you to work from. Examine what you eat; you need to eat to feed your body as well as your soul. You will nourish your life force, your essence. What you do allows you to be at your optimal functional level. Examine your rest patterns, sleep patterns, exercise patterns. This is an excellent time to start to exercise and eat well. Shamanic work requires being in shape. To dance all night or to pray on a vision quest takes a body in good basic health and shape.

You are cleansed during major life experiences of suffering. To have deep wisdom, you suffer many life experiences that include illness and pain. The power of shamanic healing comes from time. You give your whole life to this path. If you are a mother with children, you may not be able to function at this level at this time, but you are building a powerful experience to cultivate your own shamanic path.

The traditional Native American vision quest involved a fast of from one to four days, without food and sometimes without water, too. This produced a cleansing that was significant in body and mind. The cleansing also was from suffering and from painful visions. When you are strong you can vision without fear of body pain, discomfort or fear. You can do ritual and ceremony that involves physical endurance. The shaman and the yoga master were both physically strong and in good shape. To dance for four hours in a ritual requires a high level of physical training.

DO BODY WORK

Choose a body work method to ground you. It can be massage, yoga, network chiropractic, Alexander, Feldenkrais, acupuncture, shiatsu—any method that appeals to you. To choose, let your body be your teacher. The way you learn in your body will help you be with another person in his or her body. Your own healing modality stays, but complementing your healing with other healing work is essential. You need to be strong, healed, healthy to heal. You need to go from a place where you are centered and can be effective in other people's lives. You need to clear out your own sickness and unconscious issues. They emerge when you do body work. Do shamanic body work with a shamanic healer. Watch what the healer does as he or she helps you heal. Let your body be a workshop for healing and learning. Every time you go to a healer, you are learning how to cultivate the healer within. Shaman healers use body work as part of healing. They use touch, moving healing energy, massage, and medicines.

Guided imagery to see and heal your issues

Make yourself comfortable. You can be sitting or lying down. Loosen tight clothing, uncross your legs and arms. Close your eyes. Let your breathing slow down. Take several deep breaths. Let your abdomen rise as you breathe in and fall as you let your deep breath out. As you breathe in and out you will become more and more relaxed. You may feel feelings of tingling, buzzing, or relaxation; if you do, let those feelings increase. You may feel heaviness or lightness; you may feel your boundaries loosening and your edges softening.

Now let yourself relax. Let your feet relax, let your legs relax. Let the feelings of relaxation spread upward to your thighs and pelvis. Let your pelvis open and relax. Now let your abdomen relax, let your belly expand, do not hold it in anymore. Now let your chest relax, let your heartbeat and breathing take place by themselves. Let your arms relax, your hands relax. Now let your neck relax, your head, your face. Let your eyes relax; see a horizon and blackness for a moment. Let these feelings of relaxation spread throughout your body. Let your relaxation deepen. If you wish, you can count your breaths and let your relaxation deepen with each breath.

Now you will look at your own issues concerning shamanic practice. Invite yourself do this with compassion and love. Release judgment. Do this as you would do it to someone you love deeply—your child or someone you are working with. Now in your mind's eye picture yourself doing your healing work. Picture it in detail. See your body, the room or place, the other person, what you are doing.

Now surround yourself with love, surround the scene with love. Now, from within this love and light, let any fears emerge. Invite them to come to you as you would invite a child to come. Let them emerge into love, into care, into welcome. What do you see? Let your fear, lack of confidence, doubts, confusion, and depression come. Now look around you. Let scenes from your childhood or from times when you were hurt emerge. See if you can see the roots of your fear, the germ of your lack of confidence. See scenes from your life that could have contributed to the fear.

Now in those scenes, bring in your love light and compassion. Right now, bring in any helpers you have—guides, teachers, God—to support you in the place where you were hurt. Let the light and love surround you in the place where you were hurt. Now see yourself growing stronger there. Right now, go to the scene where you were hurt, and let yourself grow there and increase in power. In that place, be a person of power, a shaman. Take your animals, helpers, guides, teachers with you to be with you in that time of hurt and fear. Now, when you come out into your life, bring the strong person with you and leave the fear behind. Let it drift away. When it returns, it will be smaller and manageable. Each time you do this exercise you will get stronger and more powerful.

When you are ready, return to the room where you are doing the exercise. Grounding is essential. First move your feet and then move your hands. Move them around and experience the feeling of the movement. Press your feet down onto the floor, feel the grounding, feel the pressure on the bottom of your feet, feel the solidity of the earth. Feel your backside on the chair; feel your weight pressing downward. Now open your eyes. Look around you. Stand up and stretch. Move your body; feel it move. You are back; you can carry the experience of the exercise outward to your life. You will feel stronger and be able to see deeper. You will be in a healing state. Each time you do the exercise you will be more relaxed and be able to go deeper and be more deeply healed.

KUNDALINI FOR SHAMANIC POWER

Kundalini is the ancient term for the serpent energy that sleeps at the base of the spine and rises to heal. Traditional shamanic healing used energy experienced as body heat to burn away illness. As the heat rose, the energy rose. The fires within burned the suffering away. It accentuated it and then allowed the person to break through negativity and burn through the fire and darkness and get to the other side.

Kundalini yoga is an ancient Indian tradition of moving healing energy for spiritual enlightenment. Kundalini is the coiled energy of the goddess that lies asleep at the base of the spine. She is coiled tightly like a serpent, latent until awakened. When she rises, she completes the polarization of the body through the union of opposites. Kundalini is the female aspect located at the bottom of the spine, while Siva is the male aspect located at the top of the head.

The goal of kundalini yoga is to awaken and raise the kundalini until she is united with Siva. In this union, this world of dualities dissolves and enlightenment is reached. Mircea Eliade wrote about kundalini yoga in his book *Yoga, Immortality, and Freedom*. He noted that the ascent of kundalini is characterized by intense heat. As the kundalini energy moves up through the body, she heats each area she moves through and leaves the areas behind her cold. "The awakening of the kundalini arouses an intense heat, and its progress through the chakras is manifested by the lower part of the body becoming as inert and cold as a corpse, while the part through which the kundalini passes is burning hot." It is a powerful ascent into a place of higher consciousness. The rising intensity of energy burns into the deeper realms of our unconscious.

There are many methods used to raise kundalini, but Eliade

emphasizes the efficacy of arresting the breath (*kumbhaka*) and sexual practices. The simultaneous stopping of breath, thought, and semen awakens the kundalini from her cosmic slumber.

Vijali is an earth artist and a shaman healer. She was raised by a schizophrenic mother who often abandoned her in foster homes. As a little girl, she was so shy she could not even talk. As a teenager, she followed her own heart and went into a Vedanta monastery, then became an artist. This is her description of her kundalini experience:

> I am conscious of an intense feeling in my chest that radiates heat, becomes hotter and hotter. This internal fire becomes a blazing red hot sun slowly rising up my spine. Each breath becomes more difficult. I try to hold on; it is myself that is slipping away. My sense of self is no longer confined to my body but is expanding and expanding. My point of observation is now from a great distance—I look through a billion eyes in every direction. I must stop this force that has taken hold of me, but I can't—I am propelled by some energy beyond my control. Even though my body is frozen, I am unable to move and cannot speak; I am excruciatingly conscious. To pass out right now would be a great relief. Every detail about myself and the studio is painfully clear. My fear increases with the heat of the energy rising in my body. I panic and think I am going insane! I am dying! The flaming sun-force moves up through my neck and into the center of my head. I see blinding light. My perception changes—everything becomes radiant light: my body, the pillows, the floor I sit on, the space itself. The table, cushions, hanging plants, and my body breathe, quiver, melt into one boiling pulsating ocean of light. The world I am accustomed to dissolves into open space. This blasting force moves through the crown of my head out into the space above my body. The world continues in a new frequency . . . pulsing, merging, uniting.

The uncoiling of the unconscious is essential to becoming a shaman. It is a rebirth, a new way of living and being in the world. Since ancient times, it has been symbolized as a serpent rising up the spine. This is a literal interpretation of a physical reality as it actually happens. The sleeping snake at the bottom of spine rises when called in a crisis. In a crisis, for example, there might be a shift. With the shift, the snake uncoils, it comes up, the person is filled with energy, and his or her life is totally changed. When the serpent reaches the head, the person awakens spiritually, the third eye opens, there is a subtle shift. The person goes from being asleep, deadened, to being awake and on fire and in the present. It is like awakening from sleep, from a dream, to a new and vivid and enhanced reality where you see completely differently. When the third eye opens, you can focus and see things in a totally new way, and you will be directed to walk ahead into the mystery.

Kundalini rising can be frightening and disruptive because it fractures the conventional and contrived reality that has been created in our lives. Letting energy loose and manifesting a new reality will definitely change your life, and the old reality will be changed. A person who is attached to the past will need to adapt to the present. Power surges of energy need to be directed. The energy flows up into you and takes your life. If it is not used, emotions are freed and illness can result. So the energy needs to be directed. When you are a shaman, your energy goes toward that work. The direction of this powerful awakening is profoundly expressed in creative work.

Guided imagery to raise kundalini

In your mind's eye, imagine there is a coiled-up snake sleeping at the bottom of your spine. Look into the center of your own life force and imagine there is a tree that grows up through the center of your spine. Now imagine the snake twining up the tree. Under the tree there is a spring that flows up from the earth. Within this tree there is a force like a lightning rod that has the capacity to take the energy from above and connect it to the energy from below. You become that powerful force and become electrified. This life force acts like a vortex of energy, a coil of energy. As it uncoils, you tap into your healing power. You can access this energy and work with it as a healer. The first step is healing yourself, cleansing yourself. In this process you will become clear enough to activate the force. There are many things you can do to balance the energy so you become healthy and stronger and it does not overpower you. Energy work on your body cleanses you and heals you. You can do meditation or body work, practice yoga, do meditation exercises, change your diet. It is important when you create the experience that when the sleeping snake at the base of spine uncoils and slithers up the right lightning rod, your core center intertwines and becomes the snake. You see out of the eyes of snake, and when you do you will see the aspects of your own death and shed the old skin, the old baggage, and be reborn from the old self to the new self. The new self is the healer who lives in the world for others.

4

SHAMANIC LOVE

STORY: THE EARTH SPEAKS AS THE CRESCENT MOON

Mary, as medicine woman, tells us this story:

The crescent moon reflected in the river comes to me with a slight shimmer and I am taken. She tells me that it is about being inside desire. Being in the sensations of it, seeing it feeling it.

She says to me: "Go into the crescent moon on the river, go into the reflections, go into the shimmer, the shadows. Watch the shadows on the water, see the bears, the lions. Children can see them. These imaginary playmates are hard for adults to see. Go into the wind. Go into the water. Make love as the wind, make love as the water. That is why making love is the best way to do anything—it is the deepest trance you can take into the sensations of your body. Watch the water drop. Become absorbed and move around things. Sink into the ground, fall like the rain. That is the way it always has been done. Talk to the spirits of the rain, of the wind, of the river. Inside her body you will see things, see what to do. She will always show you the ritual. It starts with making love and then spreads to your whole life."

You need to be there. To see out of the ancient ones' eyes,

you need to put yourself in the places that they looked, to see what they saw. Your body tells you what to do next, because it has the same feeling that they had. You are them, you become them. They made masks of the wind, the moon, the sun. She takes you into her body.

THE *AYAMI* AND THE *ABASSY*

In many cultures, there is a female spirit, an *ayami,* who makes the shaman. This tutelary spirit chooses the shaman and teaches him his work. It is not about gender; the *ayami* can be a man who teaches a woman. The *ayami* gives the shaman helping spirits, his *syven.*

This is an old Eskimo story of a woman spirit coming to an ordinary man to make him into a shaman.

> Once I was asleep. A woman came to me in my dreams. She was very beautiful. She said, "I am the *ayami* of your ancestors' shamans. I taught them shamanism, and now I will teach you. I have no husband; you will be my husband. I will give you healing spirits." She lives in the hut by herself and comes to me in the night. She comes as a beautiful woman, an old woman, a tiger—she comes in many forms. I mount her and fly to villages. I see much. She gave me three spirit animals that come in my dreams. If they don't come, she makes them come to me. When I heal, the *ayami* and spirits come. They penetrate me like vapor. She speaks through my mouth. She does everything. When I eat, it is she that is eating.

Eliade also speaks of the importance of sexual energy in shamanism. Because the legends of a woman making a shaman are so basic, many researchers believe that a primary element in shamanism is sexual spiritual energy. There are many stories of *abassy,* spirits of young women or young men, who enter shamans of the opposite sex and put them to sleep. The *abassy* make love to them. Yakut Eskimo stories tell that once a shaman sleeps with an *abassy,* the man or woman can only sleep with an *abassy,* not with a human anymore. The shaman's female tutelary spirit is his celestial wife. She helps in instructions and ecstatic experience; she sleeps with him in heaven and on earth. She is also the Great Mother of the Animals, the Mother of the Sea, Sedna the sea goddess, the female spirit.

FALLING INTO THE BODY OF THE BELOVED

Being a shaman healer is seeing your life work as falling into the body of your beloved. What is it that makes you get up in morning? What is it that you have dedicated your life to? What is your beloved and what is the work you are doing? Falling in love is falling into the essence of your beloved. In the discovery of what you are passionate about, you look into the full face of your beloved. You see the mystery; something deep within you fills with the desire to get into the place of knowledge and be immersed in it. With the awe of discovery you venture into the unknown and go into places you have never been before.

When you are in synchrony with what you are doing, you fall into a spiral of your beloved where you connect with other people. A new reality manifests, a reality greater than your own. This shifts reality. You become a shape changer, you create realities, you move from your own personal space to the world, a world greater than your own world. The catalyst for change becomes powerful. Aesthetic beauty yearns toward what you desire.

This experience happens in a second. In one second, time expands to become huge and spacious. In one moment, in an encounter with another person, between the seconds, you can expand, dance, shift realities, by intention. It is only a moment. Intention takes only a second; it has to do with you being very large.

Love creates the moment in your busy life where you take time to go to a place within your practice where the spiritual dimension is illuminated. The self in that place is spiritual presence. You can resonate with it. It only takes a moment. There are windows in any action, and you can access this; you can be with other people in a way that invites something more.

It comes from a place of dropping into an altered state. You relax, you get large; your body opens, vibrates, is within resonance; you see and hear into visionary space; your intuition awakens. Being in love does that. You slow down time and expand space, you are acute and still. It is like taking a photo, a snapshot into life. It is a pause in the sequential movement of time. You can feel it in your body. Do not let these momentary opportunities pass you by.

When you feel love, act—it starts a process of a feedback loop. It is being revealed. It can be taught; everyone is capable of teaching it. You can tap into the velocity of energy in your life. Love creates powerful changing acts in our culture. Do it for good and for healing. The mysteries of life unravel themselves. For love we go into the mystery that is the future, the mystery in front of us. You discover the mystery in your beloved. This empowers people to change reality; then they do. You ask, "How did I find you?" This creates the catalyst to give birth to new stars.

SPIRIT WANTS TO BE LOVED AND TO LOVE

Spirit wants to see love and acknowledge love. Spirit wants to be seen, be loved, and be acknowledged. Spirit yearns for union with God and people it loves. Spirit wants to be present and comfortable and at peace. Spirit needs you to restory yourself to acknowledge spirit and the movement of spirit inside of yourself. In dreams and in astral travel we see spirit. In altered states we have experiences of being with loved ones, as in visitations. These are possibilities of people's experiences the healer needs to know.

When you are in love you are filled with healing energy and compassion. You find it within yourself and the person you are working with. It comes from the source of love, from the divine. It comes within patience, silence, in your openness to listen. As a shaman in love, you become sensitive to auras, the luminous light that surrounds each living being. You see colors enhanced, crisper and clearer, as if they are in better focus and more intense. You can cultivate this way of seeing with your eyes—seeing color, lines, detail, and hearing silence. It is a way of being in an intimate level, a caring encounter that is something more. It comes from a feeling within rest and calmness, being totally present with the intention to heal. The fullness of the person, of what you are doing in the moment, is the essence.

Within this transcendence, you see the spirit of another. It is a gift of angels from God to you, to see another's spirit. This nourishes you, heals you, feeds your own soul. It helps you retrieve your own soul in your own practice. It makes your work meaningful, makes clear the sacred path you are on as a healer, brings your practice back to the spiritual. It is waking up your intuitive powers as a healer and increasing your ability to see spirits. You become turned on, awake. In one moment you can see sacred blasts of energy. It is practice as embodied prayer.

Something calls to you in the landscape around you. You have the experience of moving toward something, like moving toward a flaming tree. You feel as if compared to this, all others trees are ordinary—you see this one as a tree on fire. You go toward the fire; that is the ecstatic journey. In a moment the world changes; there is a tremendous sizzle, a crack, energy is released. It moves you. You are drawn to it on your own. It feels as if your feet are not even on the ground. This is the call to your destiny. Life changes when it merges with fire. Go into the flaming tree, which burns away old things. You shed your old skin and move into your own fire. Then your own fire becomes ignited. Your own life force becomes ignited and it ignites you. You find your beloved, your work, your deepest relationship, in such a place. When you connect to your own fire, the light within you is ignited. This brings you love, warmth, fire, compassion, and surrender.

Guided imagery for falling into your beloved
Make yourself comfortable. You can be sitting or lying down. Loosen tight clothing, uncross your legs and arms. Close your eyes. Let your breathing slow down. Take several deep breaths.

Let your abdomen rise as you breathe in and fall as you let your deep breath out. As you breathe in and out you will become more and more relaxed. You may feel feelings of tingling, buzzing, or relaxation; if you do, let those feelings increase. You may feel heaviness or lightness; you may feel your boundaries loosening and your edges softening.

Now let yourself relax. Let your feet relax, let your legs relax. Let the feelings of relaxation spread upward to your thighs and pelvis. Let your pelvis open and relax. Now let your abdomen relax, let your belly expand, do not hold it in anymore. Now let your chest relax, let your heartbeat and breathing take place by themselves. Let your arms relax, your hands relax. Now let your neck relax, your head, your face. Let your eyes relax; see a horizon and blackness for a moment. Let these feelings of relaxation spread throughout your body. Let your relaxation deepen. If you wish, you can count your breaths and let your relaxation deepen with each breath.

Now in your mind's eye see yourself deeply in love. You can be in love with your work, with a project, with a person. You can be in love with God, Jesus, a teacher, or a guru. Let whatever you are in love with come to you now. See what you are in love with in detail, see the shape, form, smell, texture, feeling. Be there with your beloved now. Feel your own body. How do you feel when you are with your beloved? Let yourself go into those feelings deeply now. Give yourself time to be with your beloved in visionary space.

Now go into the body of your beloved. Move into what you love, merge with it, swirl around inside it, be there. Now in your mind's eye, let yourself go. Surrender to your beloved. Give yourself to what you love as a sacred offering. Say to yourself, "I give this offering to my beloved." The offering can be time, an object, a thought, or even your life. If you are in love with God or a celestial figure, you can rise to Him or Her on a beam of light from your heart.

In surrender, open your heart and flow into your beloved. Let yourself go completely into the process that you are involved in. If your beloved is your work, surrender in an intentional act to it. If it is a person, teacher, or God, surrender to your beloved completely in sacred offering.

When you are ready, return to the room where you are doing the exercise. First move your feet and then move your hands. Move them around and experience the feeling of the movement. Press your feet down onto the floor, feel the grounding, feel the pressure on the bottom of your feet, feel the solidity of the earth. Feel your backside on the chair; feel your weight pressing downward. Now open your eyes. Look around you. Stand up and stretch. Move your body; feel it move. You are back; you can carry the experience of the exercise outward to your life. You will feel stronger and be able to see deeper. You will be in a healing state. Each time you do the exercise you will be more relaxed and be able to go deeper and be more deeply healed.

EXPERIENCING SELF-LOVE

A body worker told us:

> Doing this work has to do with being able to experience self-love. It is really important that you love who you are and what you do. Self-love gives me the hands of confidence. No matter how sophisticated my technique is, the major part of healing is being able to bring with me the experience of self-love. I experience self-love fully.
>
> When I walk in the room, I bring this and envelop the person in my own love. He or she becomes embraced in it. Love is the energy that heals.

Self-love is a state of being. It feels gentle and warm; it feels like a flowing and fluid state where you feel your openness. Imagine a beautiful fluid; it feels like a gentle pink light around you that radiates from your body outward, that comes from the very center of who you are and envelops you. When you have powerful self-love you envelop the person you are working with and they feel loved, as though they are within a sphere of love.

You will not be able to channel God's love, the Creator's love, if you are filled with self-hate, confusion, and doubt. When you are able to feel God's love and to give it to the person you are with, you allow the love to flow through you as if you are an open vessel. If you are healing someone and all you think about is a problem, a fear, a confusion, a doubt, the love that could come through you is blocked.

Self-love is also about acceptance. The first step is to accept who you are in the moment as being right for your path. After acceptance is seeing your own beauty. Seeing that you are loved is the easiest way to self-love. Validation of who you are by others is helpful, but the true love must come from within. Obviously this takes work and time; it is the resolution of childhood issues about mothering, fathering, abandonment, and/or abuse. It is confidence in yourself, in the method of healing you use, in the process, but most of all in the source of the healing.

FORGIVE YOURSELF

In self-forgiveness you find the ability to create sacred space and clarity. In self-forgiveness you give yourself room to be truly human. To be human is the framework from which you practice shamanic medicine. Forgiveness is active, not just loving. A grudge is the opposite of forgiveness and breeds endless strife. Acting out of love can heal your life. Compassion leads to self-healing. Seeing yourself with compassion heals the pain and darkness in your own life.

To forgive yourself, it is necessary to look at what you have done and not done. First forgive yourself for not being the person you want to be. Forgive yourself for your apathy, your lack of concern, your turning away from people in need. Forgive yourself for doing business and not making enough time for family and loved ones. Forgive yourself for not feeding the hungry and working for peace.

An adversary tells us what we need to forgive. If you look out of the eyes of your adversary, you see yourself in a different way. If you are consumed by hate and carrying a grudge, self-love is blocked. Honor your own body, honor your beauty, honor your ability to love. A way to self-love is being around others who love and have self-love.

Guided imagery to experience self-love

Make yourself comfortable. You can be sitting or lying down. Loosen tight clothing, uncross your legs and arms. Close your eyes. Let your breathing slow down. Take several deep breaths. Let your abdomen rise as you breathe in and fall as you let your deep breath out. As you breathe in and out you will become more and more relaxed. You may feel feelings of tingling, buzzing, or relaxation; if you do, let those feelings increase. You may feel heaviness or lightness; you may feel your boundaries loosening and your edges softening.

Now let yourself relax. Let your feet relax, let your legs relax. Let the feelings of relaxation spread upward to your thighs and pelvis. Let your pelvis open and relax. Now let your abdomen relax, let your belly expand, do not hold it in anymore. Now let your chest relax, let your heartbeat and breathing take place by themselves. Let your arms relax, your hands relax. Now let your neck relax, your head, your face. Let your eyes relax; see a horizon and blackness for a moment. Let these feelings of relaxation spread throughout your body. Let your relaxation deepen. If you wish, you can count your breaths and let your relaxation deepen with each breath.

In your mind's eye, picture yourself. Then go to a place in the center of your body. It can be your belly, your heart, your spine. In your center is a light. It is a flickering, soft light, like a candle flame. Now in your imagination, see this light glowing brighter and brighter. See the sphere of light expand. Feel this light expand around your fingers, feel it expand down to your toes. Feel this soft, warm, translucent, golden light surround you and embrace you. Now in your imagination, feel the light expanding around your body, see the glowing light growing, see your entire body glowing. See the light move beyond the boundaries of your skin, see it expand around you from one foot to two feet away. Feel the light swirling gently, moving. It has a beauty, an ebb and flow. It is soft. It has a rhythm that pulsates like your heart.

Now imagine that this light becomes transformed into the energy of love. Your body is immersed in the glow of this living light and you are being healed, cleansed. You are being loved. The source of this love is a pulsation from within you. Now imagine that this light, this love, and this energy are you. In your mind's eye, expand this light to about four feet around you. Now it is interfaced, merged, with the light from others around you. You are interconnected and your love blends with those around you. The light brightens as it interfaces; it becomes magnified in its intensity and flows out of your body. It is spinning, soft, beautiful. Your love is spinning around your own body and the other. You are in a relationship. It is easy. You are in grace and total peace. All you have to do is breathe.

When you are ready, return to the room where you are doing the exercise. First move your feet and then move your hands. Move them around and experience the feeling of the movement. Press your feet down onto the floor, feel the grounding, feel the pressure on the bottom of your feet, feel the solidity of the earth. Feel your backside on the chair; feel your weight pressing downward. Now open your eyes. Look around you. Stand up and stretch. Move your body; feel it move. You are back; you can carry the experience of the exercise outward to your life. You will feel stronger and be able to see deeper. You will be in a healing state. Each time you do the exercise you will be more relaxed and be able to go deeper and be more deeply healed.

Guided imagery to raise compassion
In your mind's eye, picture yourself. Let the love you feel come to you and surround you. Be in the love and compassion you have from the universe. Now imagine you are the most compassionate person you have known, heard of, read about, or imagined. It can be Jesus, the Dalai Lama, Buddha, God. Go up into that person, merge with him or her, and be in the person's heart. Let the love you are merge with the love the other

person is, and be one. Now look at the yourself with pure compassion. Look at yourself through the eyes of the compassionate one. Look at yourself through the eyes of your deepest love and compassion.

GOD'S LOVE AND HEALING

The process of the making of a shaman is about cultivating power within the body. It is about cultivating self-love and developing the capacity in every person to manifest the divine. It is about cultivating a visionary life and seeing the visions that inform life and give power.

All the shamanic healers we interviewed told us that the basis of all their shamanic power is the Creator. The divine flows through you from the source. Love flows from within, from the God within you. We are channels for energy to move from within us to the other. This happens when we tap into the source within us. We have our own sun within us. Within us is a radiant sun, within us are the seasons. The sun gives birth to life. Within us is the source of love. Our universe is the tool and the vehicle for healing. Our lived experience of life is our universe. The source of that universe is our love. The source is the tool from which we heal. The Creator is the power behind each shaman. The framework of shamanism has always relied on the Creator God as the source of healing power.

Shamans know they are the source of love; they simply mirror God's love. They see themselves in everyone. Within their universe, all exists. Shamans are as large as the universe. They have the ability to embrace the universe and the people they are working with, in love. They are the oracle for the others to change and heal. They are the guardians of the threshold to change. They act to catalyze change; they do the last little bit to create the shift. The power in the shamanic shift is tremendous. The concept of the shaman as large—the foundation of the shaman as the experience of love and of the universe within divine—is critical to shamanism. Shamans know that God's love flows through them and that they are divine.

Exercise: Feel God's love come to you

In the ancient Tibetan Buddhist Powa practice, a root guru is the spiritual teacher or figure you love or admire most. Picture your root guru above you. It can be Jesus, God, the Creator, Nature, a mountain—anything. Now imagine a beam of light coming from the guru to your heart. Go up the beam of light and merge with the guru as one.

HUMILITY

The shaman learns from the practice of humility as a teacher. Native Americans have the expression "We are only pitiful two-leggeds." It is a reminder to them about being humble. We have personalities. We are only human and there is beauty in that humanness. It takes time to completely open, to open your eyes, to open your heart. Return to work with great humility. Understand more deeply how to pause, deeply connect, and see into another person's world.

> The Creator, the spirits, and the patient take credit for healing, the shaman is only with them. Native Americans won't say they are shamans or that they do the healing. We need to be humble or the spirits leave us. The patient does 70 percent of the work to get well, the Creator does 20 percent, I do 10 percent, which is barely worth mentioning. Most of what the patient does to get well is make the firm decision to *be* well. This is where the medicine person steps in, by taking seriously a vision of the sick person as healthy when no one else can or does. He or she creates with the patient a shared story of a mutual spiritual quest.

5

SACRED COMMITMENT
AND MINDFULNESS

Sacred commitment is a process. It underlines shamanic healing and anything else you do in life that is spiritual. The
process relies on mindfulness. Because the shaman takes
images from the visionary mind and makes them real in the
outer world, the shaman needs to work with mind in a very
clear way. The process of mindfulness starts with presence,
moves to intent, and then focuses your energy to be able to
heal with commitment.

Michael's teacher, Rolling Thunder, taught him that the
clarity of intent is crucial. He taught Michael to help patients
be clear about their intent for healing, to be clear about their
view of their illness, and, most important, to be clear about
their prayer of what they want from the healing. Then the
healer focuses on the process and, with full commitment, acts.
When Rolling Thunder healed, he first told patients to state
their illness and then to ask out loud for what they wanted, to
state the intent clearly in words. Rolling Thunder was fully
present for them and he had full intent to heal them. Next he
focused on the healing and removed illness from the person.
The whole process together was one of sacred commitment to
heal. This pure commitment was the center of Rolling Thunder's life as a shaman.

THE MOUNTAIN STORY

Imagine you are on the top of a mountain and the whole world is spread out below you in a 360-degree panorama. The wind blows in your face, the sun warms your forehead. You are going to go on a hike and you are going to start to walk to a specific destination. You take out your map, you orient yourself to the directions, and you look at the distant landmarks. You see from the map that there is a mountain to the south, a river to the west. You find your goal is a compass setting that leads to a distant meadow. You read the compass and only then do you start to walk. The first steps go in one direction—they are in one compass bearing. You look far into the distance to your goal and you realize that if you deviated one degree from your path now, when you are just starting out, you will be off by many miles later. The message of this story is that when you want to start a project, to make a change in your life, you need an intent, an organized plan. The closer you can be to knowing what you want and how to head toward it, the closer you will be to your goal when you arrive. Of course, you can change directions as you walk to make your path more precise. We may not know our goal fully, so we can change our path with feedback from our intuition as we feel where we are going. But intent makes the walk easier and makes our path more direct.

By taking practice seriously and moving though space and time with the intentionality to heal, you make every movement an embodied prayer. Change your view of your healing work to being your embodied prayer and you will see the illumination of your own spirit.

BE FULLY PRESENT

Shaman healers walk into a room and leave their personality and concerns at the door. They come in with their skills and are fully present in sacred space with the person that they are working with in the moment. Mary tells us this story of sacred presence:

A woman body worker walked into the room to do my treatment. She was a huge, beautiful woman; she looked like an Amazon warrior. She had large hands and was muscular. She did not speak. When she came in, I could feel her energy fill the whole, she was that large. Her energy was clear—I could see right through it. She embraced me energetically; my body was her focus. Her concentration was pristine yet fluid. I did not feel stuff around her. Her hands went in, touched, stroked. She felt my muscles. She was sensitive; she touched each muscle fiber. My tension went away; my breath merged with hers as she moved energy. Her presence was clear, pure, full, large. The moment she entered the room she became *the healer*. As she worked, she moved her hands and vibrated and became someone out of the ordinary. I could feel that her hands had energy coming out of them; I knew she could move energy. Her preparation was intense in one moment.

I went to another body worker who was not present. She would tell me about her kids, and she seemed annoyed, irritated. She left to answer a phone call. I could see she was thinking her own thoughts about her own concerns. I felt it as her mind chatter—she would mumble to herself. When she touched me I got scared; she seemed not connected to her hands, not centered on the present. Then I got distracted. I couldn't surrender and be open because she was detached. I didn't trust her. She was not present.

The first step to being committed to shamanic healing is being totally present, listening and watching. It is about being able to be mindful in the moment. We asked one body worker what he did that was so healing. He had a huge practice, with a three-month waiting list if you wanted to work with him. He said, "It's being with them." We asked him what he meant by being with them. He said, "It is presence. The experience of presence is most like what it felt like when I lived in the Everglades. In that beautiful swamp, I become full, open, even sensitive in a hypersensitive way. I could sense the wind in the slight movement of each blade of grass. My patient's body is like the earth. I learn about it like I learned about being in the Everglades. When I work, there is a hypersensitive feeling about all things."

The most important thing about being present is having had the opportunity to deal with your own issues. Before being with someone, you need to be able to be with yourself. You need to have dealt with your own childhood traumas and insecurities. You need to have your own issues resolved. Otherwise you bring your own issues into the healing and they get in the way of being there for other the person. Resolving your own issues is really important to be totally open and clear to someone else.

BE PRESENT

Presence comes from looking into a person's eyes and seeing who that person is. Then look beyond the eyes, look deep into the soul. People can't disregard your looking into their eyes. They see you are seeing them. You stay with them as long as there is a commitment to be there. You need to be fully present, not distracted. You need to be empty to be with the other.

To be totally present you need to shift from the state of ordinary talking in your mind. Pause, slow down, stop your mind chatter. Put aside your daily concerns; let go of thinking about who picks up your child, how much it will cost to repair your car. Put aside the things that are distracting your attention. Breathe, pause. Deliberately do not focus on these kind of concerns; deal with them later. Be present with yourself first.

Slow down your breathing, be conscious of your body, feel yourself in the moment. Look around you. Notice shapes, shadows, textures. Feel the temperature. Allow your eyes to become open to colors. Feel how saturated and differentiated the colors are. Face the individual; look at his or her face, look into the eyes. Look at the person as if this is what your life is about in that moment. You are in a moment of communion with that person and only that person. Part of being with the person is seeing him or her. See the color of the hair, see the eyes, see the skin. Watch the gestures. Allow yourself to be empty, allow the person to fill you up. Use your senses of smell, touch, sight. See the face unveiling to you. The unveiling of the person's face has to do with the unveiling of your face. You become accessible to yourself at the moment you allow the other to come forward. Presence means the other person is inside your own consciousness. Silence allows you to be filled with the person's life, voice, thoughts.

Experience the fullness of your own energy. You are empty of your own self-absorbed concerns. Fill from within; radiate your energy and attention outward. You cultivate this kind of fullness through practice. Fullness is felt presence. It comes through your eyes, your voice, your touch. Wait for the other to fill you with his or her beauty, then move forward from what he or she has given you.

Use your breath. Breath fills you up. Expand on the fullness of your breath. Come from a place of pure light. Energy has a resonance; it reverberates with soft, subtle vibrations. Feel it. It is the life force—qi, prana. This energy is what you use for healing. This energy is what you feel in your own life when you vibrate with the life force. One way to be present is to connect yourself, to be in alignment with the force of your own life.

You feel this as an inner light, as your life force energy. You are the conduit for spirit energy, for God's energy to move through you. When you heal with spirit energy you are not depleted. The energy enhances you; it connects you to the life force. When you get in alignment with the energy from above, you are revitalized as you heal others. Tap into this energy in alignment with God's light on earth, with forces that are positive. You are in a sublime balance of energy. The energy moves through you so you are not depleted.

Face-to-face, look into the other person's eyes, slip though the veil. Even though you are busy in your life, you will find clarity and then presence. Inside presence is sincerity, mutual concern for the other. Others have a concern for themselves; as a healer, you share it.

OBSTACLES TO PRESENCE

There are obstacles to presence, situations that make presence difficult. The first obstacle is being stuck in your problems, remembering family issues, financial concerns, everyday problems. Then there are triggers about your own beliefs, about being right or wrong. When the person you are working with says something you disagree with and you react with judgment, you are then not present for him or her. When something triggers your paranoid thoughts or your old prejudices, you cannot be present. Another obstacle is holding back from telling the person what you think, holding back from being your authentic self. Seeing differences rather than feeling oneness is an obstacle. Concentrating on feelings of you and the other, feeling separation, keeps you from being present. A major obstacle is not fully believing in what you are doing. When you are constantly feeling doubt about your process, you are certainly not present. If the person is suffering and not physically attractive, you can be distracted by his or her appearance. Finally, thinking, "He is sick, and I am not" separates you and blocks presence.

Exercise: Become present

There are many useful activities and exercises to become present. Practice being present with people wherever you are. Watch people. Hold people in your psychic space. Observe; don't be distracted from them as humans. Make meaningful conversation. Become fully absorbed in who they are and care about them. Find specific similarities and recognize yourself in another. Go deeper and mirror, see the reflection of your own soul in the other. Let the experience of being present become deep and full; being present is a meditation. To deepen your ability to become present, employ the Zen of seeing. Slow your eyes down. Feel and caress textures in the objects you are seeing, in the person's face. See colors, shadows, and light. Hear sounds, tones, silence, and pulsations. Go deeply into touch, understanding that this movement allows others to be embraced. Say to yourself, "I embrace you with my attention."

LEAVE THE PLACE OF FEAR

Sometimes we operate from a place of fear. Television, radio, and newspapers immerse us in fear; they keep our adrenaline up with fear-producing images. To counter this, cultivate being alone, being outside with nature, for fifteen minutes each day. Feel the earth below your feet, feel the air above you. Go outside, look for animals. Listen to the shrill call of the hawk, the soft song of the robin, the "whoo, whoo, whoo" of the owl. Listen to what they tell you. Listen to the howl of the coyotes. Listen to your inner voices when you hear them. Leave the place of fear and go into the place of love, and connect with the sensual nature of the earth.

CULTIVATE THE EXPERIENCE OF SILENCE

The learning and preparation of the shaman healer happens in a place of solitude. Rest, meditation, being alone, and being in nature are the time when visions and inner voices come to you. The teachings and the state of mind to do this work come within stillness, not from going up and down in activity. Stability and silence promote mindfulness and being present. Tools of being come with states of no activity—no reading, no television, no Internet. Activity and input can squelch the inner voices. The traditional vision quest is done by yourself, away from all distractions of modern life.

Guided imagery to be present

Make yourself comfortable. You can be sitting or lying down. Loosen tight clothing, uncross your legs and arms. Close your eyes. Let your breathing slow down. Take several deep breaths. Let your abdomen rise as you breathe in and fall as you let your deep breath out. As you breathe in and out you will become more and more relaxed. You may feel feelings of tingling, buzzing, or relaxation; if you do, let those feelings increase. You may feel heaviness or lightness; you may feel your boundaries loosening and your edges softening.

Now let yourself relax. Let your feet relax, let your legs relax. Let the feelings of relaxation spread upward to your thighs and pelvis. Let your pelvis open and relax. Now let your abdomen relax, let your belly expand, do not hold it in anymore. Now let your chest relax, let your heartbeat and breathing take place by themselves. Let your arms relax, your hands relax. Now let your neck relax, your head, your face. Let your eyes relax; see a horizon and blackness for a moment. Let these feelings of relaxation spread throughout your body. Let your relaxation deepen. If you wish, you can count your breaths and let your relaxation deepen with each breath.

Now in your mind's eye let yourself be in a scene you enjoy being in. It can be working with a person to heal, being in nature, being with something you love, being with your family, exercising—anything. Picture the scene in detail, feel it, see it, hear it, smell it, touch it. Let the intensity of the scene fill you and take you. Now as you are there, simply be there. Be aware of your thoughts, and when they roam bring them back gently to the place you are in. Say to yourself over and over again, "Be where I am, be present there, only there."

Now look very closely at exact detail. Look at the details as if they are your reason for living. Pay attention to them as if they could jump at you and eat you; be alert. Pay attention to them so you see when anything moves, changes shape or color. Look as if you are looking for the slightest movement or change to come. Go deeper now and look for feelings in you that are triggered by what you see—memories, images, visions. Then come back and look again. It is as if you are on a river. Your mind wanders, but the river calls you back. Be on the river, that is where you are. You can't see anything here if you are not here. In the scene you are picturing be on it, in it, see it; you can't see anything there if you are somewhere else.

When you are ready, return to the room where you are doing the exercise. First move your feet and then move your hands. Move them around and experience the feeling of the movement. Press your feet down onto the floor, feel the grounding, feel the pressure on the bottom of your feet, feel the solidity of the earth. Feel your backside on the chair; feel your weight pressing downward. Now open your eyes. Look around you. Stand up and stretch. Move your body; feel it move. You are back; you can carry the experience of the exercise outward to your life. You will feel stronger and be able to see deeper. You will be in a healing state. Each time you do the exercise you will be more relaxed and be able to go deeper and be more deeply healed.

CLEAR INTENTION

Your intention comes from a process you cultivate over years. When you have clear intention, your training, education, and learning become finely tuned. Your intentions take your mastery and activate your own skills. First the person presents himself or herself to you; then comes your intention to heal the person. In the event, what acts on the moment is all the preparation, the process you have been through. The point of contact is then instrumental; in that moment you are focused on one specific outcome.

Intention allows for openness, sincerity, and compassion. Intention is integral in all steps of healing. There is intention to create sacred space, intention to vision, intention to change reality, intention to move healing energy. There is intention to do each thing, to see and understand. Intention is the undercurrent of all you do in the process of living.

Intention is amplified by practice. What are your skills? Expand the possibility of your skills, go further, expand the parameters you are comfortable with. Look for new experiences and deeper understandings and embody them in your own work. Within intent, you grow.

Your skills are a vessel. They anchor your whole life process with the individual you work with. The image of intent sparks the engine to do the work. Intent is the fire within pushing you forward to your goal. What fuels your own fire, your own passion? You harness the fire within you to drive your own intention to be a powerful healer. If your intention is to be powerful, your power will grow. If your intention is to be compassionate, you will fill with compassion. Intent starts your momentum; inside intention is your momentum. Intent is volition pushing you forward to your target or goal.

As a healer, your intent is also based on who you see yourself as. If you have faith in the possibility of healing, if you believe in the paradigm you heal with, your intent grows. If you believe that you're the one who can do it—or, if it is you who is ill, you believe you're the one who can survive—intent grows. Have faith and confidence in the process and believe in the power to heal. Your intention is to empower the person you are working with to believe in the healing.

To increase your intent, list your goals clearly. Then list your skills and own them. If you are good at touch, say to yourself, "I am good at touch." Own who you are. Constantly be in the process of learning and yearning for more; lean forward to who you are becoming and what you are learning. You are not only who you are now, you are actually who you are becoming; your most healing act is taking your power from the future in pure creativity. Next, join your mastery with your creativity. Reach to the stars, to the furthest thing you can do. Make the intention be the master. Inside intent, always, have compassion and have clarity. To amplify your intent, involve your belief system—whatever story you heal within defines your specific intention. Belief is meaningfulness. If you believe spirit heals and you can channel spirit, that is the core of your intent. Finally, define your intention clearly, speak it aloud, and write it down.

There are also obstacles to intention. Overstimulation makes you confused. Being distracted by not being clear about what you have to do prevents intent; all you think about is confusion. Floating without defining what you are doing does not help. Thinking "Who am I, what am I doing?" makes intent difficult. Overcommitment, rushing, exhaustion—all stop intent. All you think about is being late or the next meeting. A conflict of appointments or interests, being scattered, makes your mind go elsewhere and clouds intent.

It is essential to do one thing a day to manifest your dream on earth. You need to do one very specific action each day to manifest the vision from your dream. It can be a phone call, a conversation. You can study, read, do research. But each day you need to do one thing. Doing one thing moves you into your own vision of what you want to create on earth; it makes the vision larger than you. You go into it, bringing it forth. It is like putting on a play: You start with a huge stage set, then each day you walk onstage and practice, and finally you become a star. You take responsibility, you are responsive, you are responding. Will changes reality.

Guided imagery to increase shamanic intent

Make yourself comfortable. You can be sitting or lying down. Loosen tight clothing, uncross your legs and arms. Close your eyes. Let your breathing slow down. Take several deep breaths. Let your abdomen rise as you breathe in and fall as you let your deep breath out. As you breathe in and out you will become more and more relaxed. You may feel feelings of tingling, buzzing, or relaxation; if you do, let those feelings increase. You may feel heaviness or lightness; you may feel your boundaries loosening and your edges softening.

Now let yourself relax. Let your feet relax, let your legs relax. Let the feelings of relaxation spread upward to your thighs and pelvis. Let your pelvis open and relax. Now let your abdomen relax, let your belly expand, do not hold it in anymore. Now let your chest relax, let your heartbeat and breathing take place by themselves. Let your arms relax, your hands relax. Now let your neck relax, your head, your face. Let your eyes relax; see a horizon and blackness for a moment. Let these feelings of relaxation spread throughout your body. Let your relaxation deepen. If you wish, you can count your breaths and let your relaxation deepen with each breath.

Now in your mind's eye, picture yourself as the healer you are. See yourself, see the place and the person you are working with. See it, hear it, smell it, feel it, touch it. Be there deeply. Now pause a moment and remember who you are, your skills, your abilities, the time you have spent preparing to be in the place you are now. Now concentrate on your intent to heal. Focus it, sharpen it. Like holding a bow and aiming at a target, set your goal as a healer and aim it precisely at the target. Clarify what you are doing and now put fire and energy behind this intent. Take a breath and power your intent deeply with all the energy that you have. Go inward to your inner voices and hear them power your intent; hear your guides and teachers power your intent to heal. Picture a fire within you that grows and makes your intent more powerful. In your mind's eye, picture your intent as a line leading from yourself to the other to heal.

Now take the intent and personal power and commit to it. In your mind's eye, say to yourself, "I am committed to being a healer and healing this person. I will give everything I have to be the healer I am." Think of an offering you will give for your intent. Let it come to you. Now give it to the earth in a promise to commit to healing work with full intention, to commit to that healing moment. If you wish, you can ask yourself how committed you are to doing this work. What would you give to do this, to heal that person? If you have worked for years as a healer, the answer is true. You have given, and are giving, a great part of your life to be the healer you are. Now give this with intent, consciously, as a decision: "I will give my fullest intent in this moment to heal and to be the vehicle and facilitator of the healing in the moment."

When you are ready, return to the room where you are doing the exercise. First move your feet and then move your hands. Move them around and experience the feeling of the movement. Press your feet down onto the floor, feel the grounding, feel the pressure on the bottom of your feet, feel the solidity of the earth. Feel your backside on the chair; feel your weight pressing downward. Now open your eyes. Look around you. Stand up and stretch. Move your body; feel it move. You are back; you can carry the experience of the exercise outward to your life. You will feel stronger and be able to see deeper. You will be in a healing state. Each time you do the exercise you will be more relaxed and be able to go deeper and be more deeply healed.

FOCUS HELPS YOU SEE DEEPLY

Intent that is aimed at a specific goal is focus. Concentration allows you to be aware of yourself and others. Focus opens clarity, makes your vision directive. It is concentration illuminated so it can be seen. When you focus a camera, it allows you to see details. Focus is a way of seeing and looking deeper so details reveal themselves to you. When you focus, you scan an image and then illuminate details. You take time, pause, then take more time to look and see deeply.

Focus allows you to cultivate your mystical skills. Inside your own body is your visionary space. Your own visionary images appear to you when you focus inside. Then your visionary space becomes open to someone else's. Inside you have your own visionary realm and dimension. It is deeper than thoughts, emotions—it is the dimension of imagery space. Our body in spirit space is a faceted body like a diamond. Physical reality is a surface inside with fractured light, dimension, and brilliance. That is what it looks like to look into a person's inner world. Each is a choice within. Allow one of these glimmers within you to reflect and become illuminated. From your own facet within you, you reflect back to the other person.

First, create sacred space about you as a shaman healer reclaiming ancient knowledge. Let the place in which you work become a shrine and temple. When you are in sacred space, you are focused. Have reverence for your work. Create the sacred work of healing. Deal with consciousness as energy, spirit and matter as one. Go into the dimension of healing at a distance, healing with your consciousness. Use the transformation within yourself from the ordinary to the extraordinary. Focus on deliberate care for the other, turning toward another human being as a creative act. Respond to the human as he or she unfolds; give special attention and look at the human as precious. Allow love to form. Return to the present moment every moment. Using the acuity of the senses helps to focus. Seeing the world as magical in any moment is a focusing tool. Seeing shapes and colors as more sensual and vivid gives an experience of being within richness. Seeing light with a beautiful clarity is focusing. Seeing like a blind person, seeing for the first time, seeing in a flood of endorphins—like after making love, or after meditation or exercise—is pure enhanced focus.

Guided imagery to focus

Make yourself comfortable. You can be sitting or lying down. Loosen tight clothing, uncross your legs and arms. Close your eyes. Let your breathing slow down. Take several deep breaths. Let your abdomen rise as you breathe in and fall as you let your deep breath out. As you breathe in and out you will become more and more relaxed. You may feel feelings of tingling, buzzing, or relaxation; if you do, let those feelings increase. You may feel heaviness or lightness; you may feel your boundaries loosening and your edges softening.

Now let yourself relax. Let your feet relax, let your legs relax. Let the feelings of relaxation spread upward to your thighs and pelvis. Let your pelvis open and relax. Now let your abdomen relax, let your belly expand, do not hold it in anymore. Now let your chest relax, let your heartbeat and breathing take place by themselves. Let your arms relax, your hands relax. Now let your neck relax, your head, your face. Let your eyes relax; see a horizon and blackness for a moment. Let these feelings of relaxation spread throughout your body. Let your relaxation deepen. If you wish, you can count your breaths and let your relaxation deepen with each breath.

In your mind's eye, look at yourself as a healer, as you have many times before. See yourself, the place, the person you are working with. Now look at the person more deeply. Focus on the face as if you were pointing a camera at him or her. Focus on the eyes as you focus the camera. Let them come into sharp focus. Now zoom in and see the color of the eyes. See the skin, feel it, touch it your mind's eye. Feel the hair, see the light on the hair, see the shadow and the light, the flashing of color, the intensity of the color. Now let yourself move out; look at the person from a distance, focus on the person from afar. See how unbelievably beautiful he or she is.

Now in your mind's eye, let your focus blur. See the person from an angle, from a sideways glance. See in a new and deeper way. See how the person looked at his or her most beautiful moment. See the person when he or she was a baby, a teenager, a young person, an adult, an old person, at the moment of death. See the person as an animal, as spirit, as God. Let these visions come to you; invite them to come. Do not force them, just invite them and let them be in your consciousness. Watch them as you would watch a movie. Watch them with love, compassion, and light. As you watch, as you focus, send your love to the person. As you look deeply in his or her eyes, send love out of your eyes to the other, send support, guidance, power.

When you are ready, return to the room where you are doing the exercise. First move your feet and then move your hands. Move them around and experience the feeling of the movement. Press your feet down onto the floor, feel the grounding, feel the pressure on the bottom of your feet, feel the solidity of the earth. Feel your backside on the chair; feel your weight pressing downward. Now open your eyes. Look around you. Stand up and stretch. Move your body; feel it move. You are back; you can carry the experience of the exercise outward to your life. You will feel stronger and be able to see deeper. You will be in a healing state. Each time you do the exercise you will be more relaxed and be able to go deeper and be more deeply healed.

COMMITMENT GIVES YOU POWER

How committed are you to your life? How committed are you to your life as a shaman? What is really important to you? What would you give up for the major parts of your life? What would you do to save a river threatened by a tire-burning cement plant? What would you do to save your life itself, your money, your child, your time, your work, your comfort? How committed are you to your relationship, your family, your job, the place where you live? What if you were to die in the next months, weeks, days, hours, minutes, seconds—how would you spend your last moments on earth in this lifetime? How far would you go to get what you are committed to? How much would you give up and how much would you do? If you are not fully committed, it will not happen.

When you make a commitment to walk a road, that commitment reminds you how to act. People may not want you to take that path; it may be unpopular. You constantly deal with choice, and each choice leads you to enlightenment. Each choice is another step to being in union with your higher self. A choice that honors your body, honors your life, honors suffering, honors pain is your choice for life. When you make a commitment to be a shamanic healer, you make a commitment to act in a certain way in each situation that comes to you. You consistently act to heal with spirit. The Hopi say that there will come a time when those who are enlightened stand apart from those who are not. There will be a time when those who are enlightened act differently from those who are not.

In commitment we can create the future. Right now is different from any other time. There is an awareness factor; we are awake. Today, people who understand their commitment to healing have an opportunity to direct people. People are paying attention, looking at their lives, examining what is important and not. We all have a part in sharing what we know so others can see it, hear it. Having knowledge is your opportunity to share what you know. If you were the enlightened one, if He or

She was no one else but you, and you were asked to give what you have to share in this important moment, what would you say? What would you tell us as the enlightened one?

STORY: ALL THE WAY WITH POSTAGE

The famous Sufi teacher Gurdjieff told this story about commitment. Once there was a lover. He loved his woman more than anyone could imagine. He loved her from morning until night, from the time he woke until he went to sleep. One day he decided to buy her a gift. Because he loved her so much, he wanted it to be the most wonderful gift he could afford. So he went to a jeweler and found an exquisite diamond. He asked how much it was. It was almost all he had in his life, but he would buy it for her to embody his great love. When he purchased it, the jeweler told him it would be another five kopecks for postage. The lover wondered if that was too much now. He thought about what to do. The extra money pushed it over— now it was too much.

Gurdjieff says without the postage the gift would not be sent. As he says, to fulfill the commitment, "You need to go all the way with postage." How committed are you to any action? Will you go the last step to make it happen, or give up because of an excuse, no matter how valid? The postage is the last thing that stops you, the event that really defines how committed you are. It is also the event that determines whether it happens and your life changes. Commitment is a challenge to you to be who you are without excuses.

To make a commitment, start with a prayer. Make the Creator part of it. Get help from the spirits, ancestors, and God in being successful in the commitment. It is not trivial; it is serious. Suffering and fear makes the commitment come to you powerfully. When you want to commit with your whole life, you cannot help it. You make the commitment to the Creator. It is a personal promise. It is not to other people, it is to yourself. You ask the Creator for help, you ask spirit for help, you have other people pray for you. It is a powerful urge and goal to make the commitment.

Finally you believe the commitment will heal and change the world. You are powerful, your actions contribute to changing the world. Your action matters. Your prayers make the sun rise. The shamans were always earth people who healed the earth. The shaman's commitment was to heal himself, others, and the earth.

Exercise: Make the commitment

First, decide on what you are committed to. Write it down, state it out loud. Next, make a prayer and ritual to solidify your commitment in the world. Say, "Creator, thank you for this day. Help me become a shaman healer. I am committed to this path. I will give my life as an offering for this path. This is who I am." Then repeat the commitment to yourself often. Say it to others. Reinforce it with ritual and ceremony often. Be with others who have similar commitments. Finally, act to strengthen the commitment daily. If you are saving a river, write a letter a day, make a Web site, call a person who can make change, pray, act, to change the world.

PART TWO

SEE VISIONS

6

VISIONS OF THE SHAMAN

STORY: THE FLYING HORSE

Mary tells us this story:

> I was in between being awake and being asleep. In my visionary
> space, I was so light, I could just jump up on the horse. I
> remember feeling the horse flying. I seemed to fly forever. Day
> turned into night, night turned into day. I saw the starry sky
> whirling above me. I was flying far above the cloud line. I flew
> across the whole country and finally I was there. I reached the
> cave on the side of a mountain. It was an ancient kiva carved
> from the stone. It was built into the stone cliff. I flew right into
> the cavern on my horse. I got off the horse and looked around.
> It was ethereal. I saw tribal people in the cave. There was a
> shaman there. He was wearing an open bearskin. I went inside
> him. I blew into his forehead, his chest opened, my spirit flew
> in. I found I could see out of his eyes. Then I moved into his
> entire body—I was completely inside of him. When I would
> move my hands, his hands would move. I found it was a way of
> moving healing energy throughout his body. Then I put my
> hands out through him toward other people. He moved his

hands and healed them with a light like fire that came from them. The people watched from around the fire. I could see them watching. I knew they could not see me—I was invisible to them—but the shaman knew I was there. My energy was large, and the light within the shaman and myself tripled in strength. The power of the light from within became directed and forceful, cleansing, purifying, and opening each person we worked on. The shaman worked in communion in the realm of spiritual light and power.

Michael tells this story:

I was driving to work at dawn. The frost on the grass along the side of the road shone white in the first light. In the midst of this beauty, I was worried and depressed. After my stay as a physician on the Hopi Indian reservation, I decided to change my life. Standard medicine with drugs and surgery was not enjoyable for me after seeing shamanic healing, so I took several years off from medicine and became an artist. I loved my new life. I woke at dawn and took pictures on the desolate beaches. I hung exhibitions of my work in galleries. I taught photography. On this dawn, I wondered if I had made the right choice in starting to practice allopathic medicine again. I had taken a job at Marin County Public Health Clinic doing general medicine, well-baby care, and treatment of venereal disease. I was running low on funds, and working as a physician again paid me more than I earned as an art photographer. I was building my house and needed the money for construction. The work was not perfect, but it had seemed right, so I took it. On this cold morning I wondered.

Then, from the silence of this beautiful morning drive, a voice came to me. It said, "I am with you always. I am your spirit guide. I have been with you all your life. I am here to love you and support you. I will be here forever. You can ask me questions. I am a power in the universe that is here to support you and love you." I felt a sense of great peace and calmness come over me. At the same time, I was vibrating with excitement.

I asked him his name. He said Braxius. I asked him if my

new job was right for me. He said, "Yes, it grounds you now, it keeps you in the world of forms, it keeps you with people. You will learn much there. Open your eyes, pay attention, open your mind and let the good things that will happen change you. You have an opportunity here to learn." I asked him if I could talk to him again. He said, "I am here for you always, for the rest of your life." I knew my life had changed forever. I had recently read Carl Jung's autobiography, *Memories, Dreams, Reflections,* where he told of meeting his guides. I had validation for this type of experience from a professional I respected, so I accepted the vision as real and made it a part of my life. Since then, spirit guides are as important to me as anything I do.

All shamanic healers vision. They listen and see into the nonordinary world. After they create sacred space, the next step is to see and hear. Each healer does this differently. Many look for light and darkness; others feel their body sensations and follow their own bodies as they listen and see. Some call in the spirits to be with them when they begin the healing journey. Many use guided imagery exercises, taking the person they are working with back to memories of the past. They bring the person back to childhood, to light, to darkness, taking the person through a tunnel to the past or future. This part of shamanic healing is individual and depends on who the healer is and on his or her tradition and training. The important constant is to listen and see. The information comes from you, from the person you are working with, and from the Creator.

ENTERING THE SPIRIT WORLD
THROUGH VISIONS

As a healer, you already have a visionary life you can cultivate. You have the capacity to visualize, to tap into your inner power of seeing and healing. As a healer, you have a powerful potential to visualize reality for healing. You have a potential to

create your own spiritual life as a healer. This is a doorway you
may not have entered before. You have the capacity to open
that door and expand into the other world, the spirit world.
You already know how to operate in the physical world. This
book gives you the opportunity to merge these two worlds as
you practice healing.

You can cultivate your ability to connect to the earth
though your spiritual life as a healer. This is a shift in the way
you see and live, in the way you exist in the world. It is a shift
in reality. When you see out of the eyes of the animals, of the
earth, you shift from an ordinary way of being to an extraordinary way. You connect to the authentic rhythm of the living
earth. Through visionary experience you call in the spirit animals and the powers of the directions in spirit space. It was a
shift for Michael to listen to an inner voice rather than listen to
the radio. This is completely different.

Any person can change his or her way of being to that of a
spiritual healer who heals his or her whole world. Think about
that. Heal your life, the people you work with, your family, your
community, your ecosystem, the earth. You can shift your reality so that you are in tune with the energies that manifest this
sort of healing. This book can help everyone shift to becoming
a spiritual healer to heal the world.

How do you do make this shift to sacred space to heal? You
have a visionary life that is huge. It opens you to the corridors
of your imagination, to undiscovered frontiers. The new world
is not outside, it is inside. To discover the frontiers of this inner
world, of the world of spiritual healing, you go inward into
nonordinary sacred space.

WORKING WITH GUIDED IMAGERY

Learning to see and hear in visionary space is like peeling the
skin from an onion one layer at a time. Guided imagery is a
step-by-step technique to see and hear. It is a way of seeing
into the inner world, a way to peel away layers of consciousness

to integrate words, thoughts, logic, and images. It brings together the left and right brain. Feeling images is a nonverbal way of communicating. It allows you to move into emotional ways of being, to activate ways of being in the imagistic world. That is what was known as the spirit world. With guided imagery you can invite visions. In your imagination you can see anything, you can allow whatever comes forth to come to you. This is simply the beginning of seeing the imagistic world, the visionary world. *Visionary* means "images"; guided imagery is the method for this process.

Guided imagery is the contemporary term for seeing shamanic visions. Through guided imagery you can experience visions to help you discover information and hold visions to manifest change. Images are thoughts that come in the form of lived experiences. They have the shape of the sensory modalities that feed them. They are part of real time in that they are touch, sound, sight, smell, muscle position, and taste, and are beyond real time in that they can glimpse realms that cannot be felt with senses.

Psychologists divide imagery into several categories. Memory images evoke events that took place in the past. Imagination images are not based on discrete events from the outer world; they are new images that are the result of combining memory events in creative ways, or they come from outside us, from the world of the spirit. Dream images are experienced in sleep. Hypnopompic images are the visions we see as we awaken. Hypnogogic images the images we see while falling asleep. Visions are very vivid images experienced while awake or in a trance. Hallucinations are poorly controllable images experienced while awake. *Vividness* and *controllability* are terms that show us how psychologists describe the imagery experience. When the experience of imagery is intense, when the images are bright, loud, or very attention-getting, they are vivid. When images are unbidden, cannot be gotten rid of, or cannot be changed, they are poorly controllable.

In his book on guided imagery, *Seeing with the Mind's Eye,* Michael divided imagery into two basic types: receptive and programmed. Receptive imagery comes to you; it arrives on the scene, bidden or unbidden, and rests in your mind's eye. Onto a blank screen, you invite images to come. Programmed imagery is different. You choose an image and hold it in your thoughts for a reason. The choice may be deliberate or you may choose an image that came to you from the receptive space. Either way the image affects your world. Onto a blank screen you bring in a specific image that you have seen before—a sacred figure, a shape or color, a symbol.

How do shamanic healers work with imagery? The most common technique involves picturing the inner world: picturing spirits, the person's soul, animals, and events in the spirit world. The healer or person who is ill can also picture the illness, the healing forces, and the healing process in his or her mind's eye. To do this, first the person imagines what the illness looks like, in as much detail as possible. Next, he or she imagines how the body's resources could deal with the visualized illness. This is imagined as a process over time. For example, a person can picture cancer cells, picture them in an area of the body, picture them with a certain color, shape, smell, texture. Then the person can picture killer T cells or white blood cells eating the cancer cells. He or she can picture the body's defenses advancing, multiplying, engulfing the cancer cells whole and wiping them all out. This biological imagery is more effective if it is anatomically accurate and detailed. Researchers have found that this imagery is very specific. For example, if one type of white blood cell is pictured, that type alone is found to rise in blood counts.

Next, people are encouraged to allow metaphorical imagery to form. This is the stage where little men, dogs, or white light blasts, eats, or dissolves blackness, mud, or other little men. Generally this metaphorical imagery takes place spontaneously after the biological imagery. Finally, people can hold a programmed image in mind. They can picture themselves healed, surrounded by white light, surrounded by energy, as a God, as a power animal, or as strong and secure.

The shaman healer can picture a journey, a landscape, a

cave. He or she can see figures of animals appear, and can speak to them. The healer can picture the spirit of the illness, the person's soul, an event from a person's life that was painful or caused illness. The healer can picture spirits, spirit animals. He or she can picture the person's body and look inside. The shaman can picture himself or herself going inside the person's body and working within to heal—removing something, moving energy, changing things around. The healer can sit and listen to the person's story. As the story unfolds, the healer sees into it and around it, sees the events more deeply than the person may have ever seen them. The healer sees spirit guides around the person, angels, light, and energy.

Guided imagery can be used in many ways. The images can be viewed and their balancing nature can be allowed to change a person's consciousness. Images can be used to help a person visualize a healing process or a healed state. The imagery is healing if it relaxes, allows release of tension or fear, puts a person in an altered state, opens the heart, or moves the person and gives him or her energy. Images of spirit guides or angels help a person change attitude to heal. Images of a healing process help free the body's physiology to heal.

HEALING ART

For the healing artist, there are several types of healing art: relaxing and balancing images whose presence is transformative by themselves, biological images that provide a library of images to visualize, and images of pain that are moving and result in a release of emotions. This last type of healing art provides a cathartic release, an emotional discharge. During disease, or in any major life event, stress builds up. The stress can accumulate and gets held in the body and lost inside hidden memories. Making art opens a Pandora's box of deeply held secrets. The art releases the stress like a dramatic explosion. The release causes your body to reachieve balance. All these types of healing art are powerful and effective. They all work by changing consciousness, by freeing energy, by awakening the spirit to resonate in body and mind. This is the technology of healing art, its tools, its machines.

Images made by artists can be so powerful, so filled with energy, that even though they are not personal, they, too, can be transformative. Throughout recorded history, artists have believed that images have power in themselves. Shamanic art was believed to actually have the power to change the physical world. Its shape and color were believed to be powerful in themselves, to be able to transmit and move real energy. Just standing near a piece of healing art was believed to heal. No viewing was necessary, no understanding obligatory—the experience itself brought about molecular change. This concept is difficult for many westerners to grasp scientifically, but it is not that foreign to our lives. People carry good-luck charms, relics, holy objects; people make shrines, sacred spaces, churches, and meditation rooms. Patients surround themselves with power animals, religious talismans, and crystals. The belief in the healing energy of objects is deep even in our rational, logical world.

Many healing artists have told us that the new line they draw on a blank page feels the same to them as creating a new body to heal, making new healthy cells. It is creation, making something out of nothing.

Guided imagery to have visions

The exercises below are an introduction to using guided imagery. You can use the exercises yourself or teach them to people you work with. With all guided imagery, change the exercises as needed to make them your own. We will work with a basic memory image, then an imagination image, then energy, guides, and healing. It is step by step.

Make yourself comfortable. You can be sitting or lying down. Loosen tight clothing, uncross your legs and arms. Close your eyes. Let your breathing slow down. Take several deep breaths. Let your abdomen rise as you breathe in and fall as you let your deep breath out. As you breathe in and out you will become more and more relaxed. You may feel sensations of tingling, buzzing, or relaxation; if you do, let those feelings increase. You may feel heaviness or lightness; you may feel your boundaries loosening and your edges softening.

Now let yourself relax. Let your feet relax, let your legs relax. Let the feelings of relaxation spread upward to your thighs and pelvis. Let your pelvis open and relax. Now let your abdomen relax, let your belly expand, do not hold it in anymore. Now let your chest relax, let your heartbeat and breathing take place by themselves. Let your arms relax, your hands relax. Now let your neck relax, your head, your face. Let your eyes relax; see a horizon and blackness for a moment. Let these feelings of relaxation spread throughout your body. Let your relaxation deepen. If you wish, you can count your breaths and let your relaxation deepen with each breath.

In your mind's eye, picture your bedroom. Look around this familiar place. Look at the walls and ceiling, see the room's shape and size, look at where the windows are, see where the doorway is. Give yourself time and let your inner eye wander slowly around this room you know so well. See the furniture, see your bed, see the chairs, see the dressers. See the paintings on the wall, sculptures, things you love. Now smell its special aroma, feel the bedspread with your hands. Be there, using all your senses to make it real. This is a memory image, an image from your memory of what exists in the outer world.

Now you will change the room and turn the memory image into an imagination image. Let the shape of your room change. Let it get larger, let it change to being round or square, let the ceiling height change. Let your bed rise, floating up as if it were weightless. Let the windows get larger or smaller; put in plants, art, water fountains, the outdoors; let the light change; see stars and the moon through beautiful skylights. Allow your own bedroom to be a mystical place of great beauty and love, a healing garden in your life. Spend time doing this, letting the room become a work of art.

Now bring in healing energy. In your mind's eye, imagine your guides, teachers, helpers above you sending in healing energy. Imagine the stars above and earth below sending healing energy to you. Let it come down from above like a soft rain or like stardust. Let it come up from below like the earth's touch, like dew, like a rising mist. Let this energy from the Creator and from the sky and earth heal you deeply. Let it rise up into you and wash you and energize you and give you peace.

Now you can imagine you are healing another person. In your mind's eye see the healing energy that has come up into you go to a person you are working with. Touch the center of the person's forehead with your finger. Imagine healing light of any color you wish going into the person. See it opening him or her. See the person resonating with color. Let this image change. See how your own healing energy flows from you to the other.

Now look into the person's body. Scan the body in any way that feels natural to you. You can go from the head to the toes, or the other way. Move your eyes fast and see what catches your attention. See what you see. Is there darkness, shadow, light? Do you see or feel energy blocked? Do you see or feel any illness? Let whatever thoughts you have come to you. Do not judge them or be afraid; just note them and move on.

Now, imagine the person telling you about his or her life. As it is told, see the story happening in your mind's eye. See presences around the person, see the place he or she is in, see the situation unfold. If it is painful, bring in healing energy and surround the person in light. Now let the healing energy go from you to the person you are working with. See it flow into you from above or below and then move to a place that you see needs healing in the person. See its color, shape, and texture; see it move from you to the other; see it move in his or her body.

When you are ready, return to the room where you are doing the exercise. First move your feet and then move your hands. Move them around and experience the feeling of the movement. Press your feet down onto the floor, feel the grounding, feel the pressure on the bottom of your feet, feel the solidity of the earth. Feel your backside on the chair; feel your weight pressing downward. Now open your eyes. Look around you. Stand up and stretch. Move your body; feel it move. You are back; you can carry the experience of the exercise outward to your life. You will feel stronger and be able to see deeper. You will be in a healing state. Each time you do any guided imagery exercise you will be more relaxed and be able to go deeper and be more deeply healed.

Exercise: Remember a dream

In this technique, remember a dream in vivid detail. Before you go to bed, tell yourself that you will remember a dream. If you wish, you can write a note to yourself about remembering and put it under your pillow. You can even write a request for a question to be answered in your dream. Have a notebook by your bed so that when you are slightly awake you can write down the dream. Record the dream's colors, textures, space, and time, even if it makes no sense. Record the images seen, the voices heard in your dream journal. Dreams are like messages from the spirit world. Shamans have always used dreams for information. Interpret the dream yourself; the meaning will come to you in your visionary space.

Exercise: Daydream

Daydreaming is a natural way to practice seeing and listening. All of us daydream. We look out of the window, we look at the sun flashing on the leaves, and our mind wanders all over the world. When we did this in the classroom as children, the teacher stopped us, and this put an end to the daydreaming for many of us. Parents stopped our daydreaming, too, thinking it meant we were not paying attention or concentrating. Actually, it is concentrating on the inner world rather than the outer world. A sculptor told us, "When I was daydreaming in school, I was doing the real work of my life. The schoolwork was insignificant compared to my daydreams. Now, as a sculptor, my life is what I learned from those daydreams."

Practice daydreaming again now in your adult life. To do

this, let yourself relax. Allow your mind to wander. Stare out of the window or into space. Let your eyes meander around the edges of the leaves, look at clouds drifting across the sky. Let yourself leave your ordinary way of seeing shapes, color, light, and darkness. Develop your ability to see shapes, lines, and colors as symbols, spirits, and invitations to dream. Look with your physical eyes and see things anew. Let yourself daydream again.

Exercise: Walk through woods

A walk in nature is wonderful practice to see and listen. Take a walk. Let yourself listen to a waterfall. Develop your ability to enter visionary space. As you walk, let yourself go deep. Go into the sounds, the smells, the feelings. How does the wind feel on your face? How does the earth feel under your feet? Let what you see take you into your inner world. Allow emotions to come to the surface. Allow daydreams and visions to appear. Listen to the animals and birds; let them speak to you in inner voices and visions. Ask a question of the waterfall, of an animal you encounter. Thank them for coming. Listen to the thoughts that come to you. The inner voices that come to you when you walk in nature are the voices of the spirit animals, the forces of the earth, the earth herself.

Exercise: Go between worlds

In between worlds is a membrane or veil that vibrates and resonates. The membrane or veil is a shimmering presence that is physical. It has dimension, form, and time associated with it. You can see it, feel it, and move through it like you move through an airlock doorway that keeps air-conditioning in a store. Surrealist painters painted the veil in many well-known pictures. They painted a veil around their lovers and went through it to visit them in visionary space.

To practice moving through a veil, think of somebody you know well. Think of where that person may be. Imagine what he or she is touching and seeing. Experience yourself as a soft wind around the person, as translucent. Imagine where the person is.

See the person, see out of his or her eyes. As you see, feel the membrane, slide through it to the other, then slide back through it to where you are. Go through the transparent membrane to your lover, into the body of your beloved. It takes you through time and space to the other's spirit, to the heart of your love.

BODY MIRRORING

We asked one massage healer, "How do you see?" He answered, "I see with my body." He told us:

> First, I listen to their story. I just let them talk. Then I use my body as a mirror physically. My body mirrors their posture. I do what they are doing in their body—with my body. If they tilt their head, I tilt my head the same way. If they move their hips, I move mine, too. I use my own body to assess how their body is in the world. Then when my body is in the way of being that theirs is, I can feel their pain in my own body. I realize that in a few minutes, that posture produces pain. I use my own body then, and I say, "Is your pain right there?" and I point to it in my body where I hurt. I use my own body as the barometer.

Many people can use their own bodies to feel or sense hurt in another. To do this they teach themselves how to use their bodies as a reference, so when a new sensation comes to them, they realize it is not theirs. This story from an intuitive body worker illustrates using the body as a visioning tool.

> I constantly train my own body to be in alignment. I practice being in harmony, knowing a point of reference in my own body that is in balance, that I can refer to. I am a trainer in my own journey though my body. Then, from this place of balance and harmony, I can use my intuition. For example, one time I was working with someone; I had my hands on her. When my hands went to her head and I touched her forehead, I sensed a

blackness there. I could feel it, it stopped me. I experienced something that had happened. I said, "Something happened on your head that is traumatic, you are hurt here." She said, "In my last marriage, my husband beat me." There was a trauma there, and she released the memories. I felt darkness, a thud; I felt it in me. I could sense trauma there. When there is trauma, I feel it in my body as an unfocused thing. It rises in me like a flash, an event. I suddenly saw she was hit. I asked her, then the flood-gates opened, memories came out. I saw an image of the story in my own visionary space.

A NURSE SEES GOD BEHIND HER PATIENT

The nurse walked into the room to take care of the dying man. He was in the last stages of leukemia and was not expected to live more than a couple of days. She came up to him and he looked right past her. He was very alert, his face was lit up, and he seemed to be radiant. This was a big change, as for days he had been sleepy and not very responsive, but now he was intensely present. He looked directly in her eyes and said, "Do you see him?" He pointed across the room. "Do you see God standing there in the room with us?" He pointed again and bowed reverently toward that place in the room. The young nurse did not know what to do. She looked and did not see anything. But she knew that he saw.

SEE SPIRITS, CREATE CHANGE

First and foremost, the shaman is someone who sees. The shaman sees spirits, both the healing spirits and those that cause illness. Spirits have always been believed to be the cause of illness and also what heals illness. The shaman can take the person he or she is with to the inner world and show the person the healing spirits. In contemporary terms, the shaman sees into the world of the person and sees the person's energy and the events that are around the illness. The shaman sees, feels, hears, smells; all the senses are involved.

The shaman can act in the land of spirits. He or she can affect them, convince them to leave, or bring them to heal. Through ritual, the shaman can bring visions out in the world to heal. Then the person who is ill embodies the visions and incorporates them into their own story of healing. He or she sees the spirits in their own visions when the shaman tells them the story of what he sees in the spirit world. In contemporary terms, the shaman sees the events around an illness and the energy of the patient, and by guided imagery and prayer can make a change in the physical world. The person participates in the change by going into his or her own visionary state and changing body, mind, and spirit.

Finally the shaman can create change in the physical world from the visions. This is shamanic magic. Michael's teacher, the shaman Rolling Thunder, said a shaman could stop a bulldozer that was pushing down ancient trees, or bring rain. The shaman was always the figure in a tribe who would affect fertility, crops, and the hunt. In contemporary terms, the shaman is the environmental activist, the agricultural scientist, and the physician and healer—anyone who changes the world. The shamans would traditionally heal themselves, then heal others and finally heal the earth. For the shaman, the earth means his neighborhood, his people, his environment, and his world. The shaman healer can bring back a species of animal, save a river, start a movement. He is a healer in the broadest sense. In our world today, each of us can become shamanic healers and act locally and globally, too.

LISTEN IN THE OUTER AND INNER WORLDS AT ONCE

Listen to your own inner voice, allowing yourself to open to its meditative quality. Listen to someone's words in the outer world and your own inner voice, too. Let the words and images reverberate within you and create bursts of information that allow you to see more deeply into the conversation. This process is different from thinking your own thoughts at times when you think about your own schedule, what you have forgotten to do, what you need to do. This process is like a thought in communion. It gives you the echoes in the inner world from words in the outer world. In conversation, inside each word is the echo from inside the person's soul. This process allows you to listen and be deeper and let the silent echo reverberate within you.

Michael says:

When I listen, I sniff, I hunt. Rolling Thunder taught me to do that. I am relaxed, open. I allow my body feelings to come up from my inner world. As I listen, something jumps up to my consciousness, stands out, reverberates. Sometimes my hair stands on end; I have an "aha" feeling. This process has a deep vibrational quality and resonates within me. Space and time open. I am elsewhere, I have been thrown elsewhere. I know it's an important moment. I see deep into it. The thoughts come to me and tell me what to do; they give me the information to continue the healing process. I am always surprised by what comes to me when I listen with an open mind. Suddenly, a vision or image appears and I know something. I ask the patient, "Is this what you see, is this correct?" Sometimes I say, "Do you see something over your shoulder?" Then the person tells me about the angel. Sometimes, after years of doing this work, the images are quieter; instead of jumping out they are just there softly. I recognize them by their feeling state. I feel a vibration, see light edges. My experience is more vivid than ordinary thoughts.

I was once working with a man who had liver metastasis from colon cancer. As he told me his story, I saw something over his right shoulder. I gently asked him, "Do you feel something around you?" He told me he would look. The next visit he told me he saw an angel. It was his son who was killed in an accident. I closed my eyes and saw that the angel could touch his liver. I did a guided imagery with him to try it. He enjoyed it and felt a healing presence and healing energy. Each day he pictured his son touching his liver. The son's hands were made of light. He spoke to his son and his son spoke to him as the healing occurred. He looked better each time I saw him. A year later he was tumor free.

SEEING TO DIAGNOSE

Michael tells another story of shamanic visioning:

This happened in 1971 when I was co-director of Headlands Clinic, an integrative healing facility in northern California. One day a man came into the clinic. He was a psychology professor at UCLA and had become a Silva Mind Control trainer. He told us he had become dissatisfied with Silva, with its rules and politics, and he also was dissatisfied with UCLA. He went on the road and taught his original version of Silva mixed with psychology to clinics and workshops. He did a two-day workshop with all the healers in Headlands Clinic. At that time we had three physicians, an acupuncturist, a guided imagery practitioner, body workers, love healers, Native American healers, psychic healers, color healers, and more.

He gave us all a simple assignment: Choose a person in the group. Have them write on an index card an illness they have in the present or even had in the past. Do not look at the card. Then close your eyes. In visionary space, in guided imagery space, scan the person's body from head to toe. Let your eyes go from top to bottom. Then draw what you see. He asked, "What attracts you? Let your mind rest on an area. Let images come to you, without fear or judgment, and draw them or write them down. What do you see?" I drew a map of the person's body. I drew their lungs with a dark area in them. I found to my surprise that I liked this drawing process. I became absorbed completely. I drew brown, dark colors. Then I became afraid. Then I started to feel the joy of drawing again. He said, "If you are a professional healer, write down the words in your diagnostic system that come to you." I wrote down, "Tuberculosis—right lobe, healed." I picked up the person's card. On it she had written "healed tuberculosis." I asked her, "What side did you have it on?" "Right," she said.

I was bowled over. For me, the vision was as clear as an X ray and lab test. This shocked my paradigm of reality. I was young, and this type of experience was new to me and foreign to my training. Also I was obviously good at it. This was a challenge. Was I supposed to do more of this type of work? It turned out that I did and I didn't. In my life, my healing tools are guided imagery and visions. Making a visual diagnosis in Western medical terms is not important to me. X rays and lab tests can do that. The process of seeing within is what I do now.

Exercise: Envision healing

This exercise can be done with the person present or when he or she is a long distance away. You can even do it with just the person's name and age. It is easier to start with a person you know who is present. Before you do it, ask permission

Close your eyes. Picture the person in your mind's eye. Look at his or her body. You do not have to see it in detail; you can just see its outlines in the beginning. Now scan the person's body with your eyes. Start at the top and work downward in a jerky, slow motion. Scan down several times until you are comfortable. Now let your eyes fall on areas that attract you. If you see light or darkness, let your eyes rest on that area. Now look in detail at the area. Look for qualities that tell you what is happening there. You can look in detail now for cells, infection, inflammation, injury. Try not to censor what you feel. Just let it come in and note it without judgment. Do not put yourself down or say negative thoughts to yourself. When you see an illness, start to see the healing. Let healing forces come to you; see mechanisms of healing. See the process of the healing forces vanquishing the illness.

This exercise needs to be done to be believed. You can try it with only a person's name. Then verify the results. When you do this, you may want to try it often or you may never use it again. For several years while Michael was working at the public health clinic, he would look at the person's name and age on the chart on the rack outside the door to the examining room and then close his eyes and see. Then he would go into the room and talk to the person and order lab tests. The number of times he could diagnose the condition from the name on the chart was astounding. He made a game of it—he would tell the nurse he worked with what he saw, then together they would go into the room and do the history and physical. When Michael was right, the nurse would look at him and roll her eyes. They kept the secret between them.

Guided imagery to see energy

Close your eyes. Picture the person in your mind's eye. Look at the person's body. You do not have to see it in detail; you can just see its outlines in the beginning. Now scan the body with your eyes. Start at the top and work downward in a jerky, slow motion. Scan down several times until you are comfortable. Now look for light and darkness. Look for flow and movement. Let your eyes rest when you see light, which is an area of high energy, or when you see darkness, which is an area of low energy. Now move the energy with your mind. Move the light to the darkness. Let it flow. Let it flow in a clockwise direction up from the legs to the spine, up the left side and down the right side. Do this until the energy is even. You can feel it with your hands or with a feather, too. In your mind's eye, let your hands move over the person until you feel high energy as buzzing or magnetic field and low energy as a drop. Then move the high energy with your hands until the body feels even to you.

Guided imagery to diagnose psychological issues

Picture the person in your mind's eye. Close your eyes. Look at the person's body. You do not have to see it in detail; you can just see the body outlines in the beginning. Now scan the body with your eyes. Start at the top and work downward in a jerky, slow motion. Scan down several times until you are comfortable. Now let images of life events come into your consciousness. See the past, see abuse, hurt, family scenes, injury. See love, peace, rest, and calmness, too. Now go into the times of hurt and put healing energy in there. Put love and peace around the person in that painful time.

Guided imagery to regain spirit

Make yourself comfortable. You can be sitting or lying down. Loosen tight clothing, uncross your legs and arms. Close your eyes. Let your breathing slow down. Take several deep breaths. Let your abdomen rise as you breathe in and fall as you let your deep breath out. As you breathe in and out you will become more and more relaxed. You may feel sensations of tingling, buzzing, or relaxation; if you do, let those feelings increase. You may feel heaviness or lightness; you may feel your boundaries loosening and your edges softening.

Now let yourself relax. Let your feet relax, let your legs relax. Let the feelings of relaxation spread upward to your thighs and pelvis. Let your pelvis open and relax. Now let your abdomen relax, let your belly expand, do not hold it in anymore. Now let your chest relax, let your heartbeat and breathing take place by themselves. Let your arms relax, your hands relax. Now let your neck relax, your head, your face. Let your eyes relax; see a horizon and blackness for a moment. Let these feelings of relaxation spread throughout your body. Let your relaxation deepen. If you wish, you can count your breaths and let your relaxation deepen with each breath.

Now in your mind's eye, picture yourself with a person you are working with. See yourself, the place, the person in detail. Be there. Now go deeper. You can imagine going on a path into the forest. Go over a bridge and up a hill to a meadow. In the center of the meadow is a dark area. Sit near it. This is the entrance to the underworld, the world of the spirits. You will go there with intent to find out about the person you are healing, to help find his or her spirit and heal it in the underworld. Ask your spirit animal or helper to go with you, if you have one. Go down into the darkness and see what you see. Let a vision come to you. Ask for a vision of the person's spirit to come to you. See if you can find his or her soul in the world below. Follow a path, tracks; have your spirit animals go with you on this sacred journey. When you see or feel something, let the vision or inner voice come to you. When you see or feel it, let a healing come to you. Do what you feel is healing, what your spirit animals tell you is healing. If you need to take something out of the person in visionary space, you can do it. If you need to put something back into the person, you can do that now. If you think the person's soul has wandered, you can find it and bring it back.

When you are ready, return to the room where you are doing the exercise. First move your feet and then move your hands. Move them around and experience the feeling of the movement. Press your feet down onto the floor, feel the grounding, feel the pressure on the bottom of your feet, feel the solidity of the earth. Feel your backside on the chair; feel your weight pressing downward. Now open your eyes. Look around you. Stand up and stretch. Move your body; feel it move. You are back; you can carry the experience of the exercise outward to your life. You will feel stronger and be able to see deeper. You will be in a healing state. Each time you do the exercise you will be more relaxed and be able to go deeper and be more deeply healed.

You can do the same exercise by going above into the upper world. There you will find the upper spirits rather than the spirit animals. You can do this with a person you are healing in the outer world instead of doing this in imagery space. Sit with them and in your mind's eye go on the inner journey. You can say what you are doing or keep it to yourself. You can touch the person, if appropriate, and put energy in or brush energy away.

Guided imagery to see healing forces and healing guides

Make yourself comfortable. You can be sitting or lying down. Loosen tight clothing, uncross your legs and arms. Close your eyes. Let your breathing slow down. Take several deep breaths.

Let your abdomen rise as you breathe in and fall as you let your deep breath out. As you breathe in and out you will become more and more relaxed. You may feel sensations of tingling, buzzing, or relaxation; if you do, let those feelings increase. You may feel heaviness or lightness; you may feel your boundaries loosening and your edges softening.

Now let yourself relax. Let your feet relax, let your legs relax. Let the feelings of relaxation spread upward to your thighs and pelvis. Let your pelvis open and relax. Now let your abdomen relax, let your belly expand, do not hold it in anymore. Now let your chest relax, let your heartbeat and breathing take place by themselves. Let your arms relax, your hands relax. Now let your neck relax, your head, your face. Let your eyes relax; see a horizon and blackness for a moment. Let these feelings of relaxation spread throughout your body. Let your relaxation deepen. If you wish, you can count your breaths and let your relaxation deepen with each breath.

Imagine you are with a person and doing a healing. Let the person tell you a story of the illness and the process of healing he or she sees. As you hear the story, look into visionary space and see what you see. Look into the person's body and see the tissues healing. Look at energy flow, cells moving, light and darkness. See toxic wastes leaving, see new tissue growing. As you see this, put intentional energy into making it happen faster and more easily. Bring in your energy for healing. You can even go inside the person and push cells around and take things out. Now look around for guides, angels, and helpers. If you see them, you can speak to them and ask them what they are doing in the healing and what you can do to help. If appropriate, you can tell the person that you are with what you have seen and suggest guided imagery so that he or she can see it.

When you are ready, return to the room where you are doing the exercise. First move your feet and then move your hands. Move them around and experience the feeling of the movement. Press your feet down onto the floor, feel the grounding, feel the pressure on the bottom of your feet, feel the solidity of the earth. Feel your backside on the chair; feel your weight pressing downward. Now open your eyes. Look around you. Stand up and stretch. Move your body; feel it move. You are back; you can carry the experience of the exercise outward to your life. You will feel stronger and be able to see deeper. You will be in a healing state. Each time you do the exercise you will be more relaxed and be able to go deeper and be more deeply healed.

7

Spirit Animals and Guardian Figures

Mary tells us this story of something that happened years ago.

It is late one evening; I am driving out to catch the sunset in an oasis of oaks thousands of years old. As I go though the first gate, I realize that it has been a long time since I have been out here by myself. Usually I am here with other women doing ritual. Tonight I am all alone. I can see that the sun will set any minute now and I wonder when the moon will come up. The third gate is latched; I open it and I drive over a little rickety bridge. It is like a threshold. I park the car at the edge of the circle of trees. The trees are ancient and magnificent. They hover over me like ancient spirits and I get a little bit frightened. I walk into the dark circle of trees. I look to the west, where there is a beautiful solitary oak tree. As I watch the sun set, I feel a moment of sadness and confusion and I feel incredibly alone. Why do I feel lost in the world? I turn around and I understand that something inside of me has ended. I feel like I am losing something. Now it is dark; I walk slowly back into the circle of trees. I gasp. I see the harvest moon rising. The full moon fills the entire sky. I am in awe. Suddenly, out of the darkness of the forest, a great owl with a six-foot wingspan dives over my head. I feel the feathers move over my head. Oh God, it must think I am its prey. I am taken by the owl. I hear the owl's call. I realize something has shifted and changed and I will never be the same again. The moment the animal took me became an expanded moment of magic. From that moment onward, I could see into the visionary world.

Seeing spirits comes from a magical perspective. Imagine you are walking into the center of a circle. The circle can be made of anything, but for now you look around you and find you are in the center of a circle of gigantic ancient oak trees whose branches seem to reach the sun. In this circle, there is a mysterious wind circling you like a vortex of energy. Stand there in the center and pause. Close your eyes, then open them slowly. Suddenly in the center of each tree you glimpse an ancient figure. You are silent, they are silent, the silence is silent. You are in between worlds. You can see them and they can see you. They recognize you and they realize they have been seen. Since they have been seen, their ability to speak arises; their voices become audible for the first time, like the whispers in the wind. This is what happens when you stand there and you see them. In the presence of these spirits there is incredible power and humility. They know who you are. They look dead center into your eyes; they may nod to acknowledge they have been seen. Trees hold the space for spirits on the earth. Within these giant trees, the spirits are still part of the earth. They are deeply rooted in the earth and they became the earth when they died.

When you stand there you will develop the ability to see into an inner landscape, into the spirit world. It is as if you can see into a past lifetime—you can see what they saw through their eyes. You can see how they walked on the ground, how their fires cooked animals. As a woman, you can feel your hands holding the baskets, you can see the people move in their lifetime. It depends on how wide their visionary space opens to you—that is how wide you can see into their lives. The connection has to do with tapping into an ancient wisdom of the earth. Suddenly, you see your life span and how you are connected to the earth. You see into your own way of being as a way of seeing yourself. It shifts your worldview for them to become part of your world. These people were in communion and there was a freedom, a freedom of being in the earth where there was spaciousness and awareness of animals, where there was an aliveness. There was no perception of going eighty miles per hour in a metal capsule on a highway.

Their movement in space is different. You are brought into a different way of being, a different movement in time—a shift. Suddenly you are open to a wisdom, a way of knowing the earth that you have forgotten. You see how they know the animals, how they can see out of the eyes of the animals. You hear the beautiful legends of the meaning of all the spirit animals. They were the first ones to hear the animals and they say to you, "We were the first ones to speak to the animals and now we will show you how to do this." It is as if a human guide takes you there; it is as if you are connected to their experience. You have access to their memory.

Mary tells us:

When I stood in the circle of trees, I actually saw spirits. My visionary space has always been accessed through visions of ancient people; they lead me into their world. The ancient ones and living spirits of the earth are caretakers of the earth. They stand at the threshold in between worlds. I remember vividly the experience of seeing out of the eyes of the owl. I remember being taken and being able to see in the darkness. When you are taken by them, you become increasingly aware of this animal, of all owls in the vicinity. You are heightened to your own senses. If you are aware of owls, you see them in the trees in the forest. Suddenly the world is alive with animals. Not only do they call to each other, but they know you know they are there, and they call to you. There is vibration of energy of the human awake to the owl, and the owls like knowing you are their neighbor because you need to learn from them. You have never been taught to listen to them—and now you are.

And then they call to you every night as you fall asleep. And in your dreams you fly with them every night and these animals can take you to all kinds of places. They come to you and speak to you, they transport you to visionary landscapes, they are present as huge companions. You know they are there and when they appear, you know they are a gift. If you only see their shadow on the tree you know it is a gift.

ABOUT SPIRIT ANIMALS

Spirit animals are not scary, New Age-y, or weird. Most people have animals that they are attracted to in their life. They can be pets or wild animals, large animals like bears or small animals like rabbits. Spirit animals are simply specific types of visions that a shaman has in order to increase power, receive protection, and connect with the earth. The voice of the spirit animal was a visionary experience that allowed the shaman to hear the voice of the living earth and the voice of the Creator. Native peoples believed that the animals who were all around them could speak from spirit space, from the voice of the earth, and, from the Creator because they were closer to the earth. The animal spirits were older than humans and were in balance and harmony.

No shaman would go into visionary space without a spirit animal to help him or her. The spirit animals would protect the shamans and give them courage. In contemporary times, a shaman can choose to work with spirit animals as helpers, too. You can look at the spirit animal as a virtual image tool to change your consciousness to one of courage and protection. This chapter gives you the ability to do this if you wish. You can use the tools of the shaman healer without spirit animals; you can create sacred space, vision and move healing energy in these times without using animal helpers. But animals connect you to the voices of the living earth more deeply and give you a mind state of fearlessness.

GO INTO NATURE EVERY DAY

We asked a powerful body worker where he learned to use mystical and visionary tools to heal. He told us this story.

I lived on a farm as a child, and when I went away to college I worked with computers. One day I hurt my knee. I was very involved in sports. I had a bad experience. I was living in the city at the time and my life took a bad turn. I knew I was not getting where I wanted to go. One day a friend told me he had a small shack in the mountains. I was there the next day. I lived there for four months with no interactions with people. I became immersed in nature. I knew each star, I could smell an approaching storm, I could feel the wind on my face, I could hear the water in the steams, I could see each cricket catch its own food on the brink of its own survival. I did everything myself. I was totally immersed in the natural world around me. This was a life-changing experience. When I lived in the mountains, it was one of the most important experiences in my life. I could feel the expansiveness of my own life.

I needed to do this to find my destiny, to clarify what my goals were. I went into town four times to get supplies, otherwise I was in nature. I become strong, courageous. I could hear the wind rustle, the grass stems brush against each other. I was so immersed in the earth that that the quality of the experience is with me always. I cultivated a way of being in the world.

Many shamans we interviewed told us a story like this one. They told us they became depressed and then something made them go into nature. It could be a friend with a cabin, a summer home, a wilderness area with a campsite, a trailer. Then the retreat as a hermit began and their lives changed forever. Literally, nature turned them into shamans. She who makes the shaman is a spirit of the earth.

The first thing to do to hear the voices of the spirit animals is to go into nature. Most of the healers we interviewed emphasized this. It is necessary to go into nature for you to work with animal and earth energies. It is necessary to go into nature for you to become intimate with the elements of the earth. You need to actually be in nature to feel and embody the animals, the air, the seasons, fire, the sun and moon, the stars. Going into nature really expands your experience as a creature of the earth. Going into nature allows you to open and be enveloped—to see, feel, sense, and experience connectedness. Go out into nature and feel the wind, listen to the sound of the wind, feel the sun on your face, look up at the stars and the moon. Feeling the majesty in nature allows you see the majesty in your life and in the lives of people you work with. Even if you live in a city, you can go into nature each day. Walk in a park, along a river, to a hill. Feel the sun and the wind, see the soaring birds. Cities have sky and earth, wind and stars, often rivers and lakes. They also have animals when you look for them. New York City even has peregrine falcons. Go out into nature for fifteen minutes each day.

THE SENSUOUS SPELL OF THE ANIMALS

David Abrams's *The Spell of the Sensuous* has wonderful teachings about shamanism and nature. He talks about how the shaman is humble before nature. The experience of real animals fuels the shaman's spirit world. The true magic of the shaman is to be able to change his consciousness at will; the shaman changes to the consciousness of the spirit animals. In the greater view of nature all beings have souls, not just humans, as is believed in Christianity. Abrams says a shaman has the ability to slip out of his or her perceptual boundaries in order to make contact with and learn from other powers in the land. The shaman has receptivity to meaningful solicitations, to songs, cries, and gestures of the larger, more-than-human field. The animals Abrams talks about are real animals, not supernatural animals. The awareness of the shaman is propelled laterally, into the landscape—the sensuous living dream we share with the spider hawk.

The shaman is ecological, and the shamanic vision is about saving real animals and habitats. It is an exchange. If you have a spirit animal, you have the responsibility to save that animal's habitat. If you get messages from a sacred spring, in return you have to save the river. It is the basis of ecological shamanism. At death, the body returns to the earth and becomes the animals. We are connected to the animals and the spirit animals teach us to hear the voices of the living earth, which will keep us alive.

We learn from animals to be sensuous. Animals are in their body and are sensuous. We feel the wind, the water, the earth. We learn from animals which way to go home, how to build a nest, how to predict the weather. The body is a magical entity, the mind's own sensuous object. We need to stop, to pause, to see and hear in the animal world. We need to feel the wind to find a power spot. We can look at everything to find out how a power animal feels the wind, the light. To be a shaman healer we must learn to pause to be there. No one can become a shaman without being in nature in learning and absorption. The way we know is to feel.

Guided imagery to be in nature

Nature is the home of shamanism. In this guided imagery you will go deep into nature and experience the beingness of the shamanic presence of the sacred earth. Make yourself comfortable. You can be sitting or lying down. Loosen tight clothing, uncross your legs and arms. Close your eyes. Let your breathing slow down. Take several deep breaths. Let your abdomen rise as you breathe in, and fall as you let your deep breath out. As you breathe in and out you will become more and more relaxed. You may feel sensations of tingling, buzzing, or relaxation; if you do, let those feelings increase. You may feel heaviness or lightness; you may feel your boundaries loosening and your edges softening.

Now let yourself relax. Let your feet relax, let your legs relax. Let the feelings of relaxation spread upward to your thighs and pelvis. Let your pelvis open and relax. Now let your abdomen relax, let your belly expand, do not hold it in anymore. Now let your chest relax, let your heartbeat and breathing take place by themselves. Let your arms relax, your hands relax. Now let your neck relax, your head, your face. Let your eyes relax; see a horizon and blackness for a moment. Let these feelings of relaxation spread throughout your body. Let your relaxation deepen. If you wish, you can count your breaths and let your relaxation deepen with each breath.

Now, in your mind's eye, go to a place in nature that you love, a place that calls to you. It can be the ocean, a mountain, a cave, a spring, a meadow, a river. Let the place come to you. It is your place in nature, the place in your life where the shamanic voices have come to you from Mother Earth. It may be a place you went to as a child, a place you went to on a retreat to heal yourself, a place you go to now to refuel and balance. In your mind's eye go there—see it, feel it, smell it, hear it, touch it. Let all your senses fill with this special place. Now go deeper. Listen to the sounds, let them come into your body. What do they tell you? What inner message is there for you in the voices of your place? See the visions of this beautiful place. Look deeper. What do the visions show you? What do the voices say to you from the visions? What gift does this place give you? In your mind's eye, go to each direction in this place and ask for a gift from nature, from the sacred earth, to you. When you are in each direction, pause and let the gift come to you. See it, feel it, hear it, touch it, smell it. Then give an offering to this place in nature. Finally, ask the place what it tells you about your life as a healer. What lesson does this place give you?

When you are ready, return to the room where you are doing the exercise. First move your feet and then move your hands. Move them around and experience the feeling of the movement. Press your feet down onto the floor, feel the grounding, feel the pressure on the bottom of your feet, feel the solidity of the earth. Feel your backside on the chair; feel your weight pressing downward. Now open your eyes. Look around you. Stand up and stretch. Move your body; feel it move. You are back; you can carry the experience of the exercise outward to your life. You will feel stronger and be able to see deeper. You will be in a healing state. Each time you do the exercise you will be more relaxed and be able to go deeper and be more deeply healed.

Now do the same exercise in nature. Go out and go to the place or to anyplace in nature that you love. Go to the directions and ask for a gift. See the place, listen to its voices, hear its sacred teachings. Let it be your teacher on your shamanic path as a healer. The earth is our mother and our lover and our teacher. She is.

SPIRIT ANIMALS

Spirit animals and guardian figures are the voices of the living earth received by the shaman. They are visions of the oldest spiritual forms manifest; they are healing protector spirits manifest. A spirit animal or power animal is the manifestation of the spiritual energy of the animal on earth. The spirit animal is greater than the actual animal because it embodies the essence of that animal. It is not a human form of the animal or a human dressed as an animal; it is the animal spirit itself. For example, a spirit bear is the voice of all the bears that have ever lived. It is the shamanic bear. It is the bear that can see itself and speak to you. A spirit animal appears to the shaman as a vision. It is the voice of the wild, the voice of nature, the voice of the earth. This animal informs the shaman of the earth energy it holds and gives the shaman power and protection. It is a helper that assists the shaman on the journey inward.

No shaman would attempt an inner journey without the help of a spirit animal because the spirit animal conveys to the shaman and the people he or she works with an energy needed to heal. The spirit animal gives the shaman the ways to travel and the powers to vanquish spirits of illness and destruction. The spirit animal gives the shaman gifts of sight and teachings of knowledge. The spirit animal gives the shaman protection and wisdom.

Traditionally, shamans had animal helpers to go with them into visionary space. The animals protected them and gave them power. They made the space different. Eliade says that the shamans could not exist without the animal guardians. This view of shamanism is traditional; for the shaman healer, the spirit animals may not be as necessary. From ancient times, the shaman embodied the animal and had the protection of the animal. The animal brings the shaman the power of God or of the divine. The spirit animal is more accessible and can speak and journey with the shaman. In this book, we do not believe it is absolutely necessary to have animal guides. A shaman can have divine guardians or nature guardians, or simply be in harmony with the earth directly. But the tradition of spirit animals is so strong in shamanism that we offer instructions on how to get an animal guide and how to speak to ancestors or ancient ones. If this form is uncomfortable for you, you do not have to use it.

How to Find Your Spirit Animal

Anyone can find and meet a spirit animal. It is our heritage, a basic part of shamanic training for centuries. Animals are living on earth with humans. They speak to everyone, not only to Native Americans. Even through it may sound strange, finding a spirit animal comes naturally. Perhaps you are wearing an animal T-shirt or have stuffed animals or toy animals around you; maybe you collect animal fetishes or carvings, or have a favorite animal in nature or at the zoo. Perhaps you work to protect an animal or have a pet you love. You may be entranced by an animal in a movie, on TV, or in a book. You may collect fossils, bones, of ancient animals. Any of these animals might be your animal guides. In shamanic terms, these animals have been around, waiting for you to call them. Traditionally the shaman in training would go into the wilderness in solitude to receive an animal guide. Now there are several ways to have your guide come to you. Guided imagery exercises, visioning exercises, vision quests in nature, and dreams are all ways a shaman can find his or her spirit animal.

Each spirit animal is a combination of its real animal and its collective spiritual essence. It carries themes and messages that combine with your unique personality. For example, the owl has keen sight. It signifies waking up and being seen, emerging from the night, from dreams and visions, and being taken deeper. The owl for us is the combination of the real owl that sees in the dark and hunts and our vision of the owl as one who takes us and helps us see.

To ask yourself what any animal means for you, relax deeply, close your eyes and rest a moment. Ask for the animal's voice to come to you. Ask the animal to tell you who it is.

See the animal in your mind's eye. Watch it move. Walk in its footprints. Follow it along its journey. It may glance at you. If it does, look directly in its eyes. Now imagine seeing out of its eyes. Feel its body and the way it moves. Feel its balance and its grace. Feel the ground under its feet. Look around you. See what it pays attention to. Flow into the animal's way of being. Feel your own being transformed into the animal's.

Now open your eyes and write the first things about the animal that come to mind. Perhaps you can go to see your animal in the wild, in a zoo, or on TV and then write down your impressions. The more you see your animal, the more you learn about its power and spirit. After its body speaks, its spirit will sing to you in shamanic songs and visions. It begins to speak louder, it talks in poems and images, and it tells you who it is in the spirit world. It is speaking to you as your spirit guide.

Take note of the animals that live near you. Every place has its animals. In New York State, it is the bear, deer, hawk, owl, dove. Florida has alligators, snakes, dolphin, deer. Remember the animals that were there but are now gone, like the buffalo. Remember the ancient animals—the mastodon, the saber-toothed tiger. And remember the animals that are endangered, like the Florida panther. These animals will populate your own medicine wheel. Call forth the animals. Listen for their calls; hear the hawk, the owl, the crow. See their footprints; walk in their footprints.

The animals teach us about ourselves by teaching us about their special essence in the earth. For example, the eagle is independent, free. It flies high. So the eagle might teach you about your own independence. The animal's message is the nature of the animal itself in the outer world. Recognize its nature and then see what part of you is like that. The animal speaks to you in the inner world, but it speaks from within its own nature.

The following are the animals we use most as spirit animals. The descriptions are intensely personal; they are stories from our experiences of these animals in visionary space. For you, the animal will be what it is in your own experiences. These stories are a guide for you to experience your own animal visions and find your own stories of what an animal means to you. Remember, the story is a combination of a real animal's behavior and your own visionary experience. It is not nearly as powerful to simply read a story from our book or medicine cards and memorize it. Start with the stories, hang out with your animal, and then write your own story in a journal.

OWL

The owl comes out of the night at dusk and goes away at dawn. It is in the east, it is on the wind. The owl tells you the legends of the ancient owls and sings to you, "Come through my feathers, go into the darkness. I will show you what lives there. I will show you your world within." The owl brings visions to light. The owl was one of the primary shamanic animals from the earliest times of shamanism in Siberia thousands of years ago.

The owl takes you into the sacred place of your own heart, deep into your own inner world. The owl can go anywhere, can fly silently on the currents of your own dreams. The owl flies from the very tops of the trees, going inside your life, inside the tree trunk, inside the places only the owl can go. The owl looks inside you and when the owl sees you, it sees you as who you are, with no judgment. The owl is a witness in silence and clarity.

With the owl, you start in a place where you are totally seen for who you are. Everything about your life, your imagination, your spirit, is totally seen. The unconscious as seen there becomes no unconscious, no self-consciousness. When the owl looks inside you there is an important realization that you can go where you want to go even if it is into the darkness. The owl teaches you that life is not about being loved unconditionally, it is about being seen unconditionally. Owls are not evil or loving; they are about being in the world. For people, it is being where there is no emotion.

The owl looks at you with a gaze that says you are being seen in a pristine, clear, real, and truthful way. Life has a density with just being in it. That is the way the shamans start at a place where they see themselves as who they truly are—no judgment, no consciousness. You start at a place of clarity, not with intention. You only can be who you are, like a baby. A baby does not love itself.

The owl takes you into its body and you fly. You see through the eyes of the owl. You see who it sees in the darkness, hear how it hears. Flying into the darkness with such surety, it flies through branches and trees with such grace. It takes you to the place where you see your life as just flying through the darkness. The unknown becomes clear. It is as if you become part of the darkness with perfect safety. Perfection in flight, that is the bird. The bird flies through the branches, flies low and fast and silent.

The owl is about seeing past death, seeing and watching and dreaming. The reason some people fear owl is that when they see owl, their vision stops at death. The owl takes you past death into rebirth. It is about seeing through the veils of life and death.

The owl is about inner vision, about seeing deep within without fear or judgment.

EAGLE

The eagle is about going to heights from which you can see huge perspectives. As eagle, you see the landscape but are still connected to the earth. The eagle has to do with abundance. It has to do with going to the highest tree or mountain. You stand over the edge, over the abyss. You let go. You fly, you soar on the wind currents. The light is golden. There is a keenness in the landscape, and sharp edges. There is a fearlessness about being at home at this height.

The eagle is about success. The eagle builds a huge nest at a great height on the tallest tree. It carries the branches from the valley to the highest point that can be reached. There is a unique sharpness in its seeing. There is swiftness in flight, fearlessness in dives. Eagle watches with keen sight and a huge perspective. It is up so high it has a horizon of 360 degrees. The eagle is at the top of the medicine wheel axis. It is what sees in the outer world. The eagle sees the earth rotate, sees the earth rotate below.

The eagle has to do with manifestation. It weaves the electric lines of the medicine wheel above the landscape itself. It knows the landscape of power. If you can't find the places of power, follow the eagle; it will take you there. Go to the tallest tree with the eagle. It will show you the medicine wheel. If owl is darkness, eagle is light. The eagle is in the sun, is about illumination, about being the brightest light, being totally in light. Eagle is about surrounding yourself with beauty.

Eagles make love in full flight. They fly up in spirals, higher and higher, and then lock claws and stay together in free fall and make love. Double eagles free-fall in fearlessness. When they are about to hit the ground they pull out.

Under the eagle's nest is an oasis. Underneath the nest is a vast space. The eagle is a powerful, big bird. With its sharp talons, it tears apart; it is a large bird of prey. As eagle, go as high as you can, fly above the highest mountain, sit perched on the edge. You have tremendous sight, clarity; you see every detail and movement. The eagle manifests greatness and accomplishment. The eagle is about being at home at this height. The eagle is at home in its own success in accomplishment and in manifestation. Within its security it goes to the edge of itself and does a free fall. The eagle dives or falls and suddenly flies on wind currents. If eagle is your animal, say, "I can fly like an eagle, I see out of the eyes of an eagle." Follow the eagle, go to its nesting or feeding grounds. It will take you to your dreams. Eagle says, "If you can follow me and see out of my eyes, you will manifest your greatest dream." And the landscape is so vast you are never lost. Eagles partner for life, or they can be alone.

The eagle is about illumination, about seeing in clarity and light.

LION

The lion is passion, the lion is the fire. Lions call you to them. The lion calls lovers in total passion. The lion and lioness manifest power. They call in light. In high noon they harness the fire's energy of passion. The lion stories are often about lion loving. Lions take the lovers and bring them together and hold them as one. Lions show themselves to lovers, protect them, give them babies.

The lion directs your gaze not inward but outward. True introspection is affected by the sense of sight, through the physical means of the eye. We are seeing ourselves when we observe the world. We direct our gaze to see the actual owl that flies over our head on the way to work. We direct our gaze to see the actual eagle as it soars high in the sky over our heads. We direct our gaze to see the bison encaged in a lost wilderness. This is the time when we actually see the truth as it is in the outer world. We can see what is happening and what has happened. The lion can see the face of the other. Inside the lion's gaze we can see inside those faces. We see the faces of the ancestors, we see the spirit. It is in the gesture that we remember.

The lion is about grace. It is about ease in the body, it is about being at home in our body's power. The lion is about passion. Lions sleep, eat, and make love. He follows her sniffing her from behind; he follows her and mounts her. They are always lion lovers. They always have been lion lovers. Lions come to you to bring lovers together. The spirit lion is far out of time. She appears in the colors of the sunset, huge, pregnant.

He is her protector. The lion is the matchmaker. He is regal, resting, his eyes half closed. He fears nothing.

The lion is about strength and passion.

BEAR

The bear has always been about healing. The bear has always been about power. In the medicine wheel, the bear most often lives in the west; the bear is one animal that lives in its own specific direction in the stories of many cultures. In our medicine wheel, the bear is about water. The bear takes care of the quiet waters of the unconscious; the bear comes from the deep and the dark; all healing power comes from there. The bear is medicine bear; it brings you bear medicine. It brings you healing and the power to heal. It brings healing up from the dark waters of the unconscious where the images come from. Bear stories are about bringing you your healing power.

The bear ritual is about power and healing. We dance together as the bear in bearskins, given to us as a gift. When you are in the bearskin, bear spirit takes you. The bear is a very solitary dancer. The bear is aggressive and powerful. It knows the earth, knows the plants and the rocks. It knows the trails, the mountains, the rivers, and the salmon. The bear knows everything. And the bear dances. He dances with his lover and he mates, and they populate the earth with bears, and they populate the earth with life. The bear is a very intense creature.

The bear brings medicine, brings medicine in bear wisdom, in its solitary journey. In the bear dance, he and she do not speak; there is no speaking in their dancing because they are animals. We just know who they are. We just know there is a bear. And then, as they twirl and as they begin to dance together, it is like the bears become one. And as they become one, a shamanic voice and a shaman emerges, and it is the bear shaman. It is you as the bear shaman.

The bear has to do with the sense of responsibility in healing. Bears are ceremonialists par excellence. They were doing shamanic ceremony long before humans were born. Shaman bears are fun-loving and beyond powerful. They laugh and cry too. The bear put his bear face in her fur in the cave of the darkness and wetness. He dances, she hears voices. His odor is strong. He sees on a beam of light from the mountaintop. He looks up and sees the stars. He has power in his sight, you are taken.

The teaching of the bear is to save the animals and their habitats, to heal the earth, to save the bear and all the other animals. He is ceremonial and proud. He stood bringing in spirits. He sleeps, dances, makes bear babies. She is on all fours, her haunches up, her odor strong, her wetness intense. That is always his vision. Then medicine bear comes, bringing spirit and healing together. The bear dances, and knows the earth and its smells on his solitary journey.

The bear is about healing with responsibility.

TURTLE

The turtle is about being the earth. As turtle, you go within the body of the living earth. The turtle takes you in with intense grounding, takes you deeply into your job, your family, your friends, your home. The turtle is about safety, comfort, and protection, about being taken care of and taking care of others. The sea turtle is also about going deep in the waters of the earth. It is grounding in the sea. These waters are its home; they are not the dangerous waters of the unconscious. They are the soft green sea where the sea grasses move with the currents, where you graze in peace.

The turtle's grounding may not seem as romantic as the lion's falling in love. But the turtle is about doing what you feel at home doing. In the legend of Sedna the sea goddess, the turtle is about going down in Her body where the sea creatures are born. The turtle takes us there, takes us deep into the ancient legends of the night, takes us to the stories of our return to the earth and knowing who we are. Turtle says, "You are the earth, you are the four directions, you are the body of the earth itself." The turtle sings to us in perfect peace and protection, in gentleness.

The turtle is about being grounded in the body of the living earth.

SERPENT

The serpent moves in all directions. It slides around the medicine wheel; it is at home everywhere. Serpents have always been about worship, women, and healing. They are sexual, passionate, and sensual. They have always been with the goddess, and when she rises within you, the serpent rises, too. As the serpent rises, it warms itself in the sun; it is fire and, in a storm, lightning. When the serpent bites its tail or lies with another, it is about coils and figure eights, about being intertwined and as one.

The serpent is about worship, about worshipping Her in Her body. It is about healers, venom medicine, poisons, liniments, magic. Its healing power is always about the goddess. Men came to the serpent on a pilgrimage. Its tongue darts out. Its fangs bite. When you find the serpent, your kundalini rises. With its tail in its mouth, it is one. When the serpent strikes, it is lightning—it brings you your future. You stand on the mountaintop with a serpent in each hand, on the spiral of spinning fire. The serpent rises within you like passion, like fire. In the medicine wheel the serpent warms itself in the sun, winged, in union, in a circle, feathered, double like DNA. The serpent makes a circle with its head and tail—a ring, a rose intertwined and coiled. It goes down in and needs to come out. It is root energy. It spirals into the earth, is curled up in the trees. It swims under the earth, all over; its open mouth is the cave that takes you inside. The serpent surrounds you, takes you, births you. Serpent is about renewal. You have to remember renewal with snakes. Snakes shed their skin and are born anew. The next time they are larger and more powerful.

The serpent is about energy rising and rebirth.

BEAVER

The beaver is about building. The beaver acts in a deliberate way. It takes one branch at a time. It cuts down one tree at a time. It cuts one end and then another, one end at a time. In the business of productivity, the beaver does one thing at a time. It works in a soft and restful way. The beaver is about taking one step at a time to make a large journey. For the beaver, one day is one day, one hour is only one hour. In the one task is the whole life's work. For the beaver, there usually is no hurry.

In the doing of one thing is faith in completion. The beaver works without despair, always having faith in the process of its work, faith that the work will get done. The message of the beaver is "The doing of one thing at a time will get you to completion. In a day in your life you have the rest of your life." The beaver is about passion with patience, peacefulness in the doing. The beaver is about ebb and flow, letting go and moving on. Beavers can dam up a huge river. They can change the course of a river. They can make a huge lake. They can change the environment. The beaver can control the most powerful element—water. The beaver can deal with huge forces one bite at a time. The beaver is about the mastery of energy within the ebb and flow of constant movement and change.

One lesson the beaver teaches us is about softness. The beaver flows with the river, goes with the flow of the moving waters. The beaver knows the river's mastery of flow by being one with the river. The beaver knows where the river is swift and where it flows backward in the eddies. The beaver moves up or down with the river. It is not displaced or stopped by fluctuations of energy. It does one thing at a time in physical space. In its manifestation, it is not stopped by doubt or sabotage. The beaver doesn't panic under pressure. One message from the beaver to you is "Do one thing at a time." The beaver stays focused.

Beaver is a philosopher. The beaver is about biting though spiritual materialism. It is supported, it floats with pleasure.

When the tree falls, the beaver yells, "Timber." The tree makes a huge noise in the forest. Beavers make a huge noise, too. They flap their tails to make noise. The sound is clapping. The beaver laughs; the beaver's tail makes the sound of one hand clapping.

The beaver shaman is about the building of a spirit home, about the building of the first sweat. The message of the beaver shaman is manifestation though prayer. In the beaver sweat lodge, all the animals do ceremony in the four directions to heal the earth. They are all who they are, they are all seen.

The beaver made the first sweat lodge. The beaver brought all the animals together to pray. The beaver is about prayer, about manifestation, about building your life. The beaver is sensual, sexual, soft; its fur is beautiful. It swims with its webbed feet and paddle tail. Beavers drum all night in their lodges. They invite all the animal spirits in and they pray for manifestation in the world.

The beaver is about commitment and fully honoring your life as it is right now. The beaver is about taking responsibility for your life.

The beaver is about manifestation through prayer, one step at a time.

LIZARD AND ALLIGATOR

There are lizards all around you. They move their heads back and forth and look you in the eyes. They are born under the rocks of the medicine wheel. From the underside of the rocks of the earth, little lizards are born. The lizard comes from the womb of earth itself. It calls out, "Do not forget us; we are ancient; take us in, medicine wheel." In infancy, the embryo lizard gets all it needs to grow from the earth itself; it is moist and protected. Then the lizard becomes the magician. The grown lizard can change colors, be in dryness, walk up vertical surfaces, be upside down. The lizard can adapt to drought or wetness. The lizard is flexible and ancient.

The alligator is about adaptation. It is cold-blooded; it is one with temperature and can slow down its metabolism. The lizard can accommodate the change of season; it is one with the season. It slows down, doesn't need food, is able to fast. The alligator has issues of fasting. It is huge and can still eat only every six months. The lizard is not tamable. It is not like a dog. The lizard is about being wild and primitive. It often dies in captivity. The lizard has a deeper connection to the earth.

The lizard is immobile, then quick and fast. It does not move for hours, then it gets you. It takes its prey down into the darkness, into reptilian space. It takes you into the cold and the heat, into the earth itself, untamed. The lizard says, "We have been here forever, we will be here forever. Include all animals in your medicine wheel."

The lizard is about adaptation and survival.

COYOTE

The coyote is the eternal prankster, the trickster. For humans, the coyote is about silliness, about making fun. When the coyote comes to you, the message is not to take yourself seriously. Yet the coyote is immensely powerful; coyote helps make things happen. The coyote is a great adapter, with nothing to fear except humans. The coyote howls at you from an enormous distance. The coyote is returning.

Because the coyote is so much a figure of Native American stories, we will not say more. If the coyote comes to you, you know it. You suddenly laugh or make a fool of yourself, or get tricked, or are the trickster. You recognize the coyote when your wild, chaotic side emerges and you create havoc. You recognize the coyote when you create with laughter.

Read about the coyote from Native American people to find out more. They hold the story of the coyote. But the coyote says, "I come to all peoples now. I come to you always when you least expect it. I am about surprise. I come to you when you invoke me and give you power within humor." Are you brave enough to invite the coyote in? Can you stop the coyote?

The coyote is about breaking the space, about change, about disorder, breaking rules, new thought. It always causes an uproar. It is about humble arrogance, silly pride. The coyote says, "Have faith in what you are doing, even when all is crumbling around you."

Coyote is about not taking yourself seriously while you walk the earth.

WOLF

Ancient wolf time has passed. The time has passed to wear the wolf skin. The wolf is incredibly beautiful. The time has passed to kill the wolf for its power. The time has passed to kill any wolf. Let them be. The wolf is secretive, reclusive; leave it alone. The wolf needs to increase in numbers. The wolf is about not being tamable. It is about the conflict between the wild and the domestic. The wolf is the wild pack animal in nature; it is about working together to hunt. It is about the socialization of the group for a purpose. The wolf teaches you about group consciousness.

We are now domesticated animals. Our wild side, our own inner tendency toward violence, is hidden for most of us. Red excites us still—we are predators, hereditary meat eaters. The wolf reminds us of our inner violence and wildness, instead of our socialization. Humans kill wolves to stop wildness, and for generations nobody spoke about it. We have wolf memories of the hunt, of the kill, of death, of howling at the moon in wild places. The wolf is intelligent, plans ahead, works in a team to achieve a long-term goal. The wolf is ruthless, practical. The wolf stares into your eyes and takes you to your wildness and purity of vision. The wolf says, "Look into my eyes and see the earth as she was and as she will be. I do."

The wolf is about untamed wildness and beauty.

SPIDER

The spider weaves a silver tapestry connected to the source of life. The spider is about the woven tapestry of our own lives. The web is strong; it is the web of the self. The spider weaves from within itself. The web, the tapestry of life, comes from inside its body. The spider rebuilds its world all the time, is always rebuilding. Each web is new, different, and beautiful. The spider weaves art, symmetry, and beauty. The spider is the architect, the artist, the Creator, the one who captures evanescent beauty illuminated with diamonds within the morning dew.

The spider has to do with suspension, with waiting for what comes to it. The spider sits perfectly still and waits. When food comes, the spider wraps it up and saves it for later. Spider is about building, creating a structure, and waiting. The spider is about faith.

If you look at the spider's legs, it is almost as if it holds a magic wand, from which it is weaving a magic web. You can see that the spider looks deep into the center of the universe, and from the center you can see the energy go up into its hands. A magic web is woven for you. The spider catches the energy and power and weaves it into the earth. The spider sees it, can feel it. When you look closely, you can see that the spider is weaving a spiral of light, and if you look very closely at what it is weaving, you can see that it is the light from exploding nebulae that come from the deepest inner depths.

This is the moment and source of the creation of images. The spider says, "As I take the dream, I take it to each one of you and weave it into your heart. There is a string inside of each strand of my woven web. These strings go from my hand and fly up as one—to you, up into the center of your heart. You are in the place where time and space are not limited and these threads come up like spirals and you can see them go into infinity and they go up and down in the past, present, and the future." The spider holds the interlocking connections together. The spider can see us always, sees us always. And now we can see the spider weaving the web and holding the connections together.

Spider weaves the web of life for you.

DEER

The deer is very beautiful. There is a soft place where the deer nests. She gives birth to her young in the bending grasses. Deer make soft and almost invisible trails. They come to you in herds. Deer move slowly, camouflaged. They stare into your eyes. They have big eyes. Sometimes they are tame. Deer are gentle, easy to scare. Deer are about beauty and prosperity. When you see deer, it is an omen of good things. Deer are about gentle balance, ease, and softness.

You have found deer, you have seen deer. I saw deer the other morning. I said, "Let's go find the deer," and there they were. Deer surprise you like that. They are suddenly there. And they are hunted. They are the hunted. They give themselves up for food, clothing, and shelter. The deer feeds you, gives you clothing, tools, warmth, and meat; its whole body is used in ceremony. The great animal lie is that there are too many. Kill them, people say, they are overpopulated. How many do you see? The hunter waits all day for one. Too many?

Deer are proud of their strong beauty and swiftness, like the goddess Diana. Deer are about letting us fly with the wind, leap over fences. Deer are about physical agility. They have to do with fitness, agility, and grace, with light movement. Deer dance; they run in spirals at dawn. In the medicine wheel, deer run in spirals of ecstasy. At sunset, at sunrise, deer run spirals around ancient trees in joy. Deer spin the medicine wheel into movement. They make the medicine wheel into a dance. Deer leap over obstacles effortlessly. Deer leap over everything without hesitation. Deer are spirits of the dead, of the ancient ones. They run in wild spirals around the burial mounds, around the power places. Ceremonial dancing deer are the keepers of the sacred sites.

Deer are about leaping spirals of beauty.

BUFFALO

The teaching of the buffalo is specific. It is the most sacred and secret teaching. The buffalo has almost been exterminated. It takes effort to find buffalo teaching because the buffalo are gone. For you to follow the teaching of the buffalo you need to go to them, to deal with the scarcity of what was once abundant. You need to deal with the extermination of a whole people. Those who were once plentiful are now scarce. It is promised as a sacred and secret teaching. We don't say much about buffalo teaching. It is known to Native American people. Ask them.

Look into the face of the buffalo. The buffalo speaks to you. Look into its eyes. The buffalo spirits speak. The buffalo feeds itself to you in substance and provides the tribes great wealth.

The birth of the white buffalo was an event as important to Native Americans as the coming of Christ was to Christians. It was predicted, and it happened. This is the story of the birth of the white buffalo as told to us by the man whose farm she was born on.

Long ago there was hunger and war. Two men went in each direction to find game. One pair saw a woman on a hilltop. They went to her. One man asked her to make love. She turned him into a skeleton in a cloud of white smoke. She said to the other man, "Come here, I won't hurt you. Take me to your village." She gave them ceremony, the medicine bundle, the sacred pipe, tobacco. She brought them game. Before she left, she turned into a white buffalo and said, "When I return there will be harmony, peace, and plenty."

She said she would be born on a white man's land, in the center of North America. She said she would be white when she was born, and then turn the colors of the directions of the four races: white, black, red, and yellow. Then she would turn white again in her fifth year and then peace would come to the earth.

When the white buffalo was born, on August 20, 1994, in Wisconsin, the war in Central America stopped. Peace came. Now people come from all over to visit her, and elders do ceremony with her. On her birthday, 750 people came. People pray, leave medicine bundles, tie feathers on the fence where she lives.

The buffalo is the giver of all things. It feeds all things. Spirit buffalo still nurtures you, gives you abundance. The buffalo can feed the whole community.

The buffalo is about feeding, clothing, and housing the world with abundance.

DOLPHIN AND WHALE

When a dolphin or a whale comes up to you, you are entranced. They come up to you and communicate without a word. The dolphin calls you to a place deeper than words, a place closer to spirit. Dolphins are communicators, guides, and friends from a different element. They live in water and are at home in a huge space. Their world is like being in space. The sea is huge like the universe. There are no roads, no traffic lights, no density. The rhythm of the ocean is like the heartbeat. There are waves. Dolphins ride on the inner intimate heartbeat of the living earth. They move and are ancient. They take nothing, they use nothing. They give everything. They are the essence of being who you are in your pure nature. They teach that it is not about what you have or what is around you. They ride on Her heartbeat of life as a friendly guide.

If dolphin calls you and you go to it, it is huge. If you run to it and you are in deep water, you can't get there. Dolphins are the Guardians of the Threshold. If you run out to them, the dolphins watch you in the ocean. You are still a person; you can't be a dolphin. You are communicating at a deep level.

You can give the dolphin your greatest sorrow. The dolphin will take it to the bottom of the sea. The dolphin will take all your greatest sorrows to the heart of the ocean. Put them in a basket; the dolphin will take them to the abyss. The dolphin accompanies spirits on their journeys to the other side. Dolphins are psychopomps, accompanying the moving spirits. Dolphins are the guardian spirits who take the spirits to the other side. Give the dolphins an offering. Let them take your life.

The dolphin is about communication and being who you are without your material objects.

Man and Woman

When you get a man or a woman as your guide, you tap into the ancient ones, into the memory of the ancient spirits. You can get a man, a woman, a child. The guide can be old, middle-aged, young, a baby. They all are different guides. There are always the grandfather and grandmother spirits. They come out of the ancient trees; they reside in the ancient trees until called for. They live in the old-growth trees in the spirals of the growth rings. They walk toward you and present themselves in the sacred groves of nature. They will come in silence. They rest in repose, they are so old.

A man as a guide is about solving problems, about outcomes. Man penetrates. The old man can be about wisdom, about being alone, about knowledge. Middle-aged man is about building or seeking wisdom. Man can be about going on quests for enlightenment. Man can be about dealing with power or control. A young man is about enthusiasm, about energy, about hope.

Woman as a guide is about curves, roundness, about receiving. Woman is about ancient knowledge, seeing deep into the spirit world, healing. Woman is she who gardens us from above, she who makes the shaman, she who makes the world. Woman is she who seduces, she who teaches, she who is the oracle. Woman is about aspects of being. She is the young girl, the mother, the crone. She is always about the aspects within yourself. She gives birth to things; she is receptive, penetrated, taken. She is about the sensual and softness. She is about service and nurturing the earth again.

The ancient ones see the world of the past in the present. With them, you can see out of the eyes of the ones who came before you. You can see out of the eyes of the ancestral spirits who are the guardians of earth. You become an ancient one when you see yourself as one who has passed. You can see that as a present-day human. Anyone who does this work becomes someone who has come to speak from the past. Each person who reads this book is a reawakening ancient one who can see who he or she is.

Man and woman as guides are about creating an embodied experience in this lifetime where you can remember who you were as the ancient ones. They take you back to being an ancient one. You will remember it all by reuniting with the ancient ones. Their message is "Remember, you are us alive. We will speak to you. You are one of us living in our future, which is your present. Remember us, see when we were one with the earth. We were one. We lived and breathed air with connection. We were one with the mountains, the trees, the rivers; we had no sense of ourselves as separate."

The ancient ones take you back to when you were a baby and you saw yourself as one with your mother. They are about seeing yourself as one with the earth. That is what they bring you. They say, "I am the earth, there is no separation. I do not end with my skin and then another starts—we are the same." That is the message of ancient ones as man and woman.

Man and woman are about oneness and the wisdom of ancient experience.

Each culture has a different belief about the number of spirit animals and how long they stay with us. In our experience, some people get an animal for life, but for others, the animals change. The animals only stay and talk to you if you listen to them. While some people have one animal that is primary, others have many. These choices are up to you and to them. Mircea Eliade speaks of traditional peoples whose shamans have seven, fifteen—different numbers of guardian animals.

Guided imagery to meet your spirit animal

This guided imagery will help you meet your spirit or power animal. Like the ancient ones, the spirit animals come from deep within Her consciousness and are our deepest memories. We all share DNA with all the animals alive on earth. In our memories, in the memory of our very cells, we can see out of the lion's eyes. We are the animals. The animals are helpers and they are guides. They tell you what you need to know. They give you their immense energy. In traditional shamanism, no shaman would ever go into sacred space without his or her animal helpers. This guided imagery exercise can be done to find your spirit animals and to contact ancient ones.

Close your eyes. Take a couple of deep breaths, letting your abdomen rise and fall. Go into your imagery space as you have many times before. Now put yourself on a path. Feel your feet touch the earth, smell the fresh air, feel the warm breeze on your face. Walk on the path. It goes downhill slightly. The ground is hard and has small stones in the soil. It is solid and secure. Feel the ground and feel the grass that is on each side of the path. Now the path crosses a wooden bridge across a rushing stream. The bridge has stout railings. You can hear your feet echo on the bridge like drumbeats as you walk across. Perhaps you need to drop something in the water that you want to get rid of. Do that now.

After the stream, the path now goes upward slightly and comes over a rise. Below you is a large meadow. In the center of the meadow is a grassy circle. Sit in the circle and wait. Drift and dream. See the circle become magical, and feel yourself awakening to magic.

Now ask for your spirit animal to come to you for healing. Or ask for an ancient one to appear. You can see behind you, all around you in magic space. Let the animal appear and come up to you. It can come from a distance or appear right next to you. The animal looks like an ordinary animal coming out of the mist. It may appear suddenly or slowly. The animal that appears to you is your spirit animal helper. Let the animal come toward you. It may even begin to speak to you. It will speak in an inner voice that sounds to you like a thought but feels like it is not yours alone. You can ask your spirit animal questions—why it has come to you and what it will help you do. You can speak to it and tell it what you want. Spirit animals may not speak in words; they may speak in riddles or in feelings. Tell your spirit animal you will visit it, feed it, speak to it, and be with it.

You can stay in the meadow as long as you wish. Your spirit animal is part of the earth. It has tendrils that reach deep into the earth, the sky, and you, connecting them all together. If you feel comfortable, let the animal touch you, even come into your body. You can merge with your animal and see out of his or her eyes.

When you are ready to leave, say good-bye to your spirit animal. Tell your animal you would like to speak to it again. Stand up, and leave the meadow. The path goes out of the far side of the circle and you can walk farther down the path. It leads to the edge of an ancient forest of old-growth trees. Stand at the edge of the forest by a great ancient tree. Find a tree that beckons you. Now put your hand on the tree and touch its rough back. Feel its warmth, its life. Now imagine that when you put your hand on the tree, you move deep into the spiral of your own being. You spiral deep inside yourself, into your heart, and inside your body. Your heart opens with wings. A spirit eye opens within you and sees this experience. It witnesses you becoming the shaman.

Walk back to the meadow, then to the bridge, then to where you are now. Bring your spirit animal. Bring the connectedness with you. Now move your feet. Look around you. You are now on the shaman's path. You can see and hear spirit animals. You can hear Her voice telling you how to heal the earth.

The spirit animals are the wisdom keepers of the earth's energy and magic. When we see out of the eyes of the animals, we hear the wisdom that resonates within them about the earth's energy. We hear how to be in balance and harmony with the earth. We hear how to be one with the earth. That is what they tell us.

HOW TO HEAR YOUR SPIRIT
ANIMAL SPEAK

When the spirit animal speaks to you, you will feel it as thoughts that are clearer, more focused, and sound slightly different than the ordinary. They may have a new cadence of words, an accent, a new way of speaking. It is subtle. Ask for the spirit animal or ancient one to speak to you, then listen and pay attention to the thoughts you are having. If your mind wanders, as is natural, bring it back.

Your goal is to be able to receive a clear, coherent message from your spirit animal that has a teaching and a theme that you can remember and use in your life. It takes practice, but it will happen. As you listen to the voices of your spirit animal more and more, you will be able to understand it better as it calls to you in the physical world. The messages from your spirit animal come back to you whenever you remember the animal. The animal is a pointer to the message.

As you go through your day, look for animals around you. You can make this more likely if you go to a place where animals live. Even in the city, however, there are remarkable animal happenings. There are peregrine falcons in New York City; bears in Ocala, Florida, near Disney World; and mountain lions in the Los Angeles suburbs.

When you see a physical animal, look it in the eye, look at it deeply, look at it sideways. Be attentive to thoughts and feelings you have. Spirit animals will give you thoughts that are unusual. You will suddenly feel like you are slightly out of space and time. This is the experience of the animal coming to you. When you see a physical animal behaving in an unusual way, it may be a sign that it is your spirit animal. When that happens, listen carefully.

All animals are our teachers; all can be spirit animals to us. Look deeply into the eyes of an animal. Listen to your thoughts. Ask the animal to speak to you. Listen to what you are thinking, what it is telling you. Animals talk to us through our thoughts, our bodies, and our emotions. They reach that place below words, surfacing as images we can hold on to.

QUIET DOWN

To hear the voices of animals it is essential that you quiet down. You need to create a mystical silence away from the material world where you call them and invite them to come. The spirit animals say, "Quiet down. Invite us. We will come." Take a walk, paddle on a river, hike the in mountains to where the animals live. Go to a park. Then let your eyes drift, your ears listen for any sound. When you see a shape, like a cloud, let it form into a spirit. They say, "It is us coming to you. Listen with your inner ear, not to sounds. See in your inner eye, not sights. We will come to you. There is a pause, a moment of rest, then we will start telling you the story. It will sound like your own thoughts but different. It will be clearer, straightforward, like listening to a voice with its own character. It is the inner voice of the living earth speaking through the animals as your own inner voice. When we come to you it is a merging of you and us."

Listen to the stories when they come to you. They can be long. They are clearest as poetry, as a story, as a vision. They will tell you what you are to do in your life. Ask a question. Listen to your animal guide answer. Watch for signs all day. The spirit will appear as the real animal or as the shape or sound, over and over again. The hawk lands on the tree above your head and looks directly into your eyes. The hawk comes and recognizes you.

You will receive messages and teachings, but they are not always direct. They have been riddles since the beginning of time. In a riddle, there is room for you to enter, for your own voice to fill in and make it relate to your life. Then the communion of spirit animal and you happens and it is the world being created. The spirit animal will tell you what you need to know to grow and to do what you need to do in this lifetime. Because it is from spirit animals it will always be about making the world sacred, saving the animals and the earth, healing and balance. That is the voice you are tapping into. Be specific about which voice you want to hear. That is the one who will answer. If you want a voice of healing, of balance, that is who you will get. Voices of pure greed are not here. Animals speak only in balance. They take what they use; they do not amass wealth.

You will hear the spirit animal's voice and then create your own stories with your capacity for intuitive wisdom and imagination. Your thoughts will come to you like a creative idea; it can be like a voice, a vision, a thought. If it is a vision, you will see them by simply picturing them in your mind. Open yourself to these images. See the owl in a park, where it would be; look up, put it in your mind. It can be in a dream or in a waking moment. You can see an owl in your office on the back of your chair. See it fly with you from meeting to meeting. Let the owl be in the room with you. It can be outside the window in a tree. Use your imaginary eye.

Exercise: Look out of the eyes of your spirit animal

To perform this exercise, go to a sacred place near your house. It can be within a couple of hours' drive or nearer. Pick the place that is the most sacred to you, that resonates within your soul.

In this special ritual, you can only see what your animal can see. You can only go where your animal can go. All day, during this sacred ritual, you will be the animal. If you have a bear, repeat over and over again as you drive, as you walk, "I can only see what the bear can see, I can only go where the bear can go." It is like a mantra, a refrain, a chant. Look at your landscape through the bear's eyes.

You can do this in the present or in the long past if the animal no longer lives in the place where you are. Imagine the landscape as it once was, or you can leave it the way it is. You have plenty of time, so you can look out of the animal's eyes in the present and in many different times.

Now listen for the voice of your animal or even the voice of the animal shaman. They will speak to you and tell you their stories. This is when they will be at their strongest. Remember you have plenty of time. You can do your meditation all day or as long as you wish.

When you reach your destination, act like the animal. Run, play, and as you do, it will speak to you. When you walk, imagine you leave the footprints of the animal. Let it speak to you and guide your movements. The animal will direct the ritual if you let it.

Throughout the meditation chant: "I can only see what the animal can see." If you wish, you can smell and feel as the animal. Feel the breeze and breathe in the smell of the rich earth. Remember this is a sacred exercise to perform all day. If you want to, put on an animal costume; even one feather or representative object helps. The shaman of old would wear a complete bearskin and mask and that is how he or she saw out of the eyes of the bear.

As the shaman, you can only see what your animal can see. You can see out of its eyes as a shaman animal, as an actual animal or as a visionary animal. Listen carefully and see if your animal will sing a song to you or speak to you in an inner voice. Listen for the ancient shamans. They may tell you to perform a certain ritual or to do something to save that animal. They may give you prayers or chants, or tell you what they did as the animal shamans. You can only see what your animal can see.

Guided imagery to see out of the eyes of your spirit animal

This exercise lets you experience seeing out of the eyes of your spirit animal using guided imagery.

Close your eyes, make yourself comfortable. If you wish, uncross your legs and allow your body to relax deeply. Feel your body supported by your chair as it lets go of tension. Now let your breathing slow and become deeper. Feel your abdomen rise and fall as you slowly breathe in and out.

Now let your feet relax. Feel the wonderful sense of relaxation spread upward to your legs. You may feel heaviness or tingling as you relax. If you do, enjoy those feelings and let them deepen and spread. Now let your legs relax. Feel the muscles lengthen as you relax more deeply. Let your pelvis relax, your belly relax, your chest relax. Let the feelings spread to your arms and hands. Now let your neck and face relax. Let your jaw drop. Let your eyes relax by seeing a horizon and blackness. Let the top of your head relax. Let your whole body relax deeply.

Now imagine you are on a sacred river. This river is very special. It flows from sacred springs. It flows crystal-clear, from the beginning of time to the end of time. Now let yourself float out of the headwaters and drift down the river. You can be on a raft, in a canoe or kayak, or you can float on the water itself. The water is warm. It carries you and you are perfectly safe. See yourself being taken by river. Feel yourself on the river being taken by its flow. Feel the water caressing your body. If you are on a raft, let your hands go over the side and touch the water. Feel the water flowing in an easy, gentle caressing way. Feel the water supporting you. If you wish, you can be submerged in the river. See yourself diving, rising, playing in the water.

Look upward. See the trees dappled in sunshine; see them glimmer and shimmer in the reflected moving light from the river. In the trees you can see the ancient spirits. They stand by the sacred river and hold the place. Let yourself relax even more deeply as you move downriver. You are immersed in a deep feeling of comfort, embraced by sacred waters of the earth. Feel the water touch you as you are embraced by Her love.

Now see an otter on the bank of the river. See it diving and rising near the tree roots. Notice its beautiful black shiny coat. See how it moves. It is so graceful; it is in perfect harmony with the water and its environment. It seems as if the otter is one with the river, like its beautiful black coat is part of the river, its diving is at one with the river's movement. It moves with such ease. Now allow yourself to see out of the eyes of the otter. Open your inner eyes as the otter and see what it sees. Notice the bottom of the river, the pebbles, the river grasses flowing gracefully and gently in the water. See the fish, the changing bottom textures. Now feel yourself in the otter's body. Be an otter.

Feel yourself play, twirl, dive, and rise. Come up under a log, dive again under the surface. All your moves are graceful. As an otter, you are one with the river, flowing as the river flows.

Now come up and return to your own body. Rest for a moment on the riverbank. You can feel the sun on your face, kissing you. You are embraced by the love and the beauty of the earth. Now look up. In a tree on the side of the river you see an owl. The owl stares into your eyes. You can feel yourself being taken by the owl. Allow yourself to be taken. Go into the owl's soft gray feathers. Go into the owl's body. Turn around inside the owl. Now you are the owl. You can see out of the eyes of the owl. You can see the sun. Open your inner owl eyes, eyes that have clarity. Every detail is sharp and crisp. You are at ease in this powerful body. You fear nothing. You are silent and still, and you can be this way for hours.

Now, feel your body covered with feathers. They are beautiful, soft, and colored with brown and yellow stripes. You are elegant and powerful. Now turn your head around. You can turn it all the way around and see on all sides. Feel the power of your wings beating the air for takeoff. Feel yourself gracefully fly. Your wings are expansive. They are five feet across. Your body is large, and you use your power effortlessly. Gracefully and silently you fly. Now look back, see the river below you as on owl.

Now leave the owl and return to your own body sitting by the river. You feel totally at ease in your own body. You now have the gracefulness of the otter, the clarity of seeing like the owl. You are transformed. You will never be the same again. Now the river is your home. The water, the sun, the trees are your home. You are embraced by the earth; you are at ease. Now you realize how beautiful you are. Let the river take you and carry this feeling of ease with you all day.

You can create this imagery for any animal. What you will see is the story of the animal for your own personal vision quest.

HUMAN-ANIMAL TRANSFORMATIONS

Traditionally, the shaman would dress as the spirit animal and in virtual space transform into the animal. Anthropologists called this phenomenon *human-animal transformation*. In their visions, the shamans would become an animal—they would fly as an owl or dance as a bear. The shamans portrayed the experience as ritual to share with their people.

One goal of having a spirit animal is to help you experience a human-animal transformation. In sacred healing ritual and ceremony, your spirit animal takes you in human form. You create sacred space in which you can become an animal again. In human-animal transformation, you transcend ordinary time and space. You are in harmony, woven into the fabric of the earth like the animal.

Through human-animal transformation, you acquire the power of the animal more deeply. We begin by seeing out of the animal's eyes but quickly progress to becoming the animal. You see out of the owl's eyes, feel claws and feathers, imagine flying, and then become the owl. The spirit animal is all around you, and you are now part of the sacred mystery. The owl can speak to you and speak through you to others.

Seeing out of the eyes of the animal is the practice required to bring about human-animal transformation. By performing the ritual over and over again, you bring the animals to you. Each time you see out of the eyes of an animal you move deeper and deeper into the experience of the shaman.

Several groups of people have brought back the ancient bear dances for healing. They dance to wake up the bear, celebrate the bear medicine, and put the bear to sleep. The ritual is traditional and powerful. At midnight, the dancers put on their bearskins and become the bears. Before the dance, they do a sweat lodge and prepare the bear dance circle. They light a ceremonial fire and drummers sing the sacred bear dance songs. The sacred fire, the drums and songs, all take the bear dancers deep into a trance. First they offer salmon to the bear. In the fire, they ask bear spirit to come to them to heal. Men with eagle feathers and sage handle the bear dancers to keep them under control.

Michael has danced with the bear dancers. He describes the experience: "As I dance, I feel the bear come into me. He speaks to me. He takes me. Slowly, I feel my nose turn into bear's nose, I feel my nails become claws on my fingers and toes. I feel my skin become fur on my belly and back. I see out of the eyes of bear. I know how bear heals and restructures tissue to heal. I scratch the trees, I stand and growl, I come around people brought into the magic circle to be healed. I let the bear energy flow into them and see their tissues restructured to be healed."

You can do this in guided imagery. Imagine a great eagle, swooping down with talons stretched out, ready to capture its prey. Birds of prey take you. Where they take you is up to them and—sometimes—you. You can be taken into your dreams, into your fear of the darkness, into a world where things are hunted. You may go inside their cries and listen to them speak to each other. You begin to scan the landscape for sound and movement. You become a hunter, a hunter of your own visions, and eventually you find yourself. You go into your darkness, your own nature, and your own life. That is the nature of the eagle power animal, and so it is with the others as well.

The power of the animal is the true nature of that animal. It is simple. We learn the stories of the animals by looking into their eyes, dreaming about them, honoring them. There are still many animals all around us. We see them in the wild, in zoos, and on TV. You already know a great deal about your spirit animals. You have been watching them for many years. Trust your own knowledge. You do not need to read a book to know about an animal.

HUMAN SPIRIT GUIDES: VISIONS
OF THE ANCIENT ONES

The ancient spirit appears to me across the river. He says, "Ride with me on the horse's back, come with me into the darkness of the bear caves, sit by the fires of my people. We are coming to tell you our story. From all over we are coming. We are the voice of the living earth. To see us you need only to invite us to come to you. Be patient; do not judge anything. Open your eyes and open your heart." To speak to the animal spirits and the ancient ones it is important to refrain from judgment. Worry and judgment are states of mind that make it harder to speak to spirits. Worship and love are states of mind that bring the voices of the spirits to you. The spirits will come anyway, but when you worry or judge they are more difficult to hear. You always have two choices in life: to worry about something or to worship something. The choice you make completely determines your experience on earth.

To see the shadow of an ancient one or of an animal's spirit is a gift. To receive a feather is a boon. To see the spirit is a great gift. To look in the spirit's eyes is a celebration. To touch the spirit is a wonder.

Like the spirit animals, the ancient ones, ancestors, or spirit guides are the embodiment of the ancient voices of the earth. Voices of ancient spirits are another type of visionary experience that shamans use to increase their ability to see and hear. Ancient spirits speak in the collective voices of the ancestors, of the ancient peoples. They are the spirit guides, the inner voices of people on the earth. Ancient spirits are archetypal visions given form. They appear to the shamans in visions to give them messages from the earth. They come to you with the intention of communicating with you and helping you heal. Initially you see them from afar but eventually they show themselves or speak and make themselves known to you. When it is apparent that you invite them, their voices become clearer. Ancient spirits need to have a relationship cultivated to stay visible. The spirits will bring you back into the forest, deeper into nature, as they take you on their ancient paths.

All of us have ancestors. There are those who have died recently and those from generations before. The ancestors are our collective wisdom, our racial memory. They love us and speak to us like relations. The Native Americans have a term, *mitakuye oyasin,* "all my relations," which expresses how seriously they take their family and ancestors. You can ask for your ancestors to come to you as guides in visionary space. They will speak to you in the most beautiful stories and tell you who you are and what you are to do. They want to take care of you and give you their legacy. They want you to do the work they did not complete on earth.

Ancient ones are accessible to you as teachers and guides now. They are around you, waiting to communicate with you. They are part of the earth's structure and are instrumental in our healing and growing spiritually. In our view, the ancient ones are the memory of the earth. They are accessible to us in the same way our own memories are. They are the part of the consciousness of the living earth. Shamans often had ancient shamans coming to them in the spirit world, in dreams and visions. Thus the ancient ones communicated with shamans as teachers. The shamans believed in ancient ones and in spirit animals. The culture taught the children stories from an early age that instilled a belief system. Now it is different. We must re-create a belief system that includes the spirit world. Ancient ones are different from spirit animals. Each of the shaman's guides is a unique voice, just as different people have unique voices. Ancient ones sometimes are easier to understand than spirit animals because they speak in languages more like our own. They are sometimes more accessible for specific advice or questions. Shamans have another type of ancient one, the She who makes the shaman, or *ayami,* who comes to the shamans in dreams and teach them how to be shamans.

First you must open yourself up to the possibility that they exist and are around you. Next, invite them to come to you. Finally, open your eyes and look for them. They are there and they will come to you.

Michael shares this story of a spirit meeting.

One day I was paddling down the river. It was a beautiful day, but there were no animals around. I looked out of the side of my eyes, keeping a watch out for hawks, otter, bobcats. Suddenly I saw a shape in the woods that caught my eye. I thought it was a man up in a tree standing tall. He was dressed in a bearskin with the head of the bear pulled over his nose. He was about ten feet up in the tree, moving his head. I paddled over to him for a closer look. He shimmered in the forest and I could not see him clearly. As I watched him, he began to look more and more like a bear shaman, and then he spoke to me. "Welcome to my river. I am bear shaman, the keeper of this part of the river. I was the ancient shaman of this village. We have been waiting for you; we have come from far away to tell our story. We want our story told. I have a message for you today, a teaching. It is for your book, for your people to know from me. I will have a message for you each day. My message today is: We will speak to you whenever you look for us, whenever you come into our territory and call for us. Whenever you listen, we will speak. Tell your people that if they want to hear my voice, to see the ancient ones, the ancient shamans who once could change into bears, into owls, into mountain lions, into turtles, they have to want to hear us. They have to come and look for us. They have to open their eyes to us, open their ears to us. And then they have to wait and be patient and we will appear."

Go to Where the Ancient Ones and Ancestors Lived

The ancient ones were skilled in finding special places that were precious—especially sacred, powerful, and holy places where the resonances were higher and the earth's powers easier to access. That is where they did ritual and where you can most easily hear their voices. But hearing the voices of the ancient ones in contemporary times is not always easy. When we build a whole city over a sacred site, it muffles their voices, and they are harder to recognize.

Look for sacred sites in nature. Focus on the springs, rivers, mountains, caves, ancient trees. Sometimes we are fortunate enough to find sites where ceremony was done, such as mounds, stone circles, petroglyphs, temple sites, churches, or earth lines of power. Follow the paths to village sites, places of trade, old routes of travel. Ask yourself, "Is my house above or near an ancient sacred site?"

To find sacred sites, allow yourself to travel following your own keen sense of knowing. Follow your feeling of being pulled to a particular place. Trust your instinct to go in that direction. Or you can read about sacred sites, search for them on the Internet, and then follow your instincts about which one feels best. Sometimes you will discover that the place you have located is only a parking lot in front of a restaurant, but if you pause and look around, you can see what was there before. You might see an entire valley appear before you and the ancient ones will appear to you.

You can also go home to the places your ancestors lived. In these ancestral homes, the energy and resonance of your ancestors is the strongest. You can feel them as you walk the streets, see the houses, touch the earth. As you do this, listen for their voices speaking to you, telling you who you are and what you are to do. These ancestral dwellings are sacred sites to you.

CALL THE SPIRITS FORTH

When you go visit a sacred site, call the ancient spirits to come to you. Invite them, out loud or in your thoughts. All you need to do is concentrate and call them forth with intention. All traditions did this as a prayer or invocation. Most traditions involved a ritual and an offering.

Here is a prayer to bring the ancient ones to you:

Creator, come to me in my sacred work. I thank you for the earth and its directions. I thank you for this day with all its beauty. I call the ancient ones to come to me and help me with this sacred work. I invite them to come and tell me what I need to do in my life. I invite them to come to me and tell me who I am and what I am to do. I will go and receive the gifts from the ancient ones and do what I can to heal myself, others, and the earth.

Listen and wait. The ancient ones will come to you. They will speak. It may not be in words or thoughts but rather in dreams, visions, or happenings. The prayer or rituals you choose are up to you. As you become experienced in calling in the spirits, you will discover your own way of doing this. You can also invoke the ancient ones with guided imagery. Guided imagery is a prayer or a meditation that directs your mind to be receptive to certain thoughts. The exercise for meeting your spirit animal earlier in this chapter can also be used to meet an ancient one. It will call forth spirit guides as well as spirit animals. What is most important is to be open to the voices coming to you anytime. In any vision, an ancient one can speak to you.

On this path, be patient and do not judge anything. When you see the spirit, it is natural to say, "I am making this up. This is really a tree root, a branch. There is nothing there." That is a judgment. Let the spirits come to you. Invite them to come, then accept what you see. Welcome them. If you see an owl in a tree, say, "Thank you, owl spirit, for coming," and then you will see it again. If you say, "There is nothing there," next time you will see nothing. To have your world populated again by spirits, welcome them, recognize them. Invite them and see them without judgment.

Be patient during this process. When you call them, they may not come immediately. It may be minutes, hours, days, months before they appear. Then all of a sudden you see them. And they are there. There are minutes or hours when nothing much appears to be happening, but these times are punctuated by the most intense moments of visions. Be thankful for the pause. If you were in visions all the time, it would be difficult to live! Call them and they will come.

VISION QUEST TO SEE SPIRIT ANIMALS AND ANCIENT SPIRITS

A vision quest is a search for the images in your life that will heal you and make you whole. In traditional cultures, young people were sent into nature to listen to the voices of the living earth. The elders taught them to go on vision quests to find their paths in life and to find their spirit animal helpers. People on the vision quest spent days in caves, on mountaintops, on rivers, in the desert. They waited and invited voices of the spirit animals to come to them. After the prescribed number of days, they would return to their people knowing more about who they were and what they were to do. When they returned, they told the story to the shaman who led their vision quest. Many cultures believed that without the visions seen on a vision quest, a person could not function in the world, was not an adult, was not complete. A healing vision quest evokes a similar experience for people who are ill and for healers in our own contemporary culture. When you know who you are and understand your purpose, you are healed and at peace. You are effective in making the life you want and healing the earth. When you know who you are and who your helpers are, you can deal with illness.

Vision quests are characteristic of North American shamanism, which seeks visions. Asian shamanism invites visions to come to people and does not intentionally seek them. In the most common form of vision quest done today, the shaman takes the person out into nature. Traditionally it was for several days, most commonly one, two, or four, and the place was remote and isolated, chosen for reasons that applied to the particular person and his or her journey. Each vision quest is done differently, depending on the leader and tradition. Often, the person is covered only with a blanket and has no food, water, or entertainment. He or she remains there and invites sacred visions to come. The shaman protects them in physical and spiritual space during the vision quest. Vision quests are life-changing experiences for anyone who does them.

Guided imagery for the vision quest

The vision quest is the basic tool to invite shamanic visions. As a shaman healer, your whole life is a quest for visions.

This imagery exercise will take you on a specific vision quest preparing you to become a shaman healer.

Close your eyes and take several deep breaths, letting your abdomen rise and fall. Enter your imagery space as you have many times before. Now put yourself on a path. Feel your feet touch the earth, smell the fresh air, feel the warm breeze on your face. Walk on the path. It goes downhill slightly. The ground is hard and has small stones in the soil. It is solid and secure. Feel the ground and the grass that is on each side of the path. Walk down the path. It crosses a wooden bridge across a rushing stream. The bridge has stout railings. You can hear your feet echo on the bridge like drumbeats as you walk across. If you need to drop something in the water that you want to get rid of, you can do that now. You've been on this path before.

The path now goes upward slightly and comes over a rise. Below you is a large meadow. In the center of the meadow is a grassy circle. You've met animals here before. Sit in the circle and wait.

Now imagine that you are thirteen years old. Feel your body, your strength, your youth. You are on the verge of becoming an adult. Among your group of people, this age marks a rite of passage. It is a special day for you. You have been brought here by the elders to do a vision quest that will inform your life. You know what this is like from talking to older children. You have heard that they all go into the wilderness and find a spirit animal. They find their animal helpers and ancient spirits. The helpers and spirits speak to them and tell them who they are and what they are to do.

The elders speak to you. They say, "You are going on a two-day vision quest. You take only a blanket, a rattle, and sage. Find a sacred place and sit and wait. Wait for the animals to come to you. Wait and listen. Don't sleep if you can help it. When the visions come, welcome them and listen, and then you will become an adult. All adults of our people have animals as guides."

Now imagine that you walk deep into the forest. As you travel, you find a cave, a high rock, or a mountaintop. You know you are on a journey to find your own visions. You go deeper in the forest, higher up, deeper into the wild places. You have never been so far from home, alone. You find your special place and you sit and wait and wait and wait.

After a long time, an animal comes to you. It comes up to you and looks in your eyes. There are no people here, only you and the animal. It looks at you and enters your spirit. Then you start to follow it. It moves silently among the shadows, hunting. You notice how it moves, how it crouches and pounces. You think, "Maybe I am the hunter. Maybe I can camouflage myself, too." The animal teaches you to hunt and then it vanishes, in a flash. You wonder, was it a spirit animal? You are filled with awe.

After a long time you see another animal. You see out of its eyes more easily now than with the first. What comes to you if you are alone in the forest, on the mountain, on a river? The animals come and they become your teachers. They teach you about the earth, about life. When you are asleep, the animals call to you, as if offering a challenge. The animals become your guide and the teachers of the sacred wisdom of the earth. This is your vision quest.

Now return to your circle. Come back to where you started. Bring your animals with you. Move your feet. You are home. But now you are an adult. Now you have animal guides to inform your life and tell you who you are and what you are to do.

8

HEALING MEDICINE WHEELS

The medicine wheel is an ancient tool that creates sacred space, brings in visions, and manifests change. It creates sacred space by being an altar. In the process of making a medicine wheel, you pray for spirit animals and ancient ones to come to you and give you strength and guidance. It brings in visions, because as you build the medicine wheel you see. The spirit animals in the wheel are vortexes of energy that bring the animal visions to you. It manifests change because the prayer leads to action, and action forges change. The medicine wheel affects space and time in a magical way to bring you what you ask for.

THE HISTORY OF THE MEDICINE WHEEL

A medicine wheel is a way of creating a sacred space. Throughout history, medicine wheels have been built to hold ceremony, mark sacred space and time, and make a place sacred for ritual. A medicine wheel is simply a way of making sacred space more real and more visible. Ancient peoples believed that the medicine wheel itself had great power and helped create change and healing. Medicine wheels were circles that were made all over the world. They come from the most ancient cultures and remain alive today.

The term *medicine wheel* was first applied to the Big Horn Medicine Wheel in Wyoming, the most southerly one that still exists. In the classic definition, a medicine wheel is a circle of stones arranged in a particular manner. By that strict definition, there are about a hundred medicine wheels that have been discovered. Alberta, Canada, is the central area for medicine wheels. Virtually each medicine wheel has a unique form; the Big Horn medicine wheel consists of a central cairn, or rock pile, surrounded by a circle of stone. The whole structure looks like a wagon wheel laid out on the ground with the central cairn forming the hub, the radiating cobble lines the spokes, and the surrounding circle the rim. The "medicine" part of the name was given by anthropologists to designate their belief that the stone circles were of religious significance to indigenous peoples. Today, the term is used in popular culture in a broader way that includes small circles of animal carvings and large circles different from the classic defined variety.

In this book we use the term *medicine wheel* in a much broader way to define a sacred circle. Here we use *medicine wheel* to refer to a sacred circle where ritual, prayer, and ceremony are conducted for change and healing. By making medicine wheels, you join the ancient tradition of healing and become one in a long line of people who have performed sacred ritual in this ancient way.

In many medicine wheels, each direction is associated with an animal and with one type of energy. For example, in our medicine wheel, the east has the owl, which for us stands for change and the beginning; the south has the lion, which stands for passion and manifestation; the west has the bear, representing healing power and letting go; and the north has the turtle, which stands for grounding and the unknown. The center has She who gardens us from above representing the goddess and essence. Each person calls in his or her own animals, which hold or represent for that individual a particular energy and direction. The medicine wheel can be populated by any of the animals that live or have lived around you on the earth.

Most of the rituals performed by ancient people with the medicine wheel are hidden or long forgotten. Most likely they involved the hunt, rites of passage, the stars, planting, migrations, or the spirits. They were done at a community level and involved huge amounts of energy. Often the making of a medicine wheel involved moving huge stones hundreds of miles, like the making of the pyramids in Egypt. Medicine wheels or stones circles exist from Europe to North America, including those in Avebury, England, and in Chaco Canyon, New Mexico. They were certainly places of great ceremony, places for the gathering of peoples, and were often away from village sites. Sometimes they were burial sites and temples, sometimes they were astronomical devices, but they were always sacred.

The sacred sites were often at the intersection of rivers, on mountaintops, in the center of plains between mountains and rivers. People could get there via the rivers. Even today, the waterways and mountains will lead you to medicine wheels on sacred sites. They were often on the high places, points where the worshipper could see the distant landscape. In any case, these places were deeply sacred and infused with energy. Sacred sites are found at intersections of lines of power, energy lines—places where churches and later other sacred sites were built intuitively by more recent peoples. When you build your small medicine wheel in a power place it holds the potential for change.

Small medicine wheels were built for healing, fertility, and prayer, and to create sacred space. They were made of small animal carvings placed on stones or pieces of wood. They represented the animals the particular culture believed were the embodiment of the sacred energy of the directions. In this book we make our small personal medicine wheel in the tradition of peoples throughout history. You are following an ancient path when you build your own medicine wheel.

How to Make Your Own
Medicine Wheel

This is the medicine wheel that we developed for our book *Path of the Feather*. We use it to heal patients and we use it in workshops. It introduces you to the meaning of the directions, the use of the animals, and the energy of the medicine wheel. In this wheel you will place the animals you have or know in the directions.

First, choose a place that has the right energy for you to set up your medicine wheel. Choose a place that is large enough for the size medicine wheel you want to build, a place that is protected from pets or young children. It can be a tabletop, a dresser, an area of the floor, or an area outdoors. Say a prayer of thanks to the powers or teachers who guide you. Ask for the medicine wheel to create sacred space, inform you about who you are and what you are to do, manifest your dreams, and help you do right action.

Now, choose small sculptures of your spirit animals or of animals that are meaningful to you, and lay them down next to where you will build your medicine wheel. Look around your house and find Zuni fetishes, carvings, jewelry, gifts, ceramics, rubber toys—anything that can be or represent an animal. It can be feathers, bones, fur, a stone, a seashell. Then put a compass in the center of the area you have chosen. Turn the compass so that the needle points to the letter or north. Draw an imaginary circle with your hand on the surface. Choose one animal to go in each of the four directions. Let the animals tell you where they want to be. Choose an animal that represents the meaning of the direction for you.

Place one of the animals in the East on the imaginary circle. Think about the beginning, sunrise, children, change, the wind, air for the East. Think about what this animal means to you or has told you in your visions. Place the next animal in the South of the circle. Think about manifestation, noon, young adults, passion, falling in love, energy, fire for South. Think about what this animal means to you or has told you in your visions. Place the third animal in the West of the circle. Think about healing, evening, adults, letting go, water, deep dreams, for the West. Think about what this animal means to you or has told you in your visions. Place the last animal in the North of the circle. Think about wisdom, integration, elders, grounding, the unknown, family, work, what makes you feel safe, and night for the North. Think about what this animal means to you or has told you in your visions. Finally, place a woman or man figure in the center of the circle. Think about your spiritual center, your essence, about who helps you and guides you for the center of the medicine wheel, and about nurturing and love for the goddess.

You have made your first medicine wheel. Invite your first medicine wheel to begin to change your life. Invite it to make sacred space and make your life a sacred vision quest. You might ask a question and let the answer come to you from an animal in the wheel during the day as a thought or idea. You can ask for something to come to you, and ask the medicine wheel to help it manifest. You can ask for protection for those you love. Finally, you can ask for guidance in doing right action. Go on with your day and watch what gifts come to you, see who you are within the sacred space of your medicine wheel and where you are guided. Look around you for animals that appear, for a feather under your feet.

Give thanks and move into the spiral of your own sacred space. The animal spirits are your companions and teachers now. They are always with you. The animals live within the earth. Their time is your time in the past, present, and future. The animals thank you for inviting them into your medicine wheel and beginning to listen to their voices again.

PART THREE

HEAL NOW

9

RESTORYING CHANGES REALITY

STORY: HE TOOK THE BOYS TO HEAVEN

Matthew was twenty years old. He was beautiful, in the peak of his youth. He was physically fit, handsome, an artist. His blond curls lit up as he smiled. He traveled around the world trading paintings for rides on bush planes. He went to Patagonia, to remote places, and met people and painted more. He hitch-hiked across the pampas. He laughed as he told the stories. Every moment of his life was an adventure.

He came home for a vacation from his travels. He painted a picture of a bird; it was his spirit flying. One night he was hitchhiking home. The driver of the pickup truck was drunk, and the truck went off the mountain, flew over a cliff, and landed in the trees far below. The driver, his brother, a friend, and Matthew were killed instantly. Their bodies were found the next day, deep in the ravine. His mother, Beth, heard about the accident on the radio the next afternoon.

Beth told me this story:

> When I saw him at the funeral home, he looked more beautiful than ever. There was not a scratch on him. I washed him and I

held him close to me like I did when he was a baby. I dressed him in his favorite clothes. As I held him, I heard him speak to me: "Mother, do not worry about me. I did what I wanted to do. I got in the truck to take the boys to heaven. When they crashed they were so frightened. I flew as an eagle spirit and carried them upward. They are all right now. It was what I had to do. I will always love you."

Beth went on, "He was that kind of man, you know. That is what he would do."

She cried at his memorial service, but she told this story, too. She rewrote the story of Matthew's death for her, from the visionary experience she had. She could have lived with a story of drunk driving, anger, and regret. She did not mean to choose this story. Nothing in her life before this event indicated to us that she would do something like this. The story came to her and changed her life. It helped her deal with the almost impossible situation of a mother grieving for her only son. She tells me that she sees him every day in her visions as she drives to work, past the stone memorial built at the place the truck went off the cliff. She sees him as an eagle spirit carrying the boys to heaven. She sees him as a man who died helping others.

Shamanic healing involves changing reality. In sacred space, the shaman sees a vision of what a person needs to be healed. It can be anything from joint surgery to moving energy, from massage to taking out darkness in psychic space. Then the shaman acts to heal. In this section we will discuss three common ways that shamans heal: restorying reality, using creativity, and moving healing energy. We will also talk about ritual and ceremony as healing tools and dealing with the darkness and protection.

Restorying reality is our term for changing a person's belief system and instilling hope and spirit. The shaman traditionally performed a healing ceremony that had several effects. First, it convinced the people they worked with that they would get well. The authority of the shaman, combined with the shaman's connection to the Creator, changed the way the people saw reality. Suddenly, they believed they could be well again.

Second, the shaman enacted a performance ritual with creativity, through art, music, dance, and song, to help the people embody the healing process. When the people saw, felt, heard, and moved in the healing ritual, the healing went deep into their nervous system. When the shaman was a bear who took on the illness, the people saw the bear, heard it growl, felt its fur. Their bodies felt bear healing energy. It went way beyond the mind, into their ancient memories of rituals and ceremonies around fires with people they knew and trusted.

Third, the shaman moved healing energy. The shaman brought energy from the Creator to the people and touched them, rattled over them, moved feathers around them, and the people felt the healing energy inside them and around them move. This process took the illness out and put healing energy from the Creator back in.

Imagery creates reality. The shamanic healer sees an image of healing and of a healing process in imagery space and acts the image into reality, projecting the healing image into people he or she is working with. Shamanic healing involves an intentional projection into the outer world from imagery space to change physical reality and change the physical body. Whether it is surgery or guided imagery, shamanic healing is taking an inner image and manifesting it in outer reality.

Each moment we look at the world around us, we see it within our worldview. The way we see ourselves, our goals, and our ability to succeed creates our present and our future. In the research we did for *Spirit Body Healing* at the University of Florida College of Nursing and College of Medicine, we found that when patients began to tell us the stories of their illnesses, the stories were dark and painful. When they found or created new stories of themselves and their illnesses in hope and love, their lives would change and they would heal. We called the worldview or attitude "the story" and called the shamanic process of change "restorying." All people can find a new story of who they are. Then they can change their lives by making choices based on the new story.

The shaman creates reality by changing the story that reality is hinged on. This is serious magic. People who are ill believe that they need healing. The shaman gives them the faith that they will be healed. There are three simple ways to restory a person's life. The first is through language, the second by changing the way the person looks at things, the third by looking for visionary experiences. The easiest way is by helping people listen to the words they use to describe themselves and what is happening to them. Then they choose new words that are positive and show faith. For example, if they hear themselves saying, "I paid too much. I always do," they can change the words when they tell the story again. The new story could be "I found exactly what I wanted." Restorying your life by retelling your story with new words is powerful and can be done each time you remember to do it. The second way involves actually choosing the way a person can look at something. For example, if you look at your house and say to yourself, "I wish I was living in a bigger house. I am a failure," you can realize what you are doing. The next time, look at your house and say to yourself, "This is perfect for me at this time in my life." When people hear their inner words describing what they see with negativity, they put new ones in to look at the situation in a positive way. The shaman helps the people they work with see and embody a new story of their life. The shamanic magic is the new reality created. When the shaman of old told a person who was ill that the bear would take on the illness, the person had a new way of looking at the world where he or she saw the illness leaving and saw himself or herself healed for the first time. Then the body could let its healing mechanisms function at their best. Shamans do not make up stories that are not real or suggest that people use denial or not see reality. Instead they give people a new worldview, an alternative way of seeing themselves and their lives.

OUR LIFE IS OUR STORY

Each of us already has a story that frames our lives, that tells us who we are and what we want. For example, our story might be "I am successful, I am healthy, I am in love, I am getting what I want in life." Or it might be "I am never able to satisfy anyone around me, I am sick, I never have enough of what I want, I fail because I am hurt, I can't love anyone, I am in limbo."

Examples of dark stories that people have of who they are:

- I fail because I was hurt as a child.
- I am depressed because I was abused.
- I am sick because I did something wrong.
- I cannot ever find someone I get along with.
- There is always something wrong with the person I am in a relationship with.
- I can never change; it's my personality.
- I cannot fall in love; my heart is closed.
- My partner does not see me.

Almost every word you say tells the whole story of your life. When you tell a friend what you are doing, what you are worried about, you tell your story. People say, "I am in limbo, I can't act until this happens, I am fighting with my husband, we have never gotten along." In listening to words of the story, the healer and the person can hear the story and then they can heal the story.

RESTORY YOUR LIFE TO BE LOVED

The most powerful way of restorying your life is based on inviting a visionary experience to come to you. This is what happened to Beth in the story that began this chapter. For Beth, the vision of Matthew came spontaneously. The method of inviting a vision includes art, meditation, walks, prayer, ritual, ceremony, vision quests, and travel. The shaman traditionally had people invite visions with a vision quest. After a visionary experience, they rewrite their life story to include their experience. In the new worldview they can honor it, receive it, and make it part of their life story of who they are. In their peaceful moments, they hold the vision; in their dark moments, they reach for it to comfort them. For example, if in a vision or on a vision quest a person hears an inner voice telling her that she is beautiful, she then can see herself as a person with an inner voice or spirit guide and as a person who is filled with beauty. If a man with colon cancer has a vision of his son as an angel healing him, his new story is that he is a man with cancer who has his son as a healing angel.

As the story of your life grows, you keep retelling it with new words and new ways of seeing in light of things that happen. As the experience grows, the shaman shows people how to make a story of it and put themselves in as the hero or heroine. The shaman does this with words, ritual, and magic. The shaman transfers the story to the person he or she is working with by any means available. If the person is a woman with breast cancer who is making a garden to heal, her story changes from "I am a woman with breast cancer who is depressed and may die" to one in which she is the woman with breast cancer who is creating a mandala garden to heal her spirit and her life. In the process, the person restories her life in light of what she is now doing. As her story forms, she tells it, claims it, takes responsibility for it. She changes her language, the way she sees, and invites a visionary spiritual reality to come to her. This is shamanic transformation at its best. It also can be a change to making the person the shaman. The new story is "I am a shaman healer to heal myself, others, and the earth."

Examples of stories in positivity and love:

- I can succeed in my work and relationships.
- I can heal myself.
- I have guides or helpers to help me heal.
- I can see beauty around me.
- I am on the right path to become myself.
- I am learning from this and growing with each moment.
- I am being guided and taken care of.

- I am in the right place; I can love the people around me.
- I have always been loved.
- There are guardian angels around me who love me; they have always been with me, taking care of me, loving me.

Affirmations to help a person restory his or her life:

- I have choices in every moment.
- There is magnificence in action all around me.
- This is so beautiful.
- Love will heal me and those around me.
- This is meant to be.
- Each problem is a way to evolve and grow.
- My actions are guided by a greater force.

HOW TO RESTORY YOUR LIFE

To restory a life, you do not have to know where you are going in advance. In fact, you don't usually know what the new story of your life will be. You start the process and then experience the story and glimpse it as it happens. Look for the story to appear as you follow your wishes and do what you love. The method of restorying your life includes affirmations and guided imagery. It is taken from our research for *Spirit Body Healing* at the University of Florida, and is directly prescriptive.

Step 1: Find the present story

In step 1, go into your pain and get in touch with the story you are living now. To find your story, all you need to do is look at you life. In this step, you specifically look at the words you use and the way you look at things. In this step, you feel your darkness, embody it, see who you are now.

Step 2: Invite the new story to appear

This is the process, the spiral of action. You begin to use new words to describe who you are and what is happening. Choose the words with intent to be positive and to show faith in yourself. Next, choose to look at things with positivity and faith; each time you realize how you look at something, choose a new way to see. Finally, do a creative process—write, make art, travel, garden, volunteer, go on a vision quest, take workshops. Invite visionary experiences that inform you of who you are. Experience transformation; a basic restorying takes place that makes your whole life view new. Describe yourself in a new way, see yourself in a new way, and see yourself loved and cared for.

Step 3: Rewrite the story of your life

The new story emerges in the process. You see it, honor it, become it, and now tell the new story of who you are. You become the new story. You manifest what you want. You go from being lost or a failure to being a crucial part of the world and a person who helps change reality for everyone. The new story could be "I am a shaman healer. I will use mystical and intuitive tools to heal and change my healing practice."

Once people glimpse their new story, you can show them how to use the story to change their lives and heal. First, restory their past, rewriting their histories to change the way they see themselves. Take each incident that was painful and change the perception of it to be more positive. Next, help them restory the present by finding choices in each moment. This technique allows them to experience each event as part of the new story. You can also show people how to make their new future and get what they want based on the story they experience. This is about goals and defining what people want out of life. Finally, show people how to change their view of an illness if they are ill. The shaman glimpses the story the person needs to heal in visionary space, then makes up the story together with the person and it emerges like art. Then the person listens to the shaman tell the new story and suddenly his or her life is new.

RESTORY THE PAST

Part of the process of restorying is restorying the past. To do this, people go through each painful event in their past and change the way they look at it. The shaman healer uses stories or guided imagery to allow the people to get in touch with events in their past and see that there was a spiritual presence around them taking care of them, protecting them, and loving them. In that way people can rewrite the story of the painful event with the presence of the protector as part of it. Shaman healers believe that the Creator is always present, even in times of darkness. If they can get the people they work with to see this, the restorying occurs.

Again, we emphasize that the shaman does not lie, make up false stories, or suggest that people use denial or not see events that occurred. Restorying is about making a choice to see and choose a different view of reality and leave depression and self-reproach behind. This process allows people to look at their lives from a new perspective. They can look at each event in a new way. Details in events appear that did not exist before. They restory the events of the past, and they can restory their whole lives. It is a significant shamanic transformation of the past in the present. When people restory their lives, they are never the same again. The experience of illness changes as they look at it in the past. In the new story, illness becomes an opportunity for the spirit to be seen and for growth. It is not just darkness anymore. Any event has many truths. Our world-view is one truth. Traditionally, the shaman would go in a sweat lodge with a person and see the events of the person's life. The shaman would then tell the new story of the person being taken care of by the Creator and would remove the painful event by moving energy. Restorying is a contemporary form of this ancient process that any healer can use today without relying on a sweat or even a visionary space to heal.

Restorying the past, or rewriting our histories, is beautiful and life-changing. A woman who was abused as a child goes deeply back into the incidents. She sees the pain and suffering and also for the first time sees an angel looking over her and saving her life. Now in her memories of the past, it is the angel who speaks to her, not the abuser. A person can go deeply into an incident in the past, see more than he or she remembers, see through shamanic eyes, and come back with a new story. That is what Beth did in the story that began this chapter. She rewrote her history to include the visionary story of Matthew taking the boys to heaven.

RESTORY THE PRESENT

If you are waiting for someone, you can be thinking, "Why does she not come? Doesn't she love me? Am I worthless? No one loves me, no one has ever loved me." Then you become depressed and more thoughts come about abandonment and lack of love. The first thought spirals and triggers the rest. Or you can think, "I will wait a million years her. She is so wonderful. What is a moment? She loves me perfectly." Both these thoughts are stories that show you who you are and what you think of yourself in the present moment. In each moment in the present, there is a story of who you are.

If you have a thought like "She doesn't love me, that is why she is late," you can choose in that moment to substitute the thought "She loves me perfectly but is busy. I will wait and rest." The first story will lead to you being sad or getting angry and ready to fight. The second story is a meditation to learn to love the person more deeply.

For this process the shaman helps the person look at the language in his or her story and in each moment rewrite the words in positivity. The healer can help the person look for expectations in the story he or she holds. If this person is expecting a friend to come on time and then gets angry because the friend is late, the story can be written without the expectation. The new story can be "Whenever she comes is fine." A shaman healer can also help a person use spiritual ways of looking at himself or herself to reframe what is happening in the moment.

RESTORY THE FUTURE

The person's new story tells him or her a great deal about the future. The story helps make the person's goals and healing intent clear. To make any decision, a person needs to know his or her priorities. Then each choice can be made based on getting what the person wants. Restorying the future is a way of manifesting the reality you want to live in. Just as you don't know the story before you start the process, you don't know the future. It forms itself around your dreams.

Let's say a person wants to be in a loving relationship. Then that person can make the story a story of someone who is looking for her lover. The healer can show him or her how to embellish the story and make it more real. For example, the person might say the lover will love beyond perfectly and love to make him or her grow. Then, the person can go through life inviting the lover to appear. The person can even tell everyone that he or she is looking for a special spirit lover who will see and love, and can ask friends to help.

RESTORY ILLNESS

Each person has a story of his or her illness. The stories are not what you would think they would be; they are not simple or ordinary. They almost always involve what the doctor has told the person and why the person thinks he or she became ill. The stories often involve guilt or mystical events. All these parts of the story can be restoryed.

A healer who helps someone restory an illness helps the person deal with his or her prognosis. Ask, "What did the doctor say?" Then you can show how to change the story to allow for the person's own individuality, to allow for magic and for miracles. For example, if a physician gave statistics about cancer recurrence, you tell the person to remember that these numbers apply only to populations, not individuals. Even if a person's odds of being cured are low, when a person is cured, he or she is 100 percent cured. We say, "There is no reason you can't be one of the ones who are cured. The people healed are real—there is no reason it won't be you." That is an example of a change in language and a change in the way of looking at something that affects a person's whole way of seeing the world. Instead of thinking of having a 10 percent chance of survival, a person can look at himself or herself as being the one in the group who will be 100 percent cured. When you listen to a story about prognosis, find the detail that make the person you are working with special and more likely to heal. Tell that to the person as the new story.

To restory an illness, you can help people make their stories the most positive stories they can get in touch with. They can rethink the story of why they became ill. They can look for mystical events that point to healing. They can make a new vocabulary and recreate words to define your experience. For example, a woman with breast cancer told us that she called her medical team her "boob squad" and relanguaged her entire experience to be positive, humorous, and hopeful. She called her radiation therapy the magical beam of healing light. Her restorying made her problem a challenge and gave her positivity and hope.

MAKE NEW MEANING

Carl Jung tells about living a life within a story of meaning. Jung was in New Mexico visiting Taos pueblo. He and Ochiwa Biano, the chief of the Taos Indians, stood on the roof of the pueblo at sunrise. Biano pointed to the sun. He told Jung, "Without my people, without our prayers, the sun would not rise in the morning and the world would be dark." Can you imagine believing in your soul that your prayers make the sun rise? That story gives your life meaning on a level modern humans may not even be able to understand. Jung suggested that finding a new story to live by would be deeply healing for people today. He said it does not matter whether the story is true in the light of modern science. Jung says that his patients who believed in an afterlife of reincarnation did better than those who did not. He said that modern humans have lost this connection with nature and lost the personal stories that give their lives this kind of meaning.

In our research for *Spirit Body Healing,* we learned that as part of their healing and restorying of their lives, people acted in a way they believed was helping the world. Many of their new stories were based on the generosity of giving. They were proud and spiritually strong. They received gifts of spirit in their visions and shared the gifts with others. This part of the restorying process is about going out in the world from a place of personal power to make a difference in world. The people feel empowered with action, not belief—not words, but doing. It is not about sitting in your room worrying, but about entering into life's fray, taking sides, and making change. To be a shaman healer and save a river, you have to write letters, go to meetings, protest, join organizations, raise money, and act. If you believe that the river needs you for it to be saved, you have meaning in your new story. The shamans traditionally healed themselves, then others, and then the community and the earth. The healing was not complete unless it flowed outward to the earth in service and spirit. The spirit animals tied the shamans to the earth; they took the shamans out of the realm of humans and expanded the reality to include something greater of which we are part.

THE POWER OF WORDS

Words interface between the physical world and the spirit world. A word is the physical blending of the physical and the spiritual—that is why words are so powerful. What do words do? First there is a vision, then the word. The word starts a vortex of energy and moves it forward. First it resonates in the chest. The word mixes air in a physical movement. There is a resonance of energy. The energy moves outward and travels into someone's ears.

Words create a repatterning of thought in visionary space and in physical reality. Words come from spirit into the inner world; they bring the inner world outward. Words are true embodiment, energy in the body, as movement creates vibration. It is embodied experience that shifts reality in a second. The word creates form, then reality, so be careful what you say as a shaman healer. If you say a person is loved by the Creator, he or she will be; if you say the person is very ill, the person is very ill.

Michael went to his dentist with a toothache. It was a simple visit—nothing to worry about, he thought. But the dentist told him he had a large lesion and he needed to go to an oral surgeon and have it removed. That week, Michael thought, "A large lesion—what is that?" For a physician, *lesion* is an ominous word, so in his mind it grew. The lesion become larger and more frightening. Michael then felt pain all the time and found swellings under his jaw. He began to think, "I have cancer of the jaw. Will I die?" During the week he worried, his pain increased. He developed other symptoms and began to become depressed. He went to the oral surgeon, frightened and confused. This dentist looked at the films and told him it was a wisdom tooth with an infection under it and he would take it out. He could do it in a half hour and it would be healed in a week. Michael left the office a new man. A weight had been lifted from his shoulders. With two words, the first dentist had started a progression that led to fear and depression. The second one put in words and his spirit was healed.

This story is a simple one that has meaning in more serious stories. A man goes to the hospital with a stomachache. He has an X ray. A doctor comes in and does not look him in the eye. He tells him, "You have cancer. Get your things in order; you will die soon," and leaves. The man spirals down into depression. Nothing any doctor could tell him means anything. He dies in months. We often hear this kind of story. The words are like a curse. In tribal cultures, this phenomenon was called voodoo death. When people were told they would die, they often did die. Research revealed that they shut down their vagus nerve and stopped their own heart. In shamanic terms, their spirit was taken away. The first thing I do when I see a patient is listen to what words they were told by other healers and family members and restory them. The shaman restorys the curse of illness to blessing: "You will get well."

Guided imagery to restory a life

Make yourself comfortable. You can be sitting or lying down. Loosen tight clothing, uncross your legs and arms. Close your eyes. Let your breathing slow down. Take several deep breaths. Let your abdomen rise as you breathe in and fall as you let your deep breath out. As you breathe in and out you will become more and more relaxed. You may feel sensations of tingling, buzzing, or relaxation; if you do, let those feelings increase. You may feel heaviness or lightness; you may feel your boundaries loosening and your edges softening.

Now let yourself relax. Let your feet relax, let your legs relax. Let the feelings of relaxation spread upward to your thighs and pelvis. Let your pelvis open and relax. Now let your abdomen relax, let your belly expand, do not hold it in anymore. Now let your chest relax, let your heartbeat and breathing take place by themselves. Let your arms relax, your hands relax. Now let your neck relax, your head, your face. Let your eyes relax; see a horizon and blackness for a moment. Let these feelings of relaxation spread throughout your body. Let your relaxation deepen. If you wish, you can count your breaths and let your relaxation deepen with each breath.

In your mind's eye, look at the story of your own life. To do this, imagine you are writing a novel. The novel has a plot—a beginning, a middle, an end. It has characters—a hero, helpers, adversaries. It has a challenge or problem, a solution, and an ending or process. Look at your life now as your novel in progress. Let the story come to you. See how it starts, how it progresses, where it is now. Do this with as little judgment as you can. Be open and accept what you see; do not try to guide it. Remember, this is the story of your life as it is, as you see it right now.

Now examine your story. See what themes it has, see what your attitude toward the challenge is. Are you optimistic, positive? Do you feel you can succeed in this situation you find yourself in?

Now let another story come to you. Give yourself time for this new story to emerge. Let this story be a story of the life that you would like to have. Start telling yourself this story from a point of view of positivity, of optimism, of succeeding in the challenges that lie before you. Let yourself be the hero of your healing story, let yourself be triumphant. See what strategies you can use to vanquish the adversaries of your own life.

When you are ready, return to the room where you are doing the exercise. First move your feet and then move your hands. Move them around and experience the feeling of the movement. Press your feet down onto the floor, feel the grounding, feel the pressure on the bottom of your feet, feel the solidity of the earth. Feel your backside on the chair; feel your weight pressing downward. Now open your eyes. Look around you. Stand up and stretch. Move your body; feel it move. You are back; you can carry the experience of the exercise outward to your life. You will feel stronger and be able to see deeper. You will be in a healing state. Each time you do the exercise you will be more relaxed and be able to go deeper and be more deeply healed.

You can do this guided imagery with your own life or with the life of someone you love or are helping heal.

10

ART AND CREATIVITY AS SHAMANISM

SEE LIGHT AND BEAUTY IN YOUR VISIONARY SPACE

The shaman is one who sees light and beauty and lets others share that vision. When you see beauty and people can see out of your eyes, they see the beauty, too. They see themselves as beautiful; they are within beauty, looking out of God's eyes. Seeing the person you are working with as beauty, seeing his or her authentic part as beauty, is effortless for the shaman. But a person who is injured does not see his or her own beauty. The shaman restorys and manifests the new story as reality. Love sees the beauty; creativity makes the beauty manifest. Making art opens your eyes to the beauty around you. The gift of creativity lets you be love seeing beauty.

Artist healers are powerful shamanic figures in health care today. Healers can see out of the eyes of the artist and still be healers. They can see beauty and enhanced colors, shapes, and shadows, and people they work with can see out of their eyes. Healing artists as shaman healers have a process that is simple and beautiful. They are open. As artists, they can be with people's fear and gently coax them through the darkness, loving them and seeing them in beauty all the while. They go from fear to faith, realizing there is nothing to be afraid of. As a shaman healer, you offer people the gift of love. If your intention is love, it is more powerful than action. You will do the right thing. You have the intention of wanting to be helpful. A dialogue emerges: "Try painting," "No, I don't want to," "Oh, try dance," "I don't want to." Intention is where your power is. If a person rejects one medium, suggest another. Allow resistance to change on the spur of the moment; encourage constant change. Encourage people you are working with to open their bodies as if they were a painting of beauty and perfection. Encourage them to remove the gray and paint the picture. Create their body and a canvas as an artist who extracts the pain. That is seeing though the eyes of the artist. The artist leads us; there is an artist within us who leads us there. The artist leads us to moments of simple seeing of perfect beauty.

As the shaman healer, you are the one who loves the people so that they can restory their life as loved. You see them as beautiful and give them the opportunity of opening their hearts. As the shaman healer, you feel the beauty and the power of their story as they tell it; you reflect it back to them as power and beauty so they can see it and see themselves in that way. They see the light, literally. It is about being seen and loved beyond perfectly by God.

USE WRITING, ART, MUSIC, DANCE AS A SHAMAN HEALER

The shaman was and still is an artist. The first healer and the first artist were one person, the shaman. The first art was transformative—the cave painters made art to bring animals to them in the hunt. The artist uses writing, art, music, dance to change reality; that is what the shaman has always done. The shaman traditionally healed with a multimedia ceremony that is most similar to what we now call performance art. The skills of the artist are now the ones that the shaman healer can use to heal and to do ritual and ceremony. Shamans can use creativity and art to heal themselves and the people they work with. A Mexican shaman asked the people he or she was working with, "When was the last time you made art, danced, made music, wrote?" Then, before the shaman would do the healing, the shaman had the person make art. The art would bring the person back his or her soul, bring images up to the person's consciousness that would be self-healing, bring the voices of the Creator to the person. That was the first step to shamanic healing.

Shamans makes art to heal themselves. The process of making art is the process of seeing into visionary space, the same process shamans use to see as they heal. Shamans can also use art to heal the people they are working with. They are facilitators of healing; they help the people see into their own space by making art. When shaman healers facilitate a person making art, they are using the oldest tools of the shaman.

Shamanism and Art Were Once One

Anthropological studies such as the Harvard Kalahari study and research into cave paintings indicate that thousands of years ago art and healing were one. It is our belief that the shaman came from the ordinary person making art. When you make art you concentrate deeply; you go into a creative place inside you and have ideas or visions or thoughts. From these inner meditations you create a work of art. The creative trance takes you to the inner world where you are different. In the !Kung culture all the members of the tribe danced and went into a trance and felt the boiling energy come from within them. Then cultures changed. The hunter-gatherer cultures became more complicated, and people began to specialize. People did not dance three times a week because they were out hunting or building houses or gathering food for a larger group. And as the people stopped making art several times a week they lost their ability to see in the inner world. They simply got out of practice. Something else took their attention. But there were still individuals among the people who danced and made amulets and sang. There were still people who went into a trance and saw spirits in the inner world.

Human culture had gone from a place where everyone was an artist healer to a place where some people, who were naturally gifted at it, did it for the group. But two of the main characteristics of early art and healing still remained. Art and healing were still one—they just were not being done by everyone. The shaman was the first artist and the first healer. The shaman was one person who filled both roles. And in the time of the shaman, art was still transformational. Art was made to heal or to hunt, to change the world. Eventually, in tribal cultures, music and dance were combined with costumes and storytelling and with objects and paintings in the creation of a ritual that we would now call theater or performance art. In ancient times this ritual was sacred and was part of the culture's medicine and healing practices. We believe it is now time for everyone to take back the role of the shaman, of the artist healer. The transformational process is too powerful to keep in the realm of the specialist today. The earth needs everyone to become a shaman healer.

CREATIVE HEALING

In a previous book, *Creative Healing,* we discuss the field of art in healing and give specific instructions for making healing art. In this chapter we will give an overview of how to use healing art for the shaman healer. Making healing art is easy. It is one of the most powerful tools the shaman uses to heal. All of us can heal ourselves with art. There are five simple steps to begin. The steps are the same if you are healing yourself or a person you work with.

The first is to reclaim your inner artist. The second is to make a studio. The third is to create time to make art. The fourth is to choose a medium that is natural for you to begin with. The fifth is to begin to make art where you are in your life right now. Art, like a wall you build in a new house, has something there to see at the end of each day. Healing art is real, tangible, and can be seen, felt, or heard. Healing follows.

This chapter is not about how to make professional art. It is not a lesson on how to draw or dance. It is instead an invitation to do whatever you want to do to explore what you are attracted to. In art and healing, the singing of one note can be as healing as singing a choral work, the writing of a paragraph as healing as writing a novel. We want to make the process of making art as simple as possible so you can do it every day or teach a person you are working with to do it. All you need is a half hour a day. Paint for a half hour a day, write on a laptop, play the guitar. Maintain your creative work in a way that is easy and fun. That is what healing yourself with art is about. The road to get there will be your own. Any way you make art is fine. In fact, to start out, the simplest way is probably best. It will grow from there.

We can give you advice that works for all media and is general enough not to hold you back. First, it is essential to be as flexible as possible. Artists-in-residence who work in hospital programs talk about being able to bend to the situation they find themselves in. If a person you are working with is in bed and wants to dance, it can still be done; he or she just has to move in a different way than on a dance floor. Second, consistency is important in the beginning; try to have enough consistency to make art every day. Know that this work is your gift to you to be healthy. You give yourself this time to be healthy, to feel alive, full, and the most creative that you can. Value yourself enough to do it. Believe that this is simple and as important as anything else that you do in life. In our culture, where most of us work long hours, this is about being free. We need a place in our lives and in ourselves to be truly free, to be who we are, and to be ourselves.

Step 1: Reclaim your inner artist

Reclaiming the inner artist is one of the most important shifts you will ever make in your life as a shaman. This process is about realizing that inherent in life, inside of life, is the person as a shaman artist. You have always been an artist, but you may not have seen it or valued it as much as you will now. This process is about illuminating the beauty within you. Our goal is for you to be able to say, "I am an artist," or, even better, to say, "I am a healing artist," or even to say, "I am a shamanic artist healer." To internalize this concept, know that in everything that you do each day there are opportunities to be creative. An artist is a way of being, a way of seeing. An artist looks deeply at light, at shadows. An artist looks deeply into each moment. The essential step is realizing that you want to be an artist. In most people's lives, there have been barriers and obstacles that have prevented them from doing it. Often this was because of a career choice or criticism. Realize that all of us have had obstacles to passionate creativity. The obstacles will not hold you back anymore. It is worth the risk to become your inner artist now. Let go of any insecurities. The risk of your illness, depression, or lack of meaning in your life is more than what you feared in being an artist. This is an opportunity to let go of your fear. What was threatening before is no longer important now. When people who are ill start painting, they feel they are up against the wall; there is nothing else they can do. The risk of not making art is worse than the risk of making art.

First reclaim the "Yes, I am an artist" that we all have within us. In the broadest sense, the definition of *artist* is much wider than most of us think. We usually think that an artist is a painter, musician, dancer, or poet. But for healing art, an artist makes art in any and every way you can think of. We have separated ourselves from what we have done in our lives; we say we are not an artist but a mother, a physician, a gardener, whatever. We want to broaden artistry to include our whole lives. You can become clear that you are an artist in your work and in your whole life. It is a shift of who you think you are. When you reclaim your inner artist, you realize that there is an aspect of yourself that you illuminate like an artist. You reclaim a way of being that has been reserved for artists. You reclaim the shaman healer of ancient times. To be a shaman healer it is necessary to be creative.

Step 2: Make your own studio

One of the most essential parts of the process of healing yourself with art is to allow yourself to create space to make art in your busy life. One of the ways you do this is by making a studio. Your studio can be a pad of paper, a laptop computer, a corner of the kitchen, a whole room at home, or a room somewhere else. To make healing art, you make a commitment. You decide that your art is as important as anything else that you do in your life. It is as important as your children, your job, your lists, and shopping; it is as important as the most important thing you do. Making art is what will heal you, and your studio will be the space where you will go to survive and heal. It is about finding an opportunity for yourself to do exactly what you want and need for yourself.

For many people, taking care of themselves is a crucial step. This is especially true for women who care for everyone around them. The decision to make yourself the focus of your healing process is critical. Making healing art is about you healing your life. When you do this, your family, children, and friends will be taken care of because you will be whole. You deserve it. One woman who was a healer felt that she was being selfish when she made her art. She was so used to taking care of others that when she gave some pure time to herself, she felt guilty. When she developed breast cancer, she realized that she deserved to be taken care of by others now and, more importantly, that she needed to take care of herself. So she made a piece of art that showed all the hands of all the people who were taking care of her and in each palm was a message of love to her to get well. It made her cry every time she read the messages and realized she needed and deserved the wonderful care her friends, family, and caregivers were providing her. A crucial part of her art was accepting that she needed and wanted the care.

Step 3: Create a time to make art

Every day, create a routine. Make art for so many hours a day, or so many hours a week. But most important, create sacred time, a time that is undiluted by time as you ordinarily know it. Time is the most precious resource you have. When you give yourself time, it is the most useful gift for healing art that you can give yourself. You give yourself attention; you listen to yourself. In the studio you can share with others, but you need your own space. You create a boundary around yourself, walls or rugs or bookcases, and you go into that place and work. This is an opportunity to go into your own world. You take a deep breath and then go into a different flow of time and consciousness. It is a suspension of time—an experience of time that is different from everyday time. It has to do with being totally focused. You have to be focused for images to emerge. It is like giving birth: you pay total attention to what you are doing. In ordinary life you never are focused enough to be still, to go inward enough to be truly creative. The distractions are not healing. We go to a therapist to focus on ourselves; this does it better. The focus and concentration create the physiology of healing and help the immune system function at its best.

It is really about creating moments that are your own. Create a space right now in the moment. It is a deliberate conscious act that has a space and a time. The space is sacred because it is the work of your heart, the work of who you really are. Make art with letters you never mail. Steal a moment to sing a lullaby to yourself, to another. Activate the artist within.

Step 4: Choose a Medium

When we have a physical illness, a depression, or a life crisis, or when we need to grow, we start to heal ourselves with art by opening ourselves up to our inner voices of change and creativity. We allow ourselves to listen to those voices and to let their messages emerge. In this process, choosing a medium is the next priority. Resonating with the medium is resonating with the creative process. Resonating means doing a type of artistic process that will flow with your energy. What is it that you do that flows with your body's energy? Everyone has different affinities for different types of art and different processes. You do not need to worry much about which medium you will choose, because when creativity flows it becomes multimedia, but you need to start with something as the doorway, something that will allow you to have the sense of being an artist. So you could say, "I am a painter." Then the world will expand to other media.

When you use art as healing, you don't package the experience in one medium, because you are not making art to make art. You are making art to free yourself, making art to heal. When we talk about resonating with a material, the process is unique and personal for each person. Explore materials in writing, visual arts, dance, and music. See what appeals to you. Let yourself imagine using a medium and see what you like, imagine how you would feel. Or you may have chosen your medium already. You may have made art or played music before or seen yourself as making art in your daydreams. Ask yourself what you want to do. Are you a painter, a sculptor, a musician, a poet, a storyteller, a dancer? Have you ever wanted to create something and been afraid or too busy to do it? The artist is all of these people; the artist uses all media as healing.

When you close your eyes, what one medium emerges for you? There are two times in your life when you were most likely to have been an artist: as a very young child and as a teenager. As a young child, you may have had art lessons or done art in school. As a teenager—when you started to separate from your parents, to form your own identity—there were things you did naturally to become yourself. There is something from that place of individuation that can help you now. Go to what were you before you became an adult, before your roles were fully defined. We will do an imagery to go back to both of those places, to be there and see what medium resonates. But you will see more than that; you will see yourself as an artist again.

Guided imagery for choosing a medium

Close your eyes and rest. Let your breathing get deeper; let your abdomen rise and fall as you breathe. Let your body take over and take you deeper. Now go back to a moment in your life when you were a child making art. Go back in time through the past to a point in your childhood where you remember a moment of making art that was full of happiness, a moment of making art where you were the most free. Go back to that moment in your life when you actually lived making art, when you allowed yourself to be truly creative and satisfied. Go back to that moment and go into your body. Remember how it felt, remember the world around you, remember the way you experienced the situation you were in. Spend some time in your child's body and be with that child. Be in the situation where you were making art as a child and watch your hands. Remember your thoughts and what it felt like, and look at what materials you were using. Feel how they felt, and how you felt, and totally be with it. Spend some time being with the activities you were doing, feel your hands, feel your body as you were doing it. Be there and rest in its beauty.

Then go back to a moment in your life when you were in trouble, when you were sad or lonely or lost or upset. Maybe it was a time when you were a teenager newly exploring who you were, separating from your parents. Go back to a time when you were discovering who you were. Go back to a moment when you were in conflict and pain, when you experienced despair. Go back to the darkness there, experience your full range of emotions, and remember what you reached out for when you reached into yourself. Remember who you were then, what you were thinking, what you were seeing with your eyes. Remember what you talked about, what you wanted to achieve. Was it writing poetry, making sculpture, painting? How did you explore the possibilities in your life? What did you do to get away from the problems, to go deep into your privacy, into yourself? Go to that moment and see what you were striving for, what your desires were.

Now remember a time in your youth when you were still

uninhibited. What was that dream, the dream before life became so formed, when you thought anything was still possible, without any concept of failing? What were your dreams and desires? What was the glimmer of what you might resonate with? What did you do to go elsewhere and find out who you were? When you see yourself in a time of trouble, before you return, come back into the brightest place you know now in your life. Come back into the most beautiful vision that you can remember, a moment of love and joy. Let that moment of happiness wash over the moments of sadness from your past. Let them be cleansed; let yourself come out into the light and rest there now. Don't stay in the sadness after seeing it; come back now into your joy.

Next you will pick a medium, but the opportunity to integrate all the media in the process is important. We don't want to segregate the arts, to compartmentalize them into painting, music, dance, poetry, and storytelling, when in our experience it is a more integrated process. We have found that being a healing artist is about being open to all the modalities. We separate them in the beginning because it's usually one medium you choose, but we have found an integration actually occurs. The dancer, for example, uses all of the arts. In many programs we've watched healing artists as they have evolved into renaissance artists. They walk into patients' rooms and can draw, dance, and even play music. They may be best at their own medium, but the rest come forth and make them more alive.

Step 5: Make art where you are in your life right now

Finally, we make art. Next is the process itself: to draw, to move, to write, or start a song. It is really simple. As simple as breathing or being in love. The experience of art and healing can be visualized as taking place on four spirals: the spiral of lived experience, the spiral of transformation, the spiral of empowerment, and the spiral of love. This description of how art and healing takes place is not theoretical. It is real. It comes from the experiences of people who have healed themselves with art, music, and dance, and it is taken from research at the University of Florida, Gainesville, from the actual stories people have told us. It starts from right where you are now. The first spiral of lived experience starts from your illness, your depression, your problems, your joy. The four spirals of art and healing are about you starting out from your life, about making the first piece of art simply from who you are now. We think the four spirals are useful for you, because this way of seeing art and healing divides the process into four parts that you can look at separately. Its framework helps you to understand that the process is easy and automatic and yet powerful and profound.

The entire healing process can be pictured in your mind's eye in metaphorical form as a journey on a sacred spiral. The spiral down can be imagined as a concentric pathway of creativity. Spirals are concentric forces that bring a person down into their own inner creative energy. When you reach the center of these spirals you will reach the center of your heart, where you are deeply connected to the world. Within the center of the heart, an inner eye opens up, the eye of awareness and witness. From the center of your spirit, you experience your inner connectedness. As the art comes out, you see that everything comes out, and you are like everything. This is about birth. The art is what you are giving birth to. The art in this sense is an offering that heals you, an offering directly from your heart.

EXPERIENCE LIGHT AND BEAUTY

William, a cancer survivor, told us,

> When I was ill, I realized I was dealing with the fear of my own death. I was afraid. When I made it through, I realized suddenly what I was afraid of. It was the unknown behind each tree. Then I realized I had nothing to be afraid of. What was behind each tree did not matter. I was not afraid anymore. You

know, if you walk down a path in the forest, the smells change as you walk. Did you know the leaves sparkle and become illuminated at their edges and the shadows dance across the branches? Did you know you can feel the wind shift directions over your body, and you can hear each branch rustle, each acorn fall? All of a sudden, I realized I could see out of the eyes of the artist. I could see the forest illuminated, alive, and glimmering in a way I had never seen it before I started drawing. That experience was a heightened sense of being, a way of being able to experience life as an artist.

11

MOVING ENERGY, HEALING ENERGY

Good Morning America filmed Michael working with a patient for a segment on alternative medicine. This is the story of that healing:

I chose Meg for the *Good Morning America* piece because of her ability to see in her visionary space. Meg had severe rheumatoid arthritis. After years of our working together, her arthritis was almost healed. Now the work was concentrating on empowering her as a woman and letting her manifest the life she wanted. Shaman healing starts in the body, moves to the mind, goes to spirit, and then changes the person's whole life.

We have worked together for years to manifest her own personal visions of healing in the outer world. She was originally referred to me by a physician for a shamanic initiation. I worked with her inner healers, her spirit guides, and her spirit animals. Initially we did guided imagery and she had her own visions of a healer who would come out of her chest and fight adversaries. I could see this healer in my own visions when I worked with her. When I work with patients, I go into their visions and see out of their eyes. I can see their guides, can see the adversaries. I can pull them out quickly, and even move things in there to help her battle her illness. I can attack the adversary, act as her ally, and protect her; I am active in imagery space. Some healers choose to let the person image and not enter their space; that is personal style.

After years of working together, the work matured and became deeper. Recently she came to see me with her latest vision. She brought a photograph she had taken of a rose. When she looked at the photo, she saw a shadow of a bear in the petals. She told me she wanted to receive the combined power of the rose and the bear. She saw that as a metaphor for softness and smoothness and for courage and strength. I told her that the rose was a powerful ancient healing symbol; it had energy and sent out healing aroma. The bear was the most basic symbol of healing in many cultures; it stood for rapid healing and renewal of tissue structures. A bear can heal quickly after an injury and restructure the tissue so that only days afterward, no scar can be seen.

With each person I heal, first I talk to the patient and invite the person to tell me his or her images and issues, then we do guided imagery together, and then I move energy with a feather or do body work. Finally, we go out into nature and do a ceremony. I see the ceremony in my mind as the session evolves. Sometimes I send the person out in a vision quest alone. Meg and I decided to go up to the top of Mount Tamalpais with my bearskin. We would make a medicine wheel, she would lie in the center of it, I would cover her with rose petals, and then we would bring out the bear. We went out into the rose garden my wife, Nancy, had created before she died of breast cancer. We picked roses, we picked sage, we prayed and gave thanks.

At the mountaintop we found the ancient sacred circle I often used with patients for ritual. We gave thanks to the Creator and called in spirits and helpers, teachers and ancestors. We thanked the Creator for this day and for our bodies. I thanked the Creator for giving me my healing abilities. We asked the Creator to be with us in this healing. We vowed to be honest and do our best, to be humble and to pray to heal the earth and all its creatures. We prayed to bring in the energies of each of the directions. We prayed for healing forces to come to us to heal this woman, to help her be healed. We prayed for the spirits of the animals that had come to her to help her heal.

Then Meg lay down in the circle, I covered her with rose petals we had picked, and she let the rose energy come into her body to heal her. I put on the bearskin and danced clockwise around the circle. I felt bear come into me. I felt my nails turn into claws, my skin to fur, my nose become black and rough and moist. As I danced I asked bear to come into me, to bring me the power of the bear to heal. I became bear. I growled, I scratched, I saw out of the eyes of the bear. I let the energy of the bear shaman healer come into me and flow to Meg to help heal her arthritis and her life. I danced for hours as she lay there under the rose petals. As I danced the sun set—the bear was silhouetted against the mountains and the sea, dancing and healing.

Then Meg stood and I put the bearskin over her shoulders. I did this gently and with ceremony, as a blessing. She took the bear and her face changed—she became an old woman, an ancient healer. She danced as the woman and then the bear came into her and she danced as the bear. She took the power of the bear, bringing the recuperative and regenerative power into her. She restructured herself as a bear would, regenerating tissue, healing joints. She said later that there was no room for the arthritis when the bear came in. Illness and the bear could not be there at the same time.

As we left at dark, after sunset, she told me she had been totally changed by this experience. The bear had restructured her body and her life in a way she had not seen before. She had been deeply empowered. Her own vision of the rose and the bear had been manifest in the outer world. And for *Good Morning America,* the bear healer returned to be seen again by the people of the earth.

HEALING ENERGY

The shaman feels healing energy. The shaman can feel the energy of acupuncture or qi, the energy of healing and life.

Healing energy has always been a central concept in healing. Most healing systems throughout history had concepts of healing energy that were basic to how people healed. When people talk of healing, when they experience healing, they feel energy. When healers talk of a resonation of the body, mind, and spirit, they mean a freeing of energy—a buzzing, a tingling, a vibration, a hovering. The energy is felt as a sensation, a feeling. It can flow throughout the body, from body to body, from the universe to us. It has been seen by psychics and meditators and has been portrayed in art.

What is this energy, this qi, prana, kundalini, God's breath, acupuncture energy meridians, chakras, life force? It is an integral part of the human experience. Perhaps the simplest metaphor for how the shaman heals is that he or she frees our body's healing energy to flow. When the healing energy is freed by the shaman, the spirit soars, goes home, unites with the deep source, and energy is released like a torrent, like a breakthrough, like a waterfall. The bringing home releases energy. The freeing of the spirit puts you there by itself.

The shaman can see, feel, and move the vibrational healing energy in the people he or she works with. In fact, the shaman has a way of seeing the person as light or energy. The shaman is the embodiment of energy and turns the person into the same. Working with energy makes the shaman an expert in healing by laying on hands and therapeutic touch. Whether the shaman is working with his or her hands, a feather, a rattle, a scalpel, or by sucking, the shaman moves energy. The shaman can see where the energy needs to go, where it is in excess and where it is lacking, where it is illness, and where it is healing.

Each shaman works with healing energy in a different way. A shaman may not use the word *energy* or look at healing in that way. The way shamans work depends on the cultural tradition they were raised in. Since most of us have not been raised in a particular shamanic tradition, we have the opportunity to choose and create the way we work with healing energy. No way is better than another; what is best is what works for you.

Shamans see the illness in visionary space and take it out. They remove the illness with any technique they have learned. Techniques include surgery, psychic surgery, visionary tools such as guided imagery, or use of hands in therapeutic touch techniques. Then many shamans put healing energy back in with similar techniques. They use hands, rattles, drums, or feathers to take the illness out and put it in a safe place, usually a fire, and then they put new healing energy in. The whole process comes from a higher power—it is facilitated with prayer, ceremony, and calling in the higher power. The visions and healing energy come from the Creator and are accessed by the shaman. The steps to moving healing energy are: first, pray to bring in the higher power's healing energy; second, remove the illness and get rid of it; and third, put in new healing energy.

HEALING ENERGY IN MANY CULTURES

Healing energy is an ancient concept that has been used in every culture from the beginning of recorded history. It is a real lived experience of humans on earth. It is felt and seen by both the healer and the patient. In *Spirit Body Healing,* the book based on our study on how creativity heals, conducted at the University of Florida, we described how all the participants felt healing energy as a part of their healing. They described the feeling as buzzing, tingling, lightness, heaviness, movement, heat. The experience of energy by both the healer and the person being healed is a crucial part of shamanic healing.

Healing energy is critical to shamanic healing. The life force manifests itself in the human body as energy. The energy moves, creating an energy field that can be seen and utilized for healing. The energy can be defined as the life force that energizes our life and keeps us healthy. It is the life-giving and healing energy that is within each of us. Any healer can make use of healing energy in a simple and practical way. Healing energy can be incorporated into any healing practice. Each healer sees and feels the energy in his or her own individual way. We will present a simple method of feeling and seeing healing energy and moving it in the body that any healer can use.

Five thousand years ago, ancient spiritual traditions of India described a universal energy that they called prana. They believed that prana was the breath of life that moved through all forms to give life. For thousands of years, yogic healers worked with prana using breathing techniques, meditation, and physical exercise to produce altered states of consciousness and longevity.

The Kabbalah, Jewish mystical teachings written about 500 B.C., calls these energies the astral light. Christian paintings and sculptures show a halo around the head of Christ and other spiritual leaders. Similarly, we see this halo on statues and paintings of the Buddha, and also see energy or light coming from the fingers of many of the gods of India in paintings. The human energy field or the aura of the body appears in ninety-seven different cultures, according to John White in his book *Future Science*.

CHINESE MEDICINE AND QI

China has one of the oldest concepts of healing energy. Qi, pronounced "chee," is the natural energy in all life, the vital energy. All creatures in nature have this same vital life force and are all connected to one another through the life force. Qi is believed to flow and be a field within each person. Illness results from problems in qi . This broad theory of energy and illness is the basis of Chinese medicine. Qi is everywhere in the body. It moves or circulates in one direction in channels called meridians. It moves in blood vessels with blood and is within all organs. Qi meridians are not the same as the nerves or blood vessels or lymph pathways. In Chinese medicine, the organ systems are connected with meridians of qi flow. For example, the lung meridian is far beyond the lung—it goes all over the body.

Qi is said to flow or move in balance without interruption when a person is healthy. When the qi is blocked, there is illness. Everything a person does affects the qi. Qi corresponds to the natural order around a person, to day and night cycles, to emotions, food, stress, activities. It is affected by light, chemicals, radiation, magnetic fields.

The Chinese masters developed Tai Chi, Kung Fu, Qigong, and the martial arts and acupuncture. Acupuncturists insert needles, use a type of heat called moxa, or put magnets at specific acupuncture points to balance the yin and yang of the human energy field. When the qi is balanced, the person has good health. When the qi is unbalanced, the person has poor or impaired health.

Acupuncture and acupressure touch key points in the meridians of qi flow. These points can become tender during illness. Research has shown that the points conduct electricity more readily than other areas; they are like little concentrated magnetic fields.

The Human Energy Field or Aura

The human energy field is the manifestation of the universal life force that keeps us alive. The human energy field has been described for thousands of years as a luminous body that surrounds and interpenetrates the physical body. It emits its own characteristic energy vibrations, which radiate outward and can be seen and felt. It is what has been traditionally called the aura.

Many healers have believed that the physical body arises out of the spirit body's energy field. Many cultures have spiritual beliefs that thought forms give rise to material forms. Classical Hindu philosophy stated that matter came from thought. From that point of view, an imbalance or distortion in the energy field causes a disease in the physical body. Healing distortions in the field brings about healing in the physical body.

The energy field or aura has been described and drawn in many ways. The theosophists drew many pictures of the aura and characterized it with colors for different emotions and mental states. Healers believe that the human energy field is composed of many different levels. Healers often focus on seven levels, which go from within the body to outside the skin. Each level from one to seven is of a "higher frequency" or a "higher octave." Each level extends outward from the skin several inches farther than the previous one. Each practitioner sees the energy field in his or her own way. Each culture has a different way of telling the story of healing energy, a different tradition of characterizing healing energy. In this book we encourage you to see and feel the energy yourself. It is interesting to read about it, but the lived experience is key.

CHAKRAS

The chakras, from ancient India, are ways of looking at the body's energy centers. In yogic philosophy there are seven chakras that go up the spine from the base to the top of the head. The chakra is a concentration of energy, a focus of an area.

The bottom chakra is located at the base of the spine. It is known as the muladhara chakra and is the chakra for grounding. It is between the anus and the sexual organs. It deals with security and the connection to mother earth. Above it is the svadhistana chakra, which is related to the body's sexual function. It deals with food, sexual pleasure, and reproduction. The one above that is the manipura chakra, located at the navel point; it controls digestion. (In Tai Chi, the center of heat energy is just on the navel point. By focusing on deep slow breathing at the navel point, the practitioner increases his or her vitality and stamina.) This chakra deals with power, control, and freedom. The fourth chakra, the anahata chakra, at the center of the chest at the midpoint between the two nipples, is related to the respiratory and circulatory functions of the body and is often called the heart chakra. It deals with love. The fifth chakra, the vishuddha chakra, at the point of the Adam's apple in the neck, controls speech. This chakra controls all chakras below it, thus coordinating all the energies of the body. It deals with giving and receiving and with intuition. The ajna chakra, also known as the "third eye," whose controlling nucleus is located between the eyebrows, controls the mind, which is itself a microcosmic replica of the cosmic mind. This chakra deals with spiritual perception and extrasensory perception. The sahasrara chakra, the seventh chakra is located at the very center and top of the head, and is the seat of pure consciousness, the supreme entity. It deals with cosmic consciousness and the relationship with God.

In ancient Indian healing, the physical, mental, and spiritual health of the individual depends upon a proper balance between these seven chakras. Disease is caused by weakness and imbalance in the energy flow of one or more of the chakras.

Many energy healers say they can see which chakras have a health problem. They often describe the chakra as a funnel or vortex six to eight inches in diameter, containing smaller vortexes. In the Eastern tradition they are described as petals or wheels of light. The vortexes spin, pulling in life energy from the energy all around us. Each vortex relates to a particular organ. A life event that is traumatic opens the chakras, preventing the vortex from pulling sufficient life energy into the organ. Deprived of energy, those organs do not function well and illness results.

When healers look at a chakra, they often look at the vortex, follow it down to the organ associated with it, and look at the organ to see if it has the correct pulse. If the chakra is open, the organ pulses too slowly and is extremely weak. The colors are faded. If the vortex going to that organ is clogged, the organ is probably going to be clogged and dark, and need clearing.

Some healers who do spiritual and visionary healing concentrate on the chakras to help them heal. Some don't utilize this way of looking at the body. The human energy field can be perceived with all of the five senses. As a healer begins seeing auras, he or she uses more senses. The three usual ways to be aware of energy are seeing, feeling, and hearing. Seeing is experienced as being precise; intuition is usually felt as being more vague. An experienced healer claims to be able to see into the body, to see the different organs, and to see the different levels of the fields.

You can use energy healing in your practice. Sit with the person you are working with and ask what he or she wants your help for. While the person talks, look at his or her body and see what fields get your attention. As you listen, when you hear about things that are wrong, look at changes in the field. When people are concerned about what is wrong with them, they increase the manifestation in the field. Then you can work on them with body work. You will get more information as you are working.

Depending on what you perceive, you can tell the person what you saw. You can check your perception with different senses before you give information. Then you can move energy. Each healer works differently; some charge and balance the energy with hands, others with a feather or rattle. Go to the specific areas of the body that need work and begin clearing, charging, balancing, and restructuring the energy field. Restructuring involves rebuilding the specific pattern of the field in the area that's been distorted.

You can use your own energy field by clearing and balancing it. Then bring energy in through all your chakras and let it out of your hands. Use the energy you take into your body from the universe. Most healers say they bring the energy into themselves from the universe, the earth, the sky, the Creator. That's why it's called channeling healing energy in most cultures. The healer's body acts as an energy transformer during the healing. The regulation of the energy through the healer's body is important. Healers can change the frequency of the energy out of their hands and change where it goes. They can make it very specific to rebuild certain structures.

LIGHT YOUR FIRE OF ENERGY

When you heal, you create your own vortex of energy. When you create a ceremony and ritual to heal, you raise a cone of power. When you come into the fullness of your shamanic power, you bring with you your own journey into darkness and light. You feel the depth of your own soul as a significant glimmer of your own life. The vortex inside you expands and contracts; your heart holds it and spreads it out. Inside every moment it expands and contracts, letting go of wastes, taking in pureness. It happens all the time, with every heartbeat, every breath. Each organism is self-contained to heal. When it takes in the life force, it creates a circle of life energy with intention. Groups of people come together and focus on healing one individual, raising up energy. Bringing in music and dance was traditionally done in groups to focus on one person. Today, attending physicians and residents on rounds in a medical center are in groups to raise energy. Groups in medical centers focus to heal; researchers focus in huge groups around the earth to heal. Our modern-day group healing is as powerful as the ancient ways. Collectives of caregivers come together to focus their energy to heal one person. They surround the bed and the patient becomes the focus of attention. When done intentionally, it is a powerful form of healing—it ups the energy.

Guided imagery for hands-on healing

You can use your hand and the power of touch in healing. In your mind's eye, open your hands. Imagine your hand is an ethereal hand that is able to transmit energy. Visualize your hands becoming energized. Let God's energy come to them from above. Let the earth's energy come to them from below. See and feel energy flowing into them. Feel the energy as buzzing, tingling, heaviness, lightness, heat, or cold. As you feel the sensations, let them increase. Use the energy softly and deliberately in whatever healing you are doing. Your hands become transmitters of the energy; they emit energy. Open up your hand and allow the energy to pass through it, in and out.

The basic technique for using your hands to heal and for moving healing energy is massage. Shamanic healing usually employs massage, touch, or rubbing. You can use herbs, creams, and medicines while you touch. You can ground yourself in body massage. Use touch, holding, water therapy, and baths to balance the elements of water, fire, and passion in the body.

INCREASE YOUR VELOCITY

An important concept in shamanic healing is velocity. Velocity is the spinning of the vortex of energy within ourselves. We increase velocity when we raise the vortex. Part of shamanic training is being able to see the vortexes of energy in nature and use them to raise our own energy to heal. There are enormous vortexes of energy in nature—tornadoes, hurricanes, and springs all emerge with a funnel into the vortex. Healers move into the vortexes in nature to clear themselves and up their energy. When they are in a vortex, all the energy that is not healing in their life spins free. This is what happens in Sufi dancing or whirling. They become pure healing energy. Shaman healers visualize the vortexes of energy that spiral around them and take the energy into them.

Going into nature regenerates your own vortex of energy. Being in springs, letting the springs flow through you, is deeply healing. There is a vibrational energy associated with flow; it is deep, constant, always emerging. There are vortexes of energy in nature that are power places. The ancient ones found them and said, "This feels powerful." They felt vibrational energy moving through them. We have difficulty finding these places. Television and media, traffic and rushing, disturb our lives and our abilities to tune in on the pure energy. We have to be intentional to find and use energy. We come upon these places intentionally; we connect to them by going to them. They enhance our level of being connected to ourselves and to the earth. We live in the earth's body, so connecting to the earth's energy vortex is directly healing; it is like being in our own body's healing energy. It is like acupuncture, like upping the energy of our meridians by being on the earth's energy meridians. Ley lines are the earth's energy meridians. They are lines of power, of energy, that we can tap into to heal.

The velocity is related to the expansion and contraction of your energy field. When you connect to another person, your energy envelops the person; it is as though it becomes greater than the synthesis of the two. You can be bright, large, expansible. It is still your body, it is only what it is, unless you tap into the universal vortex—then it is infinite. It allows you to move energy infinitely. It is the eternal spring of creativity flowing outward from within you. When you put two people together, the energy expands and is larger than the two, much larger. That is what a healing relationship is about. In sacred space, you create an energy vortex that is powerful. You can do that. Humans move though space and time with different degrees of velocity. They move though space and time with a rhythm and harmony like breath.

Guided imagery to move healing energy in the body

Make yourself comfortable. You can be sitting or lying down. Loosen tight clothing, uncross your legs and arms. Close your eyes. Let your breathing slow down. Take several deep breaths. Let your abdomen rise as you breathe in and fall as you let your deep breath out. As you breathe in and out you will become more and more relaxed. You may feel sensations of tingling, buzzing, or relaxation; if you do, let those feelings increase. You may feel heaviness or lightness; you may feel your boundaries loosening and your edges softening.

Now let yourself relax. Let your feet relax, let your legs relax. Let the feelings of relaxation spread upward to your thighs and pelvis. Let your pelvis open and relax. Now let your abdomen relax, let your belly expand, do not hold it in anymore. Now let your chest relax, let your heartbeat and breathing take place by themselves. Let your arms relax, your hands relax. Now let your neck relax, your head, your face. Let your eyes relax; see a horizon and blackness for a moment. Let these feelings of relaxation spread throughout your body. Let your relaxation deepen. If you wish, you can count your breaths and let your relaxation deepen with each breath.

Now in your mind's eye, see your own body. See it in front of you like a painting or a map or an illustration. Now see the two-dimensional form come to life. See it in three dimensions. Now see it in four dimensions. Look inside your beautiful body and see the flow of energy inside. See bubbles, motion, light, flow, energy, light—whatever healing energy looks like to you. It looks different to each person; you will learn to see what the energy looks like for you. See the energy flow, see what color it is, see how it moves. If there is a blockage, see how the energy can get around it. Can it break the blockage, slide around it, jump over it? Let the energy move to balance your whole body. Let it move clockwise up your spine, around, and back down. If you need more energy, get it from the sky or from the earth. Ask the Creator for healing energy to come into your body from the universe.

Now find an area that is blocked or that is low in energy. Find an area that is open and is high in energy. Now with your intent, move the energy from the high-energy area to the blocked area. Move the energy around the blockage so it flows smoothly. You can do this any way that comes to you. You can move it with your hands, with your mind, with a magic wand. Any way is fine.

Now you can picture in your mind's eye moving the energy in another person. Picture the person's body. See it clearly in front of you. See it in three dimensions. See inside it outside it around it. See its aura, its energy flowing within. Now look for areas that are low in energy, areas that have a lot of energy. Look for the flow of energy around the body, look for blockages. Now move the energy from areas of high energy to areas of low energy. Move the energy around blockages, breaking them if you can. If you need more energy, get it from the sky or from the earth. Ask the Creator for healing energy to come through you into the person you are healing.

When you are ready, return to the room where you are doing the exercise. First move your feet and then move your hands. Move them around and experience the feeling of the movement. Press your feet down onto the floor, feel the grounding, feel the pressure on the bottom of your feet, feel the solidity of the earth. Feel your backside on the chair; feel your weight pressing downward. Now open your eyes. Look around you. Stand up and stretch. Move your body; feel it move. You are back; you can carry the experience of the exercise outward to your life. You will feel stronger and be able to see deeper. You will be in a healing state. Each time you do the exercise you will be more relaxed and be able to go deeper and be more deeply healed.

You can do this exercise while you are with a person, or for yourself. You can do it on the telephone as distant healing for people. Time and space do not affect this healing. We believe that you need a contract to do it with another person. You need to ask the person's permission and say that you are doing it before you start the guided imagery process of moving healing energy in the body.

Guided imagery to go in between moments in time

Make yourself comfortable. You can be sitting or lying down. Loosen tight clothing, uncross your legs and arms. Close your eyes. Let your breathing slow down. Take several deep breaths. Let your abdomen rise as you breathe in and fall as you let your deep breath out. As you breathe in and out you will become more and more relaxed. You may feel sensations of tingling, buzzing, or relaxation; if you do, let those feelings increase. You may feel heaviness or lightness; you may feel your boundaries loosening and your edges softening.

Now let yourself relax. Let your feet relax, let your legs relax. Let the feelings of relaxation spread upward to your thighs and pelvis. Let your pelvis open and relax. Now let your abdomen relax, let your belly expand, do not hold it in anymore. Now let your chest relax, let your heartbeat and breathing take place by themselves. Let your arms relax, your hands relax. Now let your neck relax, your head, your face. Let your eyes relax; see a horizon and blackness for a moment. Let these feelings of relaxation spread throughout your body. Let your relaxation deepen. If you wish, you can count your breaths and let your relaxation deepen with each breath.

Now in your mind's eye, picture an event that happened to you. You can choose the brightest event of your life, the most beautiful moment, a moment when you succeeded or had a vision or felt wonderful. It can be a moment in an outer event like the birth of a child or an inner event like a dream or vision. Go deeply into the event—see it, feel it, smell it, touch it, hear it. Let yourself be there.

Now look deeper into the event by slowing down the moments of time. In your mind's eye see your hand from the top. See your fingers touching each other, outspread in front of you. Now open your fingers, separating them so there is space in between each finger. The fingers are the moments of time and the spaces in between are the moments in between the moments of time. Go back into the event you are looking at. Now slow it down like a movie going into slow motion. In your mind's eye, see each moment of time jump and see a moment of nontime in between. Now look at your event moving in slow motion and look deeply between the moments of time. What do you see there? Look for spirit helpers, for light, for vibration, for God. Look at the wonderful bright moment in your life and see how much there is, how rich it is. See it existing in infinity, in nontime and nonspace.

Feel the peace and the beauty of that timeless moment. Feel the vibrations and the energy that surround you.

When you are ready, return to the room where you are doing the exercise. First move your feet and then move your hands. Move them around and experience the feeling of the movement. Press your feet down onto the floor, feel the grounding, feel the pressure on the bottom of your feet, feel the solidity of the earth. Feel your backside on the chair; feel your weight pressing downward. Now open your eyes. Look around you. Stand up and stretch. Move your body; feel it move. You are back; you can carry the experience of the exercise outward to your life. You will feel stronger and be able to see deeper. You will be in a healing state. Each time you do the exercise you will be more relaxed and be able to go deeper and be more deeply healed.

MOVING ENERGY IN SHAMANIC RITUAL AND CEREMONY

Moving energy is often done in ritual and ceremony. Each shaman has his or her own ritual. Ritual helps a person embody the prayer and imagery to move healing energy more powerfully in his or her body.

Physician and shaman healer Lewis Mehl-Madrona tells this story:

> Ceremonial treatment methods are the most powerful I have encountered. Time and time again I have had the experience of working for weeks with a patient to change a situation or improve a physical symptom, almost without results. Then we would do a ritual together and an immutable problem would transform itself literally overnight. Had this happened once, I might have thought the ritual was just serendipitously performed right before the symptom changed on its own, but this has happened too often to be dismissed so easily.
>
> In Arizona I started going beyond what I had learned from others; I was developing my own style. I began to take clients outdoors for sessions. Soon I began to incorporate into these sessions some of the more formal elements of ceremony I had learned. Before long I was using ritual as an integral part of my medical practice. Ritual creates spiritual awareness for a purpose. Prayer and ceremony hold a magic and power that cannot be denied. Through ritual we address metaphysical energies that surround us, protect us, enliven us, and instruct us. It is the simplest way of requesting help with our problems. The ritual state

of consciousness is a deeper state of being that isn't rooted in personality—a state of ecstatic union with nature best expressed in poetry or song. In healing ritual and prayer, the individual with a compromised spirit who invites illness and infection can heal his or her spirit.

Healing ceremonies are a group activity. The healer's colleagues, friends, and students become the helpers. How you approach ceremony is critical. Approach with respect for the Creator. With experience, you will learn how to improvise; there are no scripts for the ceremony or the healing. The only script is from divine intervention and guidance. Shamans pick and choose from different traditions, using a combination of what works for them. Holding a ceremony convinces people they will be well.

Each ritual has a basic age-old form. The ritual starts with a prayer. Then the shaman calls in the Creator and any helpers, and invites them to come to heal. He or she gives thanks to Creator and asks for help with the healing. The shaman often gives an offering—an object, food, something valuable and desirable. Then the shaman creates sacred space and usually prays to the four directions, asking for the spirits of the directions to be with him or her in the healing. Next the shaman goes into visionary space and invites the visions to come. For many cultures, including most Native Americans, the ritual involves drumming and singing. Chanting, sweat lodges, or more complex ritual structures make up the body of the ritual. During the ritual the shaman listens to the spirit voices and lets the trance deepen. In the healing there is a letting go, the illness is removed, taken out, the person releases illness. The illness is put in a fire, in water, or in another place where it will not injure someone or stay in the shaman's body. Often the ritual is followed by a ceremonial cleansing in which any traces of illness are removed. This can be a sweat lodge or prayers. In the closing the shaman gives thanks again.

HEALING RESONANCE

Whenever you do a healing ritual or look for a spirit animal, you are participating in the most ancient form of worship. For millions of years, humans have made medicine wheels and spoken to spirit animals. Animals themselves worship and have awe and, we believe, even do ritual. All you need to do is watch the mating of a bird to know how deep this ritual becomes; it is far into dance, costume, and rhythm. When you do a healing ritual you enter the realm of all those who have gone before you. Rupert Sheldrake has written about resonances, about the patterns of energy that remain after a ritual act has been done. We believe that whenever ritual has been done, its forms remain forever. When you do a similar ritual, you enter the resonances and can experience what has been done before. When you do a shamanic healing, you go into all the shamanic healings that have ever been done. When you speak to an owl, you join all the owl energy that has ever been spoken to.

This is important, especially for people who live in large cities. Before the city was built, it was a forest, a riverbank, a mountain. Before the city was built, there were bears, lions, mastodons, and saber-toothed tigers there; there were hunters, shamans, spirits. The spirits of these ancient animals and shamans are still there as resonances. We call these spirits absent animals, absent ancient ones. When you drive past a small wood in a large city you can feel the absent animals. You can feel the ancient ones in ritual. When you do a ritual there you can feel the rituals that were done forever.

It is even more obvious when you do healing ritual on an ancient sacred site such as Stonehenge or Avebury. There the resonances are louder. It is the same when you do ritual on land where animals currently live. If you go to a bear habitat and do bear ritual, the voices of the bears are more easily heard. So doing ritual or making medicine wheels are more powerful if it is done where the energy is strongest. Remember, you may be living on an ancient ceremonial site right now. This happens often. The ancient shamans sing to you, "Look for us in your memories and in your dreams."

ROLLING THUNDER DOES A
HEALING CEREMONY

Michael tells this story:

When I set up Headlands Clinic, we invited healers of all kinds to come there and work. Amongst the healers who showed up was Rolling Thunder. Rolling Thunder was not well known at that time; Doug Boyd had not yet started his biography of the healer. Bob Dylan had not discovered him for the Rolling Thunder Revue. Rolling Thunder showed up at the clinic and watched. After seeing what we did, he told me he wanted to do a healing on a man he met at the clinic. The man was a doctor whom Rolling Thunder saw needed healing. The healing was to be in a meadow on my land. Rolling Thunder had come to my place and wandered around, looking. He showed me which plants were the grandfather plants. He said, "Never touch that plant; he is the one who makes the others." He walked around my land and I saw it for the first time. I could see the light around plants and around meadows, and I could also see the darkness. He moved like part of nature, like an animal, or even more like a moving plant. The light was around him, too. He found a meadow and said that was the right place.

That night he came early. As usual, he arrived in a van with "Indian Power" bumper stickers. The driver was a young warrior. A beautiful Swedish woman sat in the front. Earlier she had phoned and said, "RT is coming." I never saw him drive or make phone calls. He went to the meadow and said prayers and gave offerings. He lit a fire in the center of the circle and put a piece of raw meat outside the circle. The people came and sat in a circle. He told women they had to leave if they were on their moon. First he went around the circle and put cornmeal on each person's forehead; he said this was for protection. Then he asked each person who was to be healed to speak. He went up to each person individually and looked into his or her eyes. He asked the person to say out loud what was wrong, what needed healing, and most of all, what he or she wanted from him. He wanted each person to state the goal and intent of this particular

healing. The people he would work on then told what their illnesses were and what they wanted to happen. Then Rolling
Thunder went up to the person he wanted to heal and sniffed
him or her. He would sniff like an animal up and down. When
he was satisfied with the sniffing, he started sucking. He sucked
with his mouth until he took out the illness. Then he ran to the
woods and vomited into the piece of meat. He threw up violently, retching and retching. Then he threw the meat into the
fire. When he sucked out the illness I could see a darkness, a
dark shape, leave the person. The individual immediately felt
better. I asked him to heal me. I told him I had a blockage in my
neck where energy could not move easily. He sniffed me; I felt a
breath of a wolf and then felt something dark and old leave my
body. It was wild and wonderful. I heard him retching violently
in the woods outside the circle. I saw him come back into the
circle and throw the meat in the fire; I saw a darkness burn and
leave up in the smoke. My neck felt better than it ever had. My
eyes were different now. I saw light and brightness, colors and
energy. He had done something profound to me.

For a while, I become his Western physician—he called me
when he needed medical care. He told people that I knew more
than any other Western doc. He started coming to my house to
visit. One time he sat in my living room and taught me deeply.
He said, "You can heal with your eyes. You look at the illness,
you look inside the person's body. When you see it, you see it
healed. You re-see it healing and healing. I did this at the Men-
ninger Clinic. They were studying me. They brought me a man
with a broken leg. I saw inside and saw the break and saw it
healed. His leg healed instantly. I vomited. They ran and got the
vomit and analyzed it." He laughed a huge laugh. "Can you
imagine that they thought the answer to what I did was something in my throw-up?" He laughed again. He told me, "You can
do this, see inside and move matter with your eyes to healing.
Let them take your vomit." He laughed again.

Another night we sat in the darkness. He told me, "One day
I saw they were going to bulldoze a forest. I went up to the bulldozer and saw into it and broke it. It will never hurt that forest.

I spoke to it. I told it what they were going to do with it. It cooperated. You can do this. You need to do each act in your life to heal the earth. Healing the earth is all that is important now."

Another time he told me he never took money for healing. "This is sacred work. If you take money for it, it ruins it. The Creator does not accept money for healing. You cannot if you want your healing to be sacred from the Creator." Since medical school, I too have never taken money for a healing or for sacred work. I know he was right.

Shaman Rituals

Each shaman has his or her own rituals for healing. These and the ones above are examples. Michael has many ritual forms to heal. Before he participates in a healing, he calls in the Creator, lights sage, and cleanses the place where he is working. The place he uses for healing has medicine wheels and spirit animal carvings, paintings and sculptures. He gives an offering and he prays. He prays to the Creator to heal the person he is working with. Michael believes deeply that the Creator heals—he is only a helper. His patient visits do not have time limits; they can be from one hour to several days. Sometimes patients come to him for several days and in these visits he works several hours a day. He listens to the patient's story and sniffs out illness, darkness, and brightness. He uses guided imagery to take patients into the darkness and the light and makes a tunnel for them to go through from darkness to light. He finds spirit guides and animals helpers with the person. He uses guided imagery to deal with the spirits of illness and healing.

As the patient speaks, Michael has visions. He often tells the visions to the patient and then does guided imagery to help the patient see the visions. The visions can be healing physiology, spirit guides, angels, spirit animal, or celestial figures. Michael speaks to them and encourages his patients to speak to guides they receive. He then does body work with a feather to move and balance energy. He takes out illness and puts it in the fire. He puts in healing energy.

He goes out into nature to mountaintops, beaches, ancient trees, springs, and ancient Indian sacred sites to heal. He creates a personal ritual in each site for each person. He looks for real animals in nature and listens to messages from the spirit animals. He does body work with his hands and with a feather. He teaches his patients to listen to spirit animal voices and teaches them to see visions. The healing is about them learning to see and listen.

Michael also uses a bearskin and feathers to heal. He dances as a bear shaman in ceremony and, if appropriate, puts the bearskin on patients to empower them to heal. Each patient healing is individual. He never knows what will happen when a patient comes to him. He sees a vision when the patient is there, and they enact the vision as a ritual together. For example, a patient can be a forest spirit and they make a costume and the patient dances in the forest. He uses art, music, writing, and dance in performance ritual to heal. He uses the medicine wheel with many patients to heal.

Michael also sends patients out on vision quests. They can be to sacred sites, to a mountaintop, to ancient trees and springs. He sends them to find spirits or receive answers. He gives them specific instructions, and when they return he processes the material with them. He also does shamanic training with health practitioners to help them become shamans.

Mary uses many ritual forms to heal. She has conducted ritual and ceremony with the artists in the Arts in Medicine program at the University of Florida, Gainesville. She takes them to nature, to springs, beaches, or lakes, and they do guided imagery to be able to listen and see. She does rituals for women when they turn fifty years old. She trains shamans by sending them out into nature and having them do spirals around sacred sites to ask for gifts from the directions about what they seek. She builds medicine wheels to heal. Mary's healing work is in relationship to others and facilitating the actual manifestation in the world. She is a healer, a visionary, and a mystic.

Lewis Mehl-Madrona, M.D., has put together his own ritual system, as do most shaman healers. His shamanic healing techniques are done to remove all doubt that the person will get well. He prays to the directions and sets up a medicine wheel. He prays with and for the person to be healed. He works in healing-intensive retreats that can be seven days long. He encourages the person to journalize and to make sacred objects. He uses guided imagery and body work. He builds a sweat lodge the fifth night and sends the patient to vision quest the next night to cry out for a vision. He often uses hikes into remote areas and worships. He also does body work along with his listening and talking.

Guided imagery to find your own healing ritual

Make yourself comfortable. You can be sitting or lying down. Loosen tight clothing, uncross your legs and arms. Close your eyes. Let your breathing slow down. Take several deep breaths. Let your abdomen rise as you breathe in and fall as you let your deep breath out. As you breathe in and out you will become more and more relaxed. You may feel sensations of tingling, buzzing, or relaxation; if you do, let those feelings increase. You may feel heaviness or lightness; you may feel your boundaries loosening and your edges softening.

Now let yourself relax. Let your feet relax, let your legs relax. Let the feelings of relaxation spread upward to your thighs and pelvis. Let your pelvis open and relax. Now let your abdomen relax, let your belly expand, do not hold it in anymore. Now let your chest relax, let your heartbeat and breathing take place by themselves. Let your arms relax, your hands relax. Now let your neck relax, your head, your face. Let your eyes relax; see a horizon and blackness for a moment. Let these feelings of relaxation spread throughout your body. Let your relaxation deepen. If you wish, you can count your breaths and let your relaxation deepen with each breath.

Now, in your mind's eye, see yourself as a healer in your

most creative space. Imagine that you could do any ritual you want to with the person you are working with. See yourself working with a person for healing in a sacred ceremony. See where you are. Are you outdoors or indoors? What are you doing? How are you dressed? You can be a healer leading a vision quest on a mountaintop, a healer on a trek to ancient Greece to a healing temple, a surgeon in an operating room playing music. You can take the person you are working with anywhere. You can be an animal spirit, be in a costume. You can lead a dream workshop, do touch, do guided imagery to fly. You can chant, sing, dance, move healing energy, pray, talk to Jesus. In this exercise, you can do anything you want to do. You can be a healing artist, a poet, a mask maker, a priest—anything. It is all possible. For this guided imagery, let yourself dream without limits. Let yourself be totally free.

When you are ready, return to the room where you are doing the exercise. First move your feet and then move your hands. Move them around and experience the feeling of the movement. Press your feet down onto the floor, feel the grounding, feel the pressure on the bottom of your feet, feel the solidity of the earth. Feel your backside on the chair; feel your weight pressing downward. Now open your eyes. Look around you. Stand up and stretch. Move your body; feel it move. You are back; you can carry the experience of the exercise outward to your life. You will feel stronger and be able to see deeper. You will be in a healing state. Each time you do the exercise you will be more relaxed and be able to go deeper and be more deeply healed.

12

HONOR SUFFERING AND DEATH

STORY: THE LITTLE BOY

The physician walks into the room of a child with leukemia who is dying. The shades are drawn, the parents are silent and extremely depressed. The child is bald and in bed. He is quiet and still. The physician is young, a first-year resident. He is earnest; he tries so hard with each interaction. He does not know what to do here, where there seems that nothing can be done. The other residents come and go. They stay in the room for a few moments, check the chart, and leave without making eye contact with the boy. The attending physician does not even come in anymore; he told them the chemotherapy was not working and there was nothing more to do.

The young resident was attracted to this room, to this boy. As a college student, he had taken yoga and Eastern religion courses and had read spiritual books, but since then he had worked hard to become a doctor. For years he had only read and studied and memorized medical textbooks. And now he found himself going into the little boy's room more and more. He would go in at night and talk to the child when the boy was often alone. They would be alone together and they would look into each other's eyes. The boy was not like other patients with leukemia. He smiled and laughed, even made jokes. His room was full of little drawings. The young resident started to draw pictures with the boy. He would sit and color and they would tell stories to each other about their lives.

Late one night the boy looked deeply into the resident's eyes. He stopped his jokes; he created stillness. He said, "I need you to do something for me. I want a favor." Then he was silent for a while. He started again: "I am asking you to tell my parents that they have to face the fact that I am dying. I am asking you to tell them that I want them to speak to me about it. I cannot make jokes anymore and pretend that everything is all right and that I am the same as I have always been. I am different now. Will you do that for me?" The resident was shocked. He looked into the eyes of the little boy and knew the moment was special and important for both of them. He looked beyond the boy and saw the boy's spirit, large and pure, beautiful and full of light. He opened and closed his eyes and it went away. Nothing like this had ever happened to him before. He was amazed. This was a new experience as a doctor, he wondered if he was all right.

The next day, in the hall, he took the boy's parents aside and told them what the boy had said, trying his best to be gentle and kind. He looked directly in the eyes of both the mother and the father. They were not much older than he was. He did not have children, so he could not share their feelings, but he could clearly see their grief and horror at what was happening to them. They listened and then let out a sigh of relief. The mother cried and the father got tears in his eyes, too. They told him that they could not keep up their front anymore, that they had done it for the little boy and that they were glad it was over. Then they shocked the resident even more. They told him they were deeply religious and that they could see the spirit of their little boy across a divide, moving back and forth, carrying something, looking at them, beckoning. The resident listened and remembered his experience of seeing the boy's spirit. He looked at the parents and reached out and touched them, and then he cried, too.

They all went into the little boy's room together and he could see the boy understood what had happened. The parents still were crying, and the boy now cried, too, and hugged them. A cloud lifted, the sun came through, the little boy told a joke, and life went on. Now, each day the parents sat and drew with their son. The resident sat with them when he could, often in silence, just watching. He felt he was blessing them, giving them space, caring for them more than he knew in a place beyond words. The little boy got worse and one night he died. The next day the parents came to the resident and told him they had seen the little boy go forth and had blessed him and said goodbye. They hugged the young doctor and thanked him for being there and for allowing them to speak of this to him. They said it changed their whole experience of the boy's illness and of the hospital. It had changed the young doctor forever. From that day on, each person he worked with was illuminated and he could see the light when he looked directly in their eyes with love.

The young physician was Michael, and this happened in 1968.

PAIN AND DARKNESS AS A DOORWAY TO HEALING

We learned in our research for our previous book, *Spirit Body Healing*, that one of the richest and most compelling parts of the healing journey comes from suffering. In suffering there is a place deeper inside you where there is something more, where your inner life is seen. Inside the place of suffering is a doorway to deep spiritual healing. Embrace suffering. Immerse yourself in suffering.

Mary tells this story:

I was doing vipassana meditation in a nine-day retreat. I was experiencing tremendous suffering in my back. I hurt, my limbs hurt, my body found places of pain. It did not stop. I tried to focus on my breathing but I only felt pain. I got headaches.

Sitting was excruciating. I went to the teacher, Christina Feldman, and told her I was suffering. She said. "Sit with it." I went back and sat. I was in darkness. I felt my inadequacy. I was in a barrage of what was happening. I thought, "Why am I the only one who can't do this?" Then I thought, "I am dying. What is my fear of death?" I dealt with my fear and anxiety. My body tightened even further.

I remember a moment when I returned to a body position that triggered the memories of when, as a teenager, I broke my back. When I got into that position, it was my peak of suffering. I remembered the torture of being in a painful place of despair in a relationship with my family and with my boyfriend. It was after this accumulation of suffering that I broke my back. When I went back to into that memory, it was almost like I broke up. I had a deeper understanding. I remembered the event in my body. I forgot I had to deal with past traumatic time. I was able to be with the pain long enough to create an insight where I could restory my life from another place.

Then there was a moment inside my suffering where I experienced myself as larger. I pushed myself to be larger than the pain, to be expansive, very large, almost detached from my pain, away from my body. I was motivated to do this because of the pain; there was motivation to leave these mind games behind. Then I experienced transcendence; I moved beyond my physical pain to stillness, oneness, and compassion. I was able for the first time to begin to understand it. I watched my body. I saw myself. I was floating inside mind. I was larger than mind.

Fifteen years after the accident, when I thought I was way past it, I found myself still dealing with it in my life. This was a major growth experience, a deepening of the understanding of who I was, what was my past, what was my history. When I let go of pain, pain went away. When I went home, I did body work, Rolfing, to deal with the issues of that pain, to get past it. If I had not been with it long enough, it would always have been elusive. Being with it for three days was intense. It taught me that being with pain allows you to reveal pain and the deepest source of the pain to yourself. That was the place from which I could facilitate my healing. Trying to make pain go away may not heal. Dealing with it more deeply may.

There is a place inside pain. It is a most intense experience; it is a place of essence that you will hold on to. Pain takes you deeper into the inner world of the ecstatic trance than anything else. Nothing takes you deeper than that; otherwise you may not go there. There is no reason to go into a dark forest to find a healing spring if you are on a smooth road. People don't go off easy paths to go deeper unless they have pain. Pain takes them deeper than their habitual ways of looking at themselves. Inside pain you find your spirit. You find your spirit guides, your spirit grandmother, your spirit helpers. From pain comes the visions of God and the angels that Mary's patients taught her in the *Spirit Body Healing* research.

ALLOW THE SUFFERING TO HAPPEN

The shamanic healer needs to allow the journey into suffering happen. When people have the most pain they have the most powerful visions. When they look into the face of death and go through suffering they get to a place of more intensity. One woman told us, "These are visions that resonate with me—with my entire life and become the foundation of my own life. You could drug me and eliminate that. That would ease my pain and suffering but when it is there, I use it."

The pain is like the shell of a nut; it is a physical reality. Inside the nut is the seed of the tree. If you look at the nut, there is space in there. It is empty and not empty; there is balance inside. Inside is the seed with tremendous potential for growth. You need to nurture pain like a seed, giving it what it needs to grow. Don't take it away or it will never grow. You can bury a nut in fertile ground and a tree will grow. It breaks open and grows—a transformative process in which a seed becomes a tree. The metaphor of the tree is so important. Pain is our seed to growth. It is part of what gives us character, definition, and beauty. Each of us needs to say, "This is the character of who I am. I am not a perfectly straight tree. I am me."

A shaman healer creates the space for pain to manifest. Don't turn away from suffering. Listen to the story, face it. Listen deeply. Close your eyes and go into the space that resonates from inside your own self. Be at home in your own body so you can listen to the other's story. Do not be threatened. You do not need to fix it. The lesson is: You can't fix it. There is a lesson in it not to be avoided.

In the making of a shaman, a person's own issues always emerge. Fear, childhood experiences, self-esteem, confidence— all come to the surface as a person becomes a shaman. The shamanic process brings these things out. Owning yourself as a shamanic healer is a big part of it. It requires confidence, which requires that you say, "This is what I am." You need to know how you got there, what you need to be shaman. That takes you into pain, into the suffering of your own childhood issues. It takes you into power, self-confidence, love, self-love, being in nature, stillness, and finding a teacher.

Guided imagery to honor suffering

Make yourself comfortable. You can be sitting or lying down. Loosen tight clothing, uncross your legs and arms. Close your eyes. Let your breathing slow down. Take several deep breaths. Let your abdomen rise as you breathe in, and fall as you let your deep breath out. As you breathe in and out you will become more and more relaxed. You may feel feelings of tingling, buzzing, or relaxation; if you do, let those feelings increase. You may feel heaviness or lightness; you may feel your boundaries loosening and your edges softening.

Now let yourself relax. Let your feet relax, let your legs relax. Let the feelings of relaxation spread upward to your thighs and pelvis. Let your pelvis open and relax. Now let your abdomen relax, let your belly expand, do not hold it in anymore. Now let your chest relax, let your heartbeat and breathing take place by themselves. Let your arms relax, your hands relax. Now let your neck relax, your head, your face. Let your eyes relax; see a horizon and blackness for a moment. Let these feelings of relaxation spread throughout your body. Let your relaxation deepen. If you wish, you can count your breaths and let your relaxation deepen with each breath.

In your mind's eye, picture yourself with a person you are healing. Let the love you feel come to you and surround you. Be in the love and compassion you are given from the universe. Now imagine you are the most compassionate person you have known, heard of, read about or imagined. It can be Jesus, the Dalai Lama, Buddha, God. Go up into that person, merge with him or her, and be in his or her heart. Let the love you are merge with the love the other person is and be one. Now look at the person you are with in pure compassion. Look at him or her through the eyes of the compassionate one. Look at the person through eyes of deepest love and compassion.

Now imagine that the person you are healing tells you a story of great suffering or pain. You can remember a story that you have heard or let a new one come to you. As you hear this story, let your love and compassion surround you and the person you are with like a blanket from a mother to her baby. Let the love flow into the person—from the compassionate one into you, from you into the person. While you do this, do not interrupt the person's story, do not stop him or her from crying. Just be there with the person in perfect peace. You can touch the person if appropriate, but do not interrupt the story or the life. Let the suffering emerge into a sea of pure love.

When you are ready, return to the room where you are doing the exercise. First move your feet and then move your hands. Move them around and experience the feeling of the movement. Press your feet down onto the floor, feel the grounding, feel the pressure on the bottom of your feet, feel the solidity of the earth. Feel your backside on the chair; feel your weight pressing downward. Now open your eyes. Look around you. Stand up and stretch. Move your body; feel it move. You are back; you can carry the experience of the exercise outward to your life. You will feel stronger and be able to see deeper. You will be in a healing state. Each time you do the exercise you will be more relaxed and be able to go deeper and be more deeply healed.

PROTECT YOURSELF

Shamans have traditionally worked to protect themselves when they do healings. The traditional view was that the illness could leave the person being healed and go to the healer if the healer was not protected. Another belief is that the spirits that caused the illness could hurt the healer, too. This view is similar to experiences in transpersonal healing where the healer can see the visions of the person being healed. It is also similar to stories in Western medicine where a medical student gets the symptoms of the illnesses he or she learns about. Many healers have the experience of getting symptoms of the person they are treating; some even use this to diagnose when they understand and can control this phenomenon.

Michael's teacher, Rolling Thunder, emphasized protection and told him that not all spirits out there were friendly. Rolling Thunder said that the illness could stay around and go into the healer during the healing or days later. He put cornmeal on the forehead of anyone at a healing and had the illness go into a real physical fire that he lit next to the healing.

Exercise: Protect yourself

In your mind's eye, imagine a protective shield around yourself. You can picture it like a bubble of transparent glass or plastic. Imagine that any illness cannot get through it and bounces off of it.

FACE DEATH

Part of becoming a shaman is to see death face-to-face and not look away. Death is a powerful teacher. Experience your own death like a snake sheds its skin. Afterward, it is different; you die to the old way of being and are born to a new way. Physical illness or traumatic life events move a person into the place of greatest fear or darkness. The shaman goes through this darkness to be able to journey with others. Throughout history, shamans were the wounded healers. First, they used their visionary ability to heal their own sickness and deal with their own near-death experiences. When you deal with physical illness and see your own death, you come through with the perspective of what is important in life. You know life is precious, you know spiritual experience is precious, you know light and visions are crucial. When Michael's wife, Nancy, was dealing with her own death, she used to say, "There are no atheists in foxholes." When you are about to die, you may choose or receive a different way of being. When you experience pain you change. When you experience pain as a teacher, in its richness and sensuality, you become larger and grow. Learn from pain as a shamanic healer.

Mary tells us this story of when she was a young nurse:

I sat at the bedside of the old woman. The woman was ninety-three; she had led a full life and she was dying. I saw her spirit hovering over the bed, ready to leave. I also saw the woman's body holding on to life and the spirit holding on to the body like a prized possession. As I sat, I realized that since I was a little girl, I had been able to see people from the other side. This was the first dying person I sat with. Now I knew I could see the spirits of patients who were passing over. The spirits were truly beautiful. They rose like smoke wafting gently upward to heaven. I said to the old woman, "It is OK, my love. Your spirit is in the room with you. Your angels are waiting to take you to heaven." Saying this was as natural to me as breathing. I also knew I had to comfort the old woman's body as her spirit left. I knew that her spirit was attached to her body and her body was holding on. As a nurse, I felt as if I was the guardian of the threshold for this old woman. I could see her spirit standing in the room. I could see space and time fracture around it. I attended her body as her spirit left. I was in my physical space

with her body. I told her, "I will hold your body. I will take care
of it. You can leave now." You know, dying people are attached
to their bodies like they are attached to material possessions—
they do not want to let go. I felt a wise woman talking though
me as a young nurse, saying, "You can leave; I will hold your
body, I will see it is returned to the earth. I will hold and love
your body. I will set your spirit free so it can go to the other
side."

This story is a story of a transcendent moment in caring. Not
many people know how to comfort a body as the spirit leaves.
Healers need to be taught these things. The shaman healer can
be the one to do this. The shaman is the one who can see and
speak to spirits around death. The shaman is the healer who
can go to the other side—to death, to face death.

This book is a training guide for people to do spiritual healing around death and dying. It is a guide for people to go into
the darkness and listen. Allow people to go into pain, to honor
sadness and grief. No matter how dark it is, do not look away.
Be strong and listen to their story. Look into eyes of death like
a warrior. When you work with people who are going to die,
you need this skill. You are without a choice; you are the mid-
wife to their deaths.

Be the one to help people you work with deal with death.
Help them and their families deal with the afterlife, spirits of
loved ones, passages, dreams and stories of death—all the
events that are real and are present around a death. The healer
usually misses this because he or she is not open to the spiritual
space. As a shamanic healer, you can invite people you are
working with to go into a spiritual realm. You can be the one
who invites people to make altars and see visions. To do this,
you not need do anything. Just tell them what is possible and
validate their experience as healing. See deeply what is possible.
Healers can see and understand the mechanism of disease.
They can also be the ones who in the same posture deal with
spirit in the body. For all of human history, the healer was the

expert in both dimensions. We want to return the healer to that role.

What does spirit want? To see, to be loved and acknowledged. Spirits yearn for union with God and people they love. When the healer can be present and comfortable, spirits appears. The healer needs to know about the spirit's need to re-language self, to acknowledge spirit and the movement of spirit inside of self.

Healers need to know about the possibilities of people's spiritual experience so they can validate it and encourage it. All healers need to do is be present and aware of signs of a spiritual experience from the people they are working with and then encourage it. Being aware of a person's dreams, stories of astral travel, and spiritual visions allows healers to enter that realm and speak about spirit and find out what is happening in a person's life. Being aware of a person's or family's beliefs about death, spirits, and the afterlife means that you can help them go deep and change the whole experience of dying for the person and their family.

13

HEAL YOUR
COMMUNITY AND
THE EARTH

Vijali is an earth artist and shaman healer who builds sacred healing sculptures around the earth. She had been a studio painter in Los Angeles and had a vision that she should go to the wilderness and become a hermit. She moved up to a tiny trailer in the mountains outside of Los Angeles and lived alone. There the rocks spoke to her. A rock opened and showed her how to find the light within. She saw that she was to go around the earth and stay with people and make art to heal. She went to nine countries in seven years in her world wheel project. In each country she would ask three questions: What is your essence? What is holding you back from being it (that is, what is your illness)? What can we do to achieve who you are (that is, what is your healing)? Then with the local people she would do an earth carving and performance piece that embodied the answers to the questions. She would live with the people for months and fall in love with them and their lives. She would heal them as a community by making the piece with them and sharing in their healing. She says, "My work right now is global healing. Embodied prayer and my wheel are one."

THE SHAMAN CREATES COMMUNITY

The shaman creates community, which enhances ecstatic states of healing. The shaman facilitates huge ecstatic states that transform the whole world. The shaman healer cultivates people's intent to heal and uses a combination of scientific research and indigenous techniques to bring life back to healing. We all have skills; now we need to restory community healing as a spiritual path. With each act, we can heal our community; each act can be restoried to be spiritually healing.

How is shamanism related to Judeo-Christian religious forms? The relationship between shamanism and contemporary religions is deep. Shamanism was the form that underlay the mystical and visionary experiential part of any religion. The form of the ancient shamanic religion Bon came from Buddhist and Sufi ritual, and it flowed into the ecstatic Jewish Kabbalistic and Christian mystical practices.

CLEANING UP A RIVER

She was depressed. She had been ill. One day, to get out of her house, she took a walk next to the river. She heard its voice. It told her to clean up the river and write about it in a journal. It told her to go to schools and speak to children about her vision and her work. She started a project to clean up the Rio Grande. Each week she took a bag and walked the riverbank, filling the bag with the trash she found. As she walked, she prayed and meditated. She heard the voice of the river and wrote down what it said in her sacred journal. She wrote soft, beautiful, spiritual poems and read them to children all over the state. She called herself a Heartist. Her work became her art and her prayer. The river told her who she was and what she was to do.

Dominique tells us her story:

> I am a ceremonialist and lover. I love the earth. I have seen her through the eyes of a river, and a river is the eye of the earth. That's what I know and communicate. Six years ago, I had the

vision of the great cleansing of the Rio Grande. Every month, on the seventeenth, I did my ritual performance. I began at the Santa Fe River, a small tributary of the Rio Grande. I made my way through the trickle, the trash, the disrespect and despair, filling up uncountable garbage bags. I was walking toward the great river, sending her energy. I was listening, learning to hear the silences, making an art prayer.

As I walked, picking up one can from the river and then another, on and on, doing countless rosaries, I realized that what matters is the depth of my relationship with the river, my awe at the miracle of her beingness, her creativity, our oneness, our moment, our co-creation.

The walking dictates the story. The walking is a dance. The walking dance is syncopated by gestures: picking up a can from the river, then another. Gifts are bestowed, found objects, encounters, or soul imprints. Walking motion, water, life . . . it is body and mind dancing through heart. The walking in the river is a gift received, a gift to be shared.

All rivers are connected; I have learned that frequenting my river. They feed each other or connect though currents of invisible energy. They are memory carriers of the interconnection of all life. People function in the same way. One way to activate these currents is through ritual. Rituals are icons of connections, they are the art of our lives.

Dominique became a shaman. She heard a clear and deep voice that knew the way the river flows. The shaman has an experience unique to people. She is deeply connected to nature. She is part of the way the river flows. She has patience, love, and grace. She sees beauty and knows, "I have something to teach from my life." She connects with the aspect within herself that is connected to the natural flow and grace of being in her body. That allows her to do what she does with confidence and strength and to make a difference in the world. Every human heals in her connectedness to the oneness of life; when you cure a mother with breast cancer, you give a mother to the earth. When you teach a woman how to restory her life, she restorys the community. Articulate a voice of power based on experience and wisdom that merges with the knoll of the earth. She is the wisdom keeper, beautiful and mysterious, her poetry brings the ancient ones' voices in.

The shaman healer lives in a community of fellow workers. There is power in those communities that cultivate skill, knowledge, commitment, and dedication. It is the creative mind thinking—thinking about healing, dreaming about it. Creative research scientists are shaman healers, environmentalists are shaman healers. They have intention, and the spirit of transcendence leads them there. They create new ideas; they create from the dream, the mystery. They cultivate their way of being as a spiritual practice. Shamanism restorys these skills as spiritual practice.

PRACTICE SERVICE

Compare being a shaman with the journey of the bodhisattva. The shaman, like the bodhisattva, surrenders, gives up his or her life to the shamanic way of being, to help all sentient beings. One medicine woman told us, "I am that which is beyond desire." We need many shamans now. In ancient times, there was an average of one shaman per tribe of fifty people. The shaman was the healer to heal the individual, the community, and the earth. Today we need one shaman to exist per five hundred people to save the earth. We need this number of shamans. We need people who use visionary consciousness to heal their community and the earth. We need to cultivate the concept that anyone can heal their community and the earth.

The ancient shamans were based on where they were in world and how it served the culture. We need to take this ancient concept and restory it today for contemporary healers. When you are a shaman healer, it changes what you do and your view of yourself. Being within the knowledge of the earth, merging with it, using creativity for healing, is knowledge of spirit. This book is a guide to doing shamanic healing; the promise is that when you read this book, you will begin to become a shaman healer.

From One to Many

The path of shaman healer is one that heals others in one-to-one interactions and then moves to expand healing practice to the collective. What you heal with one person, if it transcends the boundaries of convention and goes beyond what you know into mystery, will create new realities of healing. The first person doing a new healing expands the paradigm. Your new kind of healing with one person may change collective thinking.

What happens in one moment happens everywhere. Doing one act perfectly makes the act happen throughout space and time. Perfect attention, perfect concentration, explodes ordinary reality and leads to transcendence. Charles Darwin noticed one lizard that was different from the others. The study of that one animal led him to shift reality and change thinking forever around the world. All you have to do is focus on one thing perfectly. Through the particular, your understanding becomes a global perspective. In the same way, one person's acts change everything, one person can change history—look at Joan of Arc and Gandhi. The ripple you make on the earth floats through the earth; it expands and expands.

The last tiger that dies will change things forever; its death will change the world. That is the action realm of healing or destruction: One act changes the world. How can you prevent the last tiger in the wild from being killed? The last tiger that will be born in the wild has been born. If that is true, you know there is no place for wild tigers. That is the beginning of the end, the beginning of what happens on earth. This book is an attempt to change the road we are on. Unless we create a large number of shaman healers, unless we change reality, the earth as we know it will be destroyed. We call you forth as shaman healers to heal the earth.

14

YOUR SHAMANIC
INITIATION

The group sat in a circle. They were solemn and excited about the initiation to come. They had worked hard to become shaman healers. They had dealt with their personal issues, practiced presence and commitment, strengthed their intent, gone on vision quests to find spirit animals, and now they were ready. They lay down, loosened their clothes, the guided imagery started, the drumming started. They went on their own personal journeys. They went deep into visionary space. Their bodies were taken down to bones. They became small sacred jewels. Then they came back and were never the same again.

Shamanic initiation usually involves an experience of being stripped to the bones. The initiation is metaphoric and real at once; it honors the creative spirit of an individual and the intention to re-create his or her life. In shamanic healing the people create wellness. They re-create their world around them. When they are put in the middle of a sand painting and a new reality is made around them, they are re-created as new into that reality. The old self disappears and the new arises. It is literally creating a new matrix—a new reality is re-created in visionary space and physical space at once. The shamanic intent is to pray for reality to be different.

Guided imagery for the shamanic initiation

The shamanic life has been viewed as a calling and a choice. Shamans were called by a vision, which showed the life path ahead. Sometimes they could not stop it from happening to them. Where did the vision come from? The shaman's vision comes from the Creator, from Her, from the earth.

All shamans were initiated into their practice. The initiation was sometimes performed by another shaman and sometimes done in a vision. We have done this exercise with thousands of people in workshops all over the world. In this guided imagery, you can go as far as you want to. In this imagery, you picture your body being taken apart. Some people are not comfortable with this, but it is safe. However, if your intuition tells you to stop, please do so and perhaps try again later. If you feel safe and comfortable, you can do the whole exercise. If you want to stop anywhere along the line, stop and rest there.

Make yourself comfortable. Close your eyes. Relax. Take several slow, deep breaths. Let your breathing become slow and even. Feel your abdomen rise and fall as you breathe. Go into your imagery space as you have many times before. Now imagine that you are on a path. It is a path in the forest, a path that is mysterious and beautiful. Feel your feet touch the earth, smell the fresh air, feel the warm breeze on your face.

Walk on the path. It goes downhill slightly. The ground is hard and has small stones in the soil. It is solid and secure. Feel the ground and the grass that is on each side of the path. Now the path crosses a wooden bridge across a rushing stream. The bridge has stout railings. You can hear your feet echo on the bridge like a drumbeat as you walk across. If you need to drop something in the water that you want to get rid of, you can do that now.

The path now goes upward slightly and comes over a rise. Below you is a large meadow. In the center of the meadow is a grassy circle. Sit in the circle and wait. With you in the circle are your friends and teachers, people who support you in this work. You have come here today for a special ceremony. It is the day of your shamanic initiation. It is a day full of importance, a day you will long remember. You have been told about this day for many years, and you know what will happen. It is safe and you will be asked to do only what you can.

Now you feel hands behind you lifting you up from the sitting position in the circle. It is the elders, your teachers, tapping you to begin. You stand and they take you into the forest and guide you to a stone. It is the ceremonial stone for shamanic initiation used by many who have gone before you. You lie on the stone and close your eyes.

Your elders sing to you. You hear the melody rise and fall. Let yourself drift—upward, upward. Let yourself rise in the air. Let your body be taken upward. Let it rise slowly and then more quickly. You can picture it being taken by a force, by a hand, by a bird, by whatever you see that will take you upward on your personal shamanic initiation—it is different for each person. Let yourself rise and rise and rise.

Now imagine that your body is being taken apart. This can happen many ways. Invite the process to happen for you. Your body can be taken apart by a giant bird such as an owl or an eagle, or by a supernatural large birdlike creature. It can be taken apart by a shaman, a spirit, by a magical wind. Let your body come apart, let it separate. Each person can let it come apart to a different point. If at any time this process feels uncomfortable, stop and rest and go back. This exercise is safe. If you are comfortable, you can go as far as you wish.

First, let your skin come off, let it come off your body. Then, let your muscles come off, let them come off your bones. Then, let your bones come off, let the bones be broken and cracked into powder. As your body comes apart, you are left with its essence; you are left with something pristine and pure. That may be a jewel, a blue light, dots, energy, a crystal. Then, if you wish, let that essence, too, dissolve into endless space. Let yourself move outward to the edge of space to fly with creation itself. What is left when all has been taken is your pure shamanic center of spirit. This may look like the eternal light within.

Now turn back, let yourself come toward earth. As you do this, let your body come back together again. As each part comes, it will come transformed into the shaman's body. It will be new, powerful, and light. When you are complete, you will have a light body with the precious object in the center. Sometimes as you come together your helper will put in powerful substances to make you see deeper. Come together the opposite way you came apart. First, let your essence become clear, then let your bones come together, then your muscles, then your skin. Feel your new body, feel how light and powerful it is. Find the center and see it glow. Look for the gifts you were given as you were put back together. Now your body is back together, but it is new and it is completely different. As it was assembled, sacred objects of power were put into it. Look into you body and see the light within.

Let yourself come back to earth. Let yourself come down, down, down. When you are back on earth, it is time to rest and be fed. You can be fed by a bird, a shaman, a spirit. Let them take you to their home and feed you. If you choose a bird, such as an owl, eagle, or hawk, let it take you in its talons and carry you over the tree tops to the tallest tree. Let it put you in its nest with its babies and feed you. Let yourself grow and grow. The bird may feed you magic jewels. As you are fed, you will become brighter and brighter. You stay in the nest in the top of the tallest tree as long as you like, perhaps years. If you are fed by a shaman, rest with him or her; let the shaman feed you and take care of you until you are made anew.

Now let yourself be brought down and put back in the circle with your friends. You open your eyes and see them all around you. Now you can stand and walk back on the path to where you started. You can open your eyes and feel your feet on the ground and you are home. But you are now different. You have been initiated. Your body is magical and healthy. You are now a shaman healer.

CALLING FORTH THE SHAMAN HEALER:
AN INVOCATION

The shaman healer is awake, and each human he or she touches is awakened. You wake up all the people you are in contact with and bring them closer to health. Their eyes open, their feet touch the earth. They feel, they look around, they see what is necessary to create harmony, love, peace, and healing of the earth.

The earth's body is your body. What you do to the earth is what you do to your own body. We are deeply connected to the air, the trees, the earth, the water in the rivers. These elements run though our bodies; we are made of same elements as the earth. The DNA is the same as ancient DNA. We are one, connected to the earth. As a shaman healer, if your intention is to honor power and energy in the earth, this heals the person you are with and the earth, too. They are connected as one healing act.

With every human you heal, if you are connected to intention yourself, you heal the people and the earth. When a word resonates in you, it resonates in the person you heal. It is an intentional act to heal from a vision. The shaman healer is so deeply connected to intention, when he or she makes contact with others, the intention is manifested by the other person. The intention is so clear and powerful that it manifests in community. This is a capacity of humans, it can be used to heal or destroy. If intention is healing, if the vision is clear, it manifests. The power of the shaman healer harnesses the power within us to manifest our vision on earth. The shaman is the one in any culture who helps people bridge the ordinary world and the spirit world and get the confidence to manifest and make revolutionary change. It is about feeling power, going inward, seeing and moving energy, and coming out and healing yourself, others, and the earth. The shaman becomes visible and the earth is healed.

. . .

Each of us has the capacity to change the world. Each of us can heal ourselves, heal our loved ones, save the habitats and save species, heal rivers and heal the earth. We do not need to be professional healers to do this. We need only to use spiritual and visionary tools to heal as shaman healers. Thank you for being with us for this exciting journey. Go forth and heal and change your world.

Appendix 1

The Gathering of Medicine Women for Peace

The call to medicine women

We wrote this chapter to call medicine women together for world peace. We realized that the horrors of world crisis calls for the emergence of the medicine woman. If you are a medicine woman, a sacred healing priestess, an oracle, a dreamer, come forth and heal. In a gathering of medicine women, come together, see each other, join your powers. Change reality and heal as one huge force of feminine energy. This is a new time, suddenly the woman is called to come forth; she is called as medicine woman to change the earth again, to reestablish balance and world peace.

Who are the medicine women?

Medicine women are everywhere. A medicine woman is inside every woman. The medicine woman is the wise woman who resides within each and every woman. The medicine woman is the healer, the teacher, the lover, the giver, the mother. The medicine woman's spirit is deeply connected to the earth, to family, to friends, to animals, to the environment, to nature. A medicine woman is a woman who can see the earth deeply; she can see the earth moving through her seasons. She can feel the wind, know when nature stirs, recognize the beauty inherent in the nature of her life. The medicine woman emerges within our bodies; she is part of an ancient clan of women called the ancient mothers of the earth. These mothers gave birth to us generations ago; they are the grandmothers who still walk within our bodies. They are the ancient bones who have made our bones.

How do you know if you are a medicine woman?

The wise woman within you has a clear voice. She has spoken to you during your days of despair and pain. She was with you during your own birth and the birth of all your children. She holds you strong, steady, and still. She has a way of exhibiting herself in your life. She comes forth in mothering relationships with other women, in spiritual practices, and also through your work. If your position involves taking care of people or animals, you are tapping into the ancient knowledge of the earth. You may be a mother; you may rub the body of a child after a long day; you may be a body worker, a physician, a caterer, a pharmacist. These careers are all ways of expressing your medicine woman knowledge within.

Go on a vision quest to get in touch with the voice of the medicine woman. The medicine woman is in you as a vibrational energy that resonates in your body. The energy is exhibited individually since every woman is different. The medicine woman comes to us like a dream; she appears in the memories of our minds; she dances when we dance, she sings when we sing. She becomes stronger when we stand in a circle of other women who are medicine women, who see each other, recognize each other, and wake each other up. The medicine woman is a state of mind, a state of body; she holds the fluidity of our spirit.

The first step is to meditate throughout the day

Devote one hour a day to this goal. We do not need to even stop our lives to do this. We can be washing dishes, driving carpools, and healing at the same time. Devote yourself to world peace. The momentum will get larger and larger; the vibrational energy of the earth will shift. We can shift consciousness worldwide. Women can pray for world peace while they do other things. Women are experts in doing more than one thing at once. Be practical, keep order, and at the same time work on healing the world.

Guided imagery with the ancient mothers of the earth

The medicine woman stands in the center of the circle of women. Around her are the ancient mothers of the earth. Imagine yourself in the center of a circle. In the circle you are surrounded by the ancient mothers of the earth. They are from all over the world; there are old woman from Africa, Celtic women, old women from Sicily. In your mind's eye, see the old women from the different places of the world. See a community of women from the world's spiritualities; see Christian, Buddhist, Hindu, Jewish, and Islamic women. All these women of the world are the ancient mothers of the earth.

These women call to you; they call to you to give birth to world peace now. They are your own ancient grandmothers. They look to you as their granddaughters; you are their way of being. It has taken a long time for this to happen. It has taken this long for you to get the power to take over the world. Many of the ancient women came from little villages; they did not leave them their whole lives. You travel the earth weaving webs of peace. We are part of a lineage of ancient mothers. As we become ancient mothers, our mission is to protect our children, all the children of the earth. All children are our children, all children are our concern; the earth is our family.

Medicine women heal with Her energy

Mary says:

I have a vision of women whirling in the nighttime sky. We expand from our bodies and become tall. There is a large energy moving outward, embracing us in our aura. We women use our auric fields of energy as a force to envelop others with love and compassion. One way to do this is by prayer. You pray directly to the target with energy, not your energy, but Her energy. Use the life force. We have infinite resources available within our feminine spaciousness. We are large and bright. As medicine women, we are illuminated in the light of our world. We are awake. Presence is our power; all we have to do is be present and see through oppression, evil, and greed.

This is moving forward. Men bring organization, clarity, and linear placement of thoughts. This is essential for bridges of communication. Women whirl. As we whirl, we sprinkle stars from our own bodies. All people are born of this energy. Spiritual women twirl in the sky and give birth to stars. Light flows from within these stars and causes the birth of it all.

As medicine women, express your dreams

It is time for medicine women to express their dreams. There is a dream in every woman. For Mary it is to be a dancer. In her deepest dreams, she dances across the nighttime sky without limits. She moves freely as a transparent spiritual body; she is limber; she has no limits. "This image is freeing. It allows my spirit to soar and merge with Her. In my dream of being a dancer, She moves into me. By evoking Her, I invoke the deep, powerful, and ancient feminine force. When I feel large in visionary space, I feel swirling energy spiral through me; her life force goes in me. I feel as if I am being penetrated; she goes inside me and I get larger. It is an empowering experience as we receive."

The medicine woman acts with integrity and a full heart. She feeds the world and feeds her soul. If you do not feed your soul and if you do not receive abundance in return, you need to reevaluate your life. The medicine woman clicks into the flow. What energy or force moves through her in what she does? It is like plugging into the right circuit; it comes through you and becomes accessible to the world. Truly powerful, you become a transformer. The light of love and peace flows through you.

Women have lunar cycles in their bodies; they have the moon within their bodies. Their bodies also move with the energy of the earth. They have seasons in their bodies. As they live their lives, they respond to winds, weather, and colors. These changes are reflected in their bodies.

When I see a medicine woman, there is an intimacy of knowing her soul, of touching her soul, and reaching out woman to woman as an act of love. It is being friends before we are friends. It is seeing someone's beauty or breath. It can happen with ordinary people. It happens when you look into someone's eyes and see a beautiful person. If you want to fall in love, you can fall in love in that moment. This is intimacy.

Women can fall into the wonderful experience of caring or being cared for. Women can do this at any moment. A mother can care for a child, a nurse can care for a patient, and a makeup artist can make a connection in a department store just by touching your face and looking into your eyes. This is the power of women. These connections are made in giving and receiving. One woman is the giver and the other woman is the receiver.

The commitment to heal the earth

One of our students wrote this after 9/11:

> Breathe in, breathe out, regardless of whether bombs are showering down. Look to the sky with certainty. This is all happening for a reason. Learn. You chose this time to come to earth. There is purpose here for you to serve. Break free from the petty distractions that enchain you. Time stands still for the soulsearcher. Break down the barriers of your mind. Finding the keys to enlightenment is deep and divine. Life is too webbed and complex to wrap your mind around it. Simply let it permeate your entire being, drenching your pores with experience. You can either see the light in life, or wait and see the light that accompanies death. This is the light that shines from within you, so you choose.

If you were the enlightened one, she was no one else but you, and you were asked to give what you have to share in this important moment, what would you say?

Commitment is a simple act. You feel it resonating within your body like an essential vibrating energy. You hold on to it and know that it is an essential truth in this world, in this lifetime. It comes to you as an essential commitment to life, a feeling, a certainty. When I saw it, I felt my commitment strengthen. I felt shock and then it felt as if a wall had torn in the world, a cluster of souls were taken, a sacrifice was made to illuminate something. You have to have the ability to see what is illuminated. It is based on your own ability to see and be awake. Commitment holds true to what you understand about the world; it holds true in the moment.

The open woman

Take a long walk down a winding road. Let the wind blow in your face; feel your body moving through time; take in the sensual experience of being alive. Make a commitment in the deepest place in your soul you can reach. Be open like the open woman; everything flows through her.

Mary says:

There is a woman inside of me; I can feel her echo of the Spirit Lovers. She is visionary, mystical; I feel her existence. I see her face; she opens up my heart. I let her go in. Her spirit goes inside me, and I become large. Spirit is separate, in service to spiritual beings; she is the manifestation of love. She is the manifestation of the earth, the mother, the pregnant fairy woman. She is a real spirit looking for and returning to spirit. I stand behind her and go forward when all we have to do is go inward.

Create the open woman; open wide, let her voice come through you, otherwise you are outside of yourself. I open my life to allow love to flow in. I do not close anything; I keep everything open. It does not define any place in the external world for love to flow. I open within myself and the movement of love begins to flow within myself. It connects me with God, and with the rhythms of the earth. In love, the most important thing you can do is open your life and allow creativity to flow.

The medicine woman's dream

The medicine woman dreams of connectedness and of being the earth. She dreams about healing the earth, about knowing what to do, and about doing it. She dreams about astral travel, energy, and healing. She has accurate dreams about what she needs to do now. It is her role as a medicine woman to heal the earth in this crisis.

Healing is about love and about peace. It is an experience; it is about now; it is about doing. The world crisis has given each of us a new opening. Like an illness, it is a time for suffering, reassessment, readjusting priorities, quick spiritual learning, and action. Everyone's energy changes to spiritual energy in a moment; it suddenly becomes denser, more intense, and more alive. When a person is near death, they are more alive, more real, and more spiritual than when they are shopping.

People are slowly realizing that the solution to this world crisis is a woman's job. Women are sensitive to emotion and energy. They have a nurturing instinct that includes appreciation for the earth and its animals. They know about children, and the weak, oppressed, and innocent. Women do not cause war or go to war, but women have son's who are taken.

The world is now populated with increasing numbers of women that see. These seers—priestesses of old, witches, oracles, healers—know the future and the present, they know about energy and healing. It has been a long time coming. It is a reaction to the patriarchal system that has oppressed them for millennia.

Now women need to heal. They need to become the spiritual healers again as they were for thousands of years. I speak to all women: You are the earth. Your body needs to be healed. Clear the parasites from the earth. Do this with energy and love. With your energy you will change the structure of the earth. You have been through it all; you have done the necessary suffering and developed skills to make you a healer. From your mothering, you know how to care for everything.

There are three stages of shamanic healing. First, get rid of the illness; suck it out and throw it in the fire. Second, rest in the void of perfect openness. Feel the energy; let healing begin. Third, use healing energy from the Creator.

This is the time to turn up the volume. Do work each week with energetic connections. It looks like war is imminent, but it's really an opening. It is a losing of everything and then it is necessary to say a prayer to move energy. Each person who prays changes the whole world. Each person who prays for peace creates peace. The earth is calling out for healing. Words have been spoken that are like a toxic poison. The world prays, speaks, and calls for peace and healing.

The world crisis is the wake-up call for the woman healer to emerge. The terrorist attack on the world trade center was highly visible. I saw it; all the women on the planet saw it. The Hopi elder Thomas Banyacya told the story of man and woman walking. In ancient times, man walked ahead; woman and children walked behind, so man could protect them. Then man and woman walked ahead and protected the children. Now is the time for the woman to walk ahead. The woman must walk ahead to save the earth and clean up the mess we are in. If she stands beside her husband in this crisis, we go to war. Look into your own heart. Do you want to send your young son to die? Do you want to take him and us to where all you see is your death? The goddess gave her only son to die for the world—it's been done. Her son said, "Forgive them father, for they know not what they do." And they were forgiven.

We are an idealistic generation of free, educated, and powerful women. We will change the world; we will change human consciousness. We will move toward new creative ways of peace through communication; we will make change in balance with the earth and the animals.

APPENDIX 2

For Professional Healers

My patient's room is a temple

Michael tells this story:

> She was tall and elegant, an African American woman who exuded quiet confidence and power. She was a young doctor and had just finished training at Stanford University in internal medicine and oncology. She was attending a conference on alternative cancer care and I could see her interest in my presentation. She took me aside at a break and told me this story: "When I see a patient with cancer, I have a ritual that I do." She stopped. I could see that she was embarrassed, and hesitant to go on. I told her it was all right and that I was used to these kinds of stories, so she continued. "As I walk up to the patient's room, I pause. And then everything changes. I go into the place in my world where I am at perfect peace. I go into the stillness, the silence—into the place where I have gone to pray since I was a little girl. Time and space change all around me. Then there is a silence and a quality of light, a grayness, a radiance from within itself that is so beautiful—it takes me completely, washes me, prepares me, and purifies me.

> "In that moment, pregnant with peace, I fill it and I pray. I give thanks to God for allowing me to be a physician, for my abilities, and for this opportunity to heal. I ask God to come with me into the patient's room, to stay with me, and give me insight, healing power, and strength. I ask for the ability to heal, listen, and love. In my mind's eye I picture the patient's room as

a sacred temple. I picture columns on each side of the door, like in a Greek healing temple. I picture owls on each column for the healing Goddess Athena.

"Then I drop deeper into my center, my spiritual place of healing, and I go into the room. Inside the room, I am the physician that I have been trained to be and I do the best I can with my skills, but I am more. I have God with me, helping me. I see the patient with God's love and I feel God's love too. I am able to listen and be fully present. In this altered state I can see things, hear things, and get ideas that I don't usually get. I get ideas and see colors and light. I am so alive. In the room, I am an ordinary physician and a special one, too. Does that make sense to you? Is that what you mean in your presentation when you talk about healing?"

If you are a physician, a nurse, a body worker, an acupuncturist, a homeopathy healer, a psychic, a family therapist, a psychologist, or a student of any kind of healing, this story is an example of how to consciously expand your practice using shamanic spiritual and visionary tools. It is a way to heal and much, much more.

"Something more": Going deeper into the healing relationship

One of the main themes of this book is understanding that spiritual and visionary tools take a healer deeper and give him or her a more powerful healing modality. In nursing, this is called advanced therapeutics. Daniel Stern and the Process of Change Study Group from the Children's Hospital Boston have developed the term "something more" to describe a relationship of patient and healer that is deeper than conventional therapy. In their paper, "Non-interpretive mechanisms in psychoanalytic therapy: The 'something more' than interpretation," the study group says that by now, it is generally accepted that something more than interpretation is necessary to bring about therapeutic change in psychotherapy. The study group asked patients the question, "What healed you?" To their surprise, it was often not the psychotherapeutic process itself. Patients told them of special moments that suddenly changed their world. The doctor may not have even noticed the moment. It usually involved eye contact, words of support, or encounters of mystery that the researchers called a "something more moment."

Using an approach based on studies of mother-infant interaction and nonlinear dynamic systems and their relation to theories of the mind, the study group proposes that the something more resides in a magic moment in a relationship. They say that the relationship between the healer and the person they work on is moving and alive, and results in a deep knowing that flows from the two being one. These special moments occurring between healer and the person being healed create new organizations in the person's implicit knowledge, in his ways of being with others. The healing moments actually deeply change the person being healed from within and he or she is repatterned, newly restructured. This is what happens when a shaman brings back a soul.

The distinct qualities and consequences of these moments, which the study group calls "now moments" or "moments of meeting," change with time in a deep, magical way. They call the process "moving along." This takes place below words within the shared implicit healing relationship. A powerful therapeutic action occurs within a deep inner knowledge that comes from the two merging and being one. They propose that much of what is observed to be lasting therapeutic effect results from such changes in this relational domain. In other words, they have found it is the relationship that heals. We have found that the healer and person being healed bring in healing energy, and together are in a vortex of power that changes both and results in healing.

A "something more" moment

Elizabeth had broken her leg badly six months ago and it was not healing. She went from one orthopedic surgeon to another; she was in constant pain and nothing helped. The doctors had tried electrical stimulation, drugs, and physiotherapy, but nothing healed her broken bones.

She went to a new physician who seemed nice; he had soft eyes. He looked directly into her eyes as she spoke. She moved closer to him as she told her story; he listened with complete attention. For the first time, she told the doctor the details about the horrible accident that had taken her son's life and left her crippled. As she spoke, she cried softly. He looked like he was meditating as he listened. He looked directly into her eyes with love and care. When she stopped, he simply said, "It must be very hard being Elizabeth, since your son died."

That moment with the doctor opened her world, it was almost as if it was out of time. It felt like a dam opened within her, and from behind the dam, tears flowed. Pure water seemed to flow through her whole body; it was a huge release. She had opened her heart and shown herself. She was seen by another and had been accepted and loved. The moment was just a second long, but it reverberated deep within her and without her at once. In that moment, she felt like her and the doctor were in the hands of God.

She started healing immediately. Within days she was pain free and within weeks she was completely healed. The "something more moment" freed her healer within. She made herself available and the physician took the offering, blessed it, and send it back to her with love. It was all she needed to make herself well.

We believe that this book provides information about the "something more moment" in medical care. It gives healer and patient a presence and a connection with the divine that brings in the power of spiritual healing and love and heals deeply. The techniques in this book will teach you as a professional healer how to make "something more moments" happen and how to take advantage of them.

Put the strands together

A woman physician came up to me and asked me to be her teacher. We were sitting at lunch; I looked into her eyes. She said, "How can I take all the spiritual work I have done and use it to heal myself, to grow, to be creative, to become the healer that I am meant to be? I have wanted to be a doctor since I was nine years old. I am now a successful surgeon, but my practice lacks meaning for me. I go to work each day and it is not fulfilling; something is missing. I looked for an answer; I took workshops in therapeutic touch and meditation. Each is a strand in my life, but that is not enough; I still cannot meld my interest in spirituality with my profession a physician."

For medical students or nursing students, this book will help with growth in the spiritual dimension, which is lacking in ordinary education. People interested in medicine want to heal from deep within their heart. The spiritual power of the initial calling is often lost in technical training. We want to take the part of them that made them want to help people in their heart and let it become part of their lives as medical professionals.

The altar

Michael tells us:

> One day, a renowned surgeon asked me a question. He asked, "A woman I operated on built an altar on the window sill of her hospital room. Her family helped her. Was she using the altar to pray for healing?" In that moment, I realized the enormity of the gap between medicine and spirituality. This book will help welcome Him to one's world so He can be there in a healing way, or as the Native Americans say, in a good way.
>
> A venerable psychiatrist and researcher told me, "My life has always been split in two. I am an excellent physician and work with my patients and do my research. At home I am a spiritual man; I am deeply religious. I walk, I pray, I speak to God, to Jesus, and when I walk in nature, to the animals. I have never been able to put these two sides together. I hid my spiritual side from my medicine because I was afraid it would discredit my scientific side." As he spoke, tears came into his eyes. At ninety years old, the split could no longer be tolerated by his soul.

This book will help physicians and all healers put the strands of their lives together to expand their practice of healing to become fulfilled, spiritual, and creative. It will help any healer join the two sides that have been separate. We told the psychiatrist mentioned above to look at his next patient with prayer and love, as if he were on a nature walk. We told him to listen to his next patient like he listens to the voices of the animals he loved. That was our assignment to him, and that is what this book is about.

Shamanism leads us to spirituality in health care

Prayer has now been recognized as a major healing tool by medical centers all over the world. Doctors have found that spirit gives an element to healing that conventional medicine lacks; it enhances the healing process. As a result, there are now more than seventy-five departments of spirituality and health care in major teaching medical schools. The spirituality and health care program at the University of Florida, Gainesville, taught us much in writing this book. Mary is developing curricula to teach creativity, spirituality, and health care to nurses; Michael teaches art in healing, shamanism, and spirituality at San Francisco State University at the Institute of Holistic Studies. Because the shaman is the traditional specialist of the soul, the shaman is recognized as a major part of spirituality and health care programs.

This book has brought you, the health professional, into the world of spirituality and healing by helping you move deeper into your spiritual world and the spiritual world of others. It has created pathways to help you access the visionary world of yourself and others, and it has helped you to honor these visions. With more and more people involved in spirit, mind, and body healing, it is valuable for health professionals to be able to speak and move in that world. It is helpful in the healing relationship for the professional to be able to speak about matters of the spirit and understand a person's interests and methods of spiritual healing. Patients (and their families) are deeply involved in rituals and in prayer. In the moments they walk down hospital corridors, they are praying and imagining themselves well in their mind's eye. You can become an integral part of their spiritual healing process.

The Invitation: You are using some shamanic tools already

We honor the healing work that you already do. One of our goals is to show you how your work is already shamanic and spiritual so you can maximize that aspect of your healing work consciously. This book has taught you specific skills of shamanic healing so you can make your healing more powerful and multidimensional. The healer you are includes whatever healing you do, whatever healing path you are on already. Now you can be the healer you are—but with more spiritual skills. You can increase the power of the healer you are, and expand the healer by healing yourself, others, and earth with spirit. This is a life change; it is a new life, a new way of being that you can cultivate. This book invites you to be on this path with prayer, commitment, and intent.

Miracles: The magic wand

Bill was a professor of radiation oncology at a major medical center. He was one of the world's experts on the Gamma Knife, a particular therapy that is highly technical and advanced. This procedure destroys brain tumors that in the past were too difficult to reach with surgery. But more than that, this doctor could bring hope to his patients in a way few other physicians knew how to do.

One day he took me to his office, deep in the lower levels of the medical center. It was a room without windows near the machines he used in his treatments. He reached up to a shelf and took down a wand. He said, "I take this magic wand in with me when I see patients. Sometimes, if we become close, I will show it to them. A little boy once touched it and told me he knew he was going to get better. He told me he knew that any doctor with a magic wand was really powerful. I told him that I had the force and that I would cure him with the force, my machine, and my magic wand." The parents of the little boy said, "There is God and there is Bill. I don't know who did more, but our little boy has been healed."

How can you bring a magic wand into your own healing?

There are healing miracles. Science calls them "spontaneous remission." This means that the person gets better on his or her own. To us, it means more. The shaman healer can make miracles happen by activating the healing energy from the Creator and the healing power of the imagination.

Guided Imagery with the magic wand

Take your magic wand and go around the room. Ask each person, "In your mind, what do you wish for? Close your eyes, remember what is precious, and make a wish." Take the magic wand and tap the person's forehead. Tap their third eye and say, "Your wish has been granted. Be patient and allow the universe to give you what you want; surrender and have faith. It may not happen the way you think, but your wish will come true."

As a healer, you can always allow miracles to come to you and your patients. You can tell your patients about miracles and about previous patients who healed from the same condition. You can find several stories of spontaneous remission with the same illness. Remember stories of patients you treated who recovered against all odds. Be the healer who invites the miracle to enter your patient's life.

The shaman surgeon

The surgeon stands at the sink washing her hands. She is in a green hospital gown; her mask hangs down, ready to be raised. She washes her hands slowly; she looks at herself in the mirror. She washes each finger and each nail with a slow deliberate movement. She pictures in her mind's eye the difficult surgery she will do in just minutes. She knows that the washing is a ceremonial purification, a cleansing. She sees it as her first step in her elaborate ritual to heal. The patient has Crohn's disease, a condition of the small intestine; she needs the surgery or she will die. The surgeon enters the operating room. The operating room is her sacred space to work. It is sterile, perfectly clean, and washed and purified several times a day. She will work with a group, all gowned and masked. She speaks to her patient before starting. She tells her that she will heal her; she will make her better; she will take out the diseased parts and put her together again, whole and perfect. The anesthesiologist speaks to the patient too. He says he will take good care of her; she will feel no pain and will wake up feeling hungry and healed. The surgeon takes each part of the sacred process of her surgery seriously. She herself was healed by a shaman in Brazil when she had been very ill. She remembers his sacred space, his confidence, and his respect for what he did. She remembers his prayers, his bringing in the spirits, and his taking out her illness in psychic space.

She heals as a surgeon and a shaman healer. She will dis-member, take apart, and cut her patient; and then through manipulation she will put the woman back together healed. She prays with each patient; she prays for her hands to be guided by the Creator. She offers all the knowledge and skill she has learned during her years of hard work, as a gift to the Creator and to her patient. She prays for the young woman she is operating on to be healed. She says the same prayers she was taught by her shaman healer in Brazil. "May this woman be healed, Creator; she is a good woman. May your power come to me and help me heal. May I see what needs to be taken out and may I put her right." Then she starts. Years of learning, dedication, knowledge, and skill come to her. She relaxes knowing she is being guided and will do her best. During sur-gery she only speaks positive words; she says out loud to her patient over and over again, "You are doing well; the operation is working; you are healing. You will awaken feeling good and knowing you are all better."

She is a surgeon and a shaman healer within the traditional medical model. From the days when she was a young girl, she has been on her own vision quest to be a powerful healer. She has dedicated her life to being a surgeon, to take care of people and heal them. It has been a vigorous path. It took focus; it took years of going through her own darkness. Like the shamans of ancient time, she had to let go of herself. She had to let go of herself as a dancer, let go of her husband for years when she was a resident, and let go of the part of her that loved to travel. She had to let go of her motorcycle and let go of herself as a concert pianist. She let go of all of this to pursue her one goal, to become a surgeon. She was molded; she suffered; she stayed up every night; and she forced herself to see patients when she was exhausted. This was her shamanic initiation, to see only how to do one thing. In her residency she stayed up every second night—it was immersion. She remembered the long nights working on only one hour of sleep. It was hazing, brainwashing, a stripping. It was her descent of Ianna; she was striped to her bones; she went to the underworld and into her own suffering.

At the end she was different—a healer, but she needed more. When she became ill with a condition, Western medicine did not help. So she went to a shaman in the jungles of Brazil. He did a ceremony that replaced the pieces she had lost during her medical training. He brought back her soul. Now she had both sides—her scientific training and skill and her ability to pray, create sacred space, and see visions. She is a shaman healer today. Her combined vision gives her huge healing powers. She can manifest change in a person's body from both her visionary space in sacred space and from physical space with her hands. As she operates, she pictures energy shooting from her hands. Her results are better than those of her colleagues. If she feels they would benefit, she tells her patients about prayer. Her patients know she gives them something more. Many people come to her because she prays and has a spiritual side. Her reputation has grown; she has been interviewed and filmed while she prays with a patient and then does the best surgery that can be done. She feels she has gone into the underworld in her shamanic initiation and come back up. Her work is her sacred practice. She is shape changing, manifesting reality that is infused with her deep spiritual life.

INDEX